HOLLOW BODIES:

Institutional Responses to Sex Trafficking in Armenia, Bosnia, and India

Susan Dewey

Kumarian Press
An Imprint of Stylus Publishing

Hollow Bodies: Institutional Responses to Sex Trafficking in Armenia, Bosnia, and India

Published 2008 in the United States of America by Kumarian Press
22883 Quicksilver Dr., Sterling, VA 20166

Copyedit by Connie Day
Proofread by Marilyn Silverman
Design and production by UB Communications, Parsippany, NJ.
The text of this book is set in 11/13 Adobe Sabon.

Printed in the USA on acid-free paper by Thomson-Shore, Inc.

⊗ The paper used in this publication meets the minimum requirements of the American National Standard for Information Sciences—Permanence of Paper for Printed Library Materials, ANSI Z39.48-1984.

Library of Congress Cataloging-in-Publication Data

Dewey, Susan.
    Hollow bodies : institutional responses to sex trafficking in Armenia, Bosnia, and India / by Susan Dewey.
        p. cm.
    Includes bibliographical references and index.
    ISBN 978-1-56549-265-3 (pbk. : alk. paper) — ISBN 978-1-56549-266-0 (cloth : alk paper)
1. Human trafficking—Government policy. 2. Human trafficking—Prevention.
3. Prostitution—Government policy. 4. Prostitution—Prevention. 5. Women—Crimes against—Prevention. I. Title.
    HQ281.D49 2008
    354.15—dc22
                                            2008010158

For my son Gabriel,
whose birth made the world
a better place

Acknowledgments

This book could not have been written without the constant support, love, and affirmation my husband Robert has unfailingly given me throughout several years of challenging research. I am indebted to the International Organization for Migration (IOM) Chiefs of Mission in Armenia and Bosnia-Herzegovina, who made my research possible by allowing me access to their important work on migration and the traffic in women. I thank Neal Abraham of DePauw University for supporting my research in Sarajevo, Jim Lance of Kumarian Press for his faith in my work, and Meryl Altman for her consistent support and mentoring. I have been inspired by the stories of thousands of women who have survived injustice and abuse to hope for a better life, and I remain extremely grateful to the Armenians, Bosnians, and Indians who shared their stories of hardship with me and simultaneously reaffirmed my belief in essential human goodness.

A Note on the Use of Names and Pseudonyms

I have followed standard ethnographic practice in providing pseudonyms chosen by individuals who did not wish to be identified by name in this book, either because they feared professional repercussions or because they simply wanted to remain anonymous. I fully understand that the relatively small number of individuals who work in the field of counter-trafficking in Armenia, Bosnia, and India will make some individuals identifiable by virtue of their professional titles. I have attempted to preserve the privacy of everyone who could be negatively affected by public knowledge of their personal beliefs or, in some cases, their actions.

Contents

Preface

Feminist anthropologist from the United States: Could you please share your story with me so I can write a book that will educate others about the traffic in women?

Suada from Bosnia-Herzegovina: I was thirteen when the war spread to my city. I was kidnapped by four soldiers who locked me in a house where I was raped every day by different men for eight months. I had a miscarriage while I was there. When the war ended, soldiers wearing unfamiliar uniforms came and told me to go home, but my city had been destroyed and my family was dead. I moved to Sweden with a man I trusted, and he sold me to a pimp in Stockholm. Later the police sent me back to my country, but I am still afraid to go outside, because I worry that everyone can tell what happened just by looking at me.

Anjali from India: My family never had enough to eat. I wanted a life different from that. I met someone who promised he would find me a job in the city, but once we arrived in Bombay he left me with one of his female cousins and said that he would return very soon. He didn't come back, and a few days later I found out that his "cousin" was actually the owner of a brothel to which I had been sold. She made me accept all the men who came to me, and when I got sick as a result, she threw me out in the street. I am seventeen years old and have no money to pay for medicine. All I wanted was a better life, and now I am dying.

Sophia from Armenia: I was thirty-one and unemployed. I am a single mother with no education, and sometimes I had to sell myself to feed my daughter. I called a number from a newspaper ad seeking waitresses in Greece, and the woman I spoke to arranged a fake passport and a plane ticket to Athens for me. I am not some naïve young girl, but I thought this was my only chance. I left my daughter with my mother, and once I got to Greece the woman told me that if I did not give her money, I would go to jail because I had broken the law by using false documents to travel. So I became a prostitute in a foreign country. It was that simple.

Feminist anthropologist from the United States: What are we as a human community doing to help women like Suada, Anjali, and Sophia? How much longer will we continue to support their invisibility?

1

Sarajevo Roses: Why Feminist Questions Are Also Human Questions

A stranger walking through the city of Sarajevo may notice that parts of the sidewalk have been sharply indented to form designs that radiate outward from a circular center into a vaguely floral shape. He or she might think these indentations constitute some sort of abstract art, or a case of municipal neglect, and walk on without giving them a second thought. In fact, however, these indentations are locally known as Sarajevo roses, and they mark the deliberately unrepaired sites where residents of the city were killed by mortar and sniper fire while waiting in line for bread and water during the three-and-a-half-year siege of the city by Serb nationalist troops. It was a beautiful summer day when I first encountered a Sarajevo rose under my feet near the eternal flame in the city center, which is kept alight in memory of the Serbs, Croats, Muslims, and others who fought and died together, without regard to ethnicity or religion, to liberate the city from Fascist troops during World War II.

In the brilliant light of summer in a country that had again been torn apart by conflict and, over a decade later, was still trying to find and prosecute the criminals responsible for wartime atrocities, it was difficult to comprehend that the normal, everyday space of this sidewalk had also been the scene of unspeakable horror and grief as bullets and bombs arbitrarily tore through pavement and human bodies. Sarajevo roses are ubiquitous and unobtrusive enough that a visitor to the city might not give much thought to their meaning or what they symbolize to the city's residents who lived through the war. They may even go completely unobserved unless one is truly looking for them or, if observed by the visitor, may simply remain a story to tell about a series of unusual memorials in a city best known in the European Union (EU) and the United States for a brutal war that they both remained indifferent to until its consequences became impossible to ignore. Sarajevo roses are meant to serve as a reminder of those who were killed so that the war dead will never become invisible to the living, and yet most Sarajevo residents are so busy with their daily lives that these memorials remain unnoticed underfoot.

The traffic in women for the purposes of sexual exploitation is very similar to the Sarajevo roses in that it is easy for the vast majority of individuals to choose to ignore what they reveal about humanity. Whenever I speak on the subject of sex trafficking, the reaction of audiences and individuals alike is always the same—shock, horror, inquiries into what can be done—and yet everyone who asks these questions is at least somewhat cognizant of the existence of prostitution. The irony of this lies in how the two are distinguished by most people as polar opposites on a continuum of guilt and innocence: The prostitute is a widely reviled figure to whom it is difficult to relate, whereas the victim of trafficking is construed as uniquely deprived of agency and thus is invested with a kind of saintly "mythic resonance" (Murray 1998) that sharply divides women who engage in the exchange of sex for money into guilty whores and innocent victims. This extreme public ambivalence toward two groups who perform the same actions and largely share the same life circumstances is precisely what makes the topic a matter of such pressing social and feminist concern.

My main goal in writing this book is to demonstrate how sex trafficking and institutional responses to it are social processes supported both directly and indirectly by the complicity of societies. I was consistently struck, throughout my research in three countries, by the way bureaucracy and social discrimination consistently hinder counter-trafficking efforts in almost the same ways they directly facilitate the traffic in women. This individual and institutional complicity in the use of women's bodies as sexual objects can take a variety of forms, including the denial that trafficking is a problem; the social stigmatization of prostitutes (and, by default, victims of trafficking); and, as is discussed in detail in the three ethnographic case studies presented in Chapters 3, 4, and 5, institutional apathy, organizational paralysis, and government corruption.

This book does not obscure its discussion of institutional responses to the lives of individual women by adding to the already voluminous policy, feminist, activist, and scholarly literature that debates definitions of sex work. Accordingly, I use the terms *prostitution* and *sex work* interchangeably with the understanding that in the context of my research, both refer to the ability of some men to buy sexual services from women who belong to marginalized groups. Although this book discusses various institutional and activist definitions of sex trafficking, I have tried my best to remove myself from these debates and present a balanced analysis of how discrimination against prostitutes and victims of trafficking is institutionalized to a degree that can obfuscate the ability of organizations to truly assist either group. Sex trafficking and prostitution are not simply questions of semantics, and—like the Sarajevo roses—both are ongoing reminders of how individuals, governments, and international organizations can profoundly fail individuals despite their best-intentioned efforts to cooperate and to assist vulnerable populations.

I choose to adopt the broadest possible definition of sex trafficking in order to focus on the human issues raised by its continued existence. This book considers the traffic in women for the purposes of sexual exploitation to involve a minimum of four things: an element of movement to at least one location away from an individual's place of origin, prostitution, female gender, and a lack of life choices. All singular definitions that attempt to address extremely complex and multifaceted issues are problematic because they can never hope to encompass the manifold ways in which individuals are affected. The vast majority of cases do, however, involve relocation either across a national border or to an area outside the victim's native place. They also necessarily feature the exchange of sex for money or something of value, and this is gendered in that although men can become victims of sexual exploitation, women are in far greater demand as prostitutes for a number of sociocultural reasons. Sex trafficking is also characterized by a lack of other choices in the sense that most individual women would opt for a form of work other than prostitution if their life circumstances allowed them to do so.

The traffic in women generally, but by no means always, involves a situation of real or invented indebtedness that often serves as a trafficker's justification for paying the woman for the sexual services that she performs. It is also common for threats of violence against the woman or her family to be used as a means of control by the person who is profiting from her work. The sense of insecurity and fear that this creates is compounded by the often-illegal nature of the activities involved, such as the use of false or altered documents to cross borders, the bribery of border guards and police, and the stigma associated with prostitution even in countries where there are no laws against it. Even when a woman is entitled to be in a country because she holds a tourist or student visa, her marginal status as an illegal worker and a prostitute discourages her from approaching the police or organizations that could assist her.

Violence is often used as a coercive mechanism when women are reluctant to engage in sex work, but this is by no means always the case. General understandings of the problem employ a highly subjective caricature of brutal men abusing vulnerable women, and yet almost half of those who profit from the prostitution of others are themselves women. It is impossible to ignore the reality that sex trafficking is made possible by sexism, but it is equally important to note that many women who leave forced prostitution are able to do so because a male client assists them either financially or socially, for instance, through marriage. It is also true that women who are coerced into selling sex in other countries sometimes believe their situation is preferable to life in their country of origin and, consequently, do not want to return home.

These ironies are compounded by the fact that those who meet the various definitions of the term *victim of trafficking* often do not recognize or describe themselves as such because of the shame associated with prostitution, just as victims of sexual assault and domestic violence often blame themselves and are suspected by society of provoking the violent behavior inflicted on them. These difficulties in self-identifying with the word *victim* are also rooted in the lack of agency the term implies, a subject that we will address in depth in Chapter 2. Individuals who migrate to obtain any form of work do so because they hope for a better life, and this motivation for self-improvement is in itself a form of agency. However, the marginal circumstances and lack of social status that many unskilled migrants face when they arrive in a foreign country in search of work create a kind of social invisibility that limits the number of choices they are able to make, including the right to refuse work that they do not want to perform or that they would not have done in their home country.

Individual cases of sex trafficking underscore the difficulties faced by labor migrants and highlight the inequalities related to gender, race, nationality, social class, and age that they are forced to negotiate when confronted with a lack of sustainable opportunities in their home countries or places of origin. An employee I spoke to at a Sarajevo-based nongovernmental organization (NGO) described the case of a Bosnian teenager who had traveled to Italy on a tourist visit procured by her aunt, whom she and her family considered a benefactor. The aunt had promised to find her niece a job in an Italian office at a salary that far exceeded what she could have earned in a similar position in Sarajevo. Soon after her arrival in Italy, however, the teenager had been forced to work as a prostitute and to surrender all her earnings to her aunt.

The aunt had directly capitalized on the teenager's youth and lack of life experience not only by convincing her that she would be ostracized as a prostitute by her family and community if she returned to Sarajevo, but also by insisting she owed her aunt a great deal of money for housing and food that she had been provided with in Italy. The aunt further exploited her position of power vis-à-vis the young girl by forcing her to send regular letters to her family in Sarajevo documenting her happiness in an affluent European Union country and a level of security that never could have been achieved in Bosnia. Two years after her departure from Sarajevo, the teenager was lying in bed with an older Italian man who had become one of her regular clients when she told him the truth about the coercive nature of her situation. He was genuinely horrified by the abuse she had been subjected to and the revelation that she was only fifteen years old. He immediately took her to the police to be returned to her family in Sarajevo.

I met a middle-aged single mother of two children at a shelter for victims of trafficking in Yerevan, Armenia, who told me in an extremely matter-of-fact manner how she had traveled to Turkey using false documents prepared by a man she met through a newspaper advertisement he placed seeking "entertainers." She explained to me that although she left Armenia with the understanding that she would be paid to work as a prostitute, once she arrived in Istanbul she was informed that her travels had placed her in significant debt to the man who had arranged her journey. Her marginal status as an illegal migrant in a country that had no diplomatic relations with her own made her afraid to approach the police, and her need to support her children in Armenia convinced her that it would be better to repay the "debt" in the hope of keeping her future income after "repayment" was complete. It was only when a Turkish police raid on the Istanbul brothel in which she was forced to work to repay her "debt" revealed her as an illegal migrant that she was deported to Armenia, where she approached the shelter at which I met her.

A woman who works for an NGO that assists young women who are forced into prostitution in India shifted uneasily in her seat as she described the situation of a thirteen-year-old girl from an impoverished family of five sisters who had been traded by her parents to an affluent family in exchange for a sum of money, with the understanding that she would perform unpaid domestic labor. The NGO worker became aware of the girl's case when a mutual friend of the family informed her that the girl was quite likely being sexually abused by one of the family's sons. It was decided that nothing should be done, because the girl did not want to leave what was essentially the only stability she had ever known, and because the family was seen to be, at least in some ways, "helping" an unwanted young girl by giving her a place to stay. Although the woman I spoke to remained unconvinced that this was the right decision, she felt that the girl should be entitled to make her own choices due to the fact that government institutions would be ill-equipped to care for her.

Both the Sarajevo teenager and the woman from Yerevan, Armenia, were victims of *trafficking* by almost any definition of the term, but the case of the thirteen-year-old unpaid domestic laborer in India is much more ambiguous. The family she lived with genuinely believed that they were improving the life of a girl who had no other choices by providing her with shelter and food, and cultural taboos against speaking openly about sexuality prohibited the NGO worker and others from confirming any suspicions they had about abuse. This is of critical importance, given that even though all three cases featured the same coercive elements of poverty and social marginalization, each was handled very differently by organizations that assist victims of trafficking. Thus the specific realities of the millions of other lives affected by this phenomenon necessitate some definitions of key terms that will be used throughout the book.

The term *trafficker* describes someone who facilitates forced prostitution and profits financially from his or her actions, as did the aunt from Sarajevo and the man who promised the woman from Yerevan a paid position as a prostitute in Turkey. These cases clearly demonstrate that a trafficker can be almost anyone, including a relative, a loved one, or a stranger. *Victim of trafficking* is used to refer to a person who is coerced into prostitution by someone who benefits from her sexual labor, and although *trafficking* can also be understood to involve exploitive labor migration of men or children, in the context of this book (which deals exclusively with the coerced movement of women for the purposes of sexual exploitation), *trafficking* will be used interchangeably with *sex trafficking*. Finally, the words *prostitute* and *sex worker* will be used to describe a woman who exchanges sexual acts for something of value, usually money. Thus, all victims of sex trafficking can be described as *prostitutes* in this sense of the term, but not all prostitutes are victims of trafficking, and extremely contentious debates surround how these distinctions should be made.

This book will repeatedly demonstrate how the messy realities of life and relationships between men and women render the contemporary definitions of trafficking discussed in Chapter 2 somewhat irrelevant to the lives of women who are coerced into selling sex. The example of the thirteen-year-old girl who was essentially sold by her relatives to a wealthy family and placed in a situation of sexual exploitation in the process does not meet most definitions of sex trafficking currently in use, yet her situation was just as abusive as the experiences of the women from Sarajevo and Yerevan. Furthermore, it would be extremely unreasonable to argue for the abolition of such definitions, even though they do not always adequately characterize women's experiences.

Without definitions there would be no way to target groups, and this leaves organizations in a tense bind. They must create and enforce categories designed to be broad enough to benefit a large number of women but also sufficiently narrow and specific to produce results. Definitions are essential to the process of bringing about change from a policy and legislative perspective, and yet their meanings hold the power to determine who counts as a victim and who does not. The implications are enormous. These definitions draw on entrenched sexist stereotypes that separate women into categories of guilt and innocence; they deeply disadvantage women who do not fit the narrow set of criteria devised by international organizations, governments, and aid agencies; and they may undermine the ability of such groups to implement real change in women's lives.

These are deeply human questions that highlight the ability of powerful groups to speak for the marginalized and to define the circumstances in which they live and work. Accordingly, the central question this book seeks to investigate is twofold: How do gendered structural inequalities manifest themselves in the form of sex trafficking? And why do efforts to end the trade in women's bodies almost universally replicate the very processes of marginalization that they seek to combat? This book acknowledges that even though socioeconomic crises and political upheaval definitely contribute to the existence of sex trafficking, they are by no means the sole causes. By documenting the social and institutional contexts that shape the lives of individual victims in three very different countries, it will demonstrate that a process of institutionalizing victimization is at work by which societies become complicit in the commoditization of women's bodies at both the interpersonal and international levels. Institutionalizing victimization is by no means an accidental process and is not confined to sex trafficking; rather, it results from a number of entrenched sociopolitical forces that combine to effectively cripple many well-intentioned efforts by international, government, and activist organizations.

Sex trafficking and prostitution do not exist in a vacuum. Rather, both are part of broader socioeconomic processes that uniquely disadvantage women. The advent of an interconnected global economy, accompanied by historically unprecedented levels of labor migration by both genders, has complicated and exacerbated a phenomenon that is by no means new but has increased exponentially in scope as global socioeconomic and political crises have increasingly pushed women into migration as a survival strategy. The traffic in women is inseparable from gender inequality, migration, neoliberal economic policies, and the feminization of poverty, and these issues impact everyone, regardless of their gender, class, race, or national origin. This perspective has been well documented in Enloe's pioneering work (2007; 2004), which insists that feminists have an obligation to engage with contemporary political debates, and in Sassen's discussions of globalization (2006; 1999), which have similarly reaffirmed how crucial feminist analysis is to an understanding of the world that incorporates a genuinely human perspective. Books by Berkovitch (2002), Keck and Sikkink (1998), and Mohanty (2003) on the engagement of women's advocacy networks with international politics and policymaking further underscore that feminism is not just a question of semantics or personal lifestyle, but a way of politically engaging with the world.

A vast literature documents the feminization of poverty under the austerity measures that accompany the implementation of structural adjustment policies; see especially articles by Connelly (1996), Lawson (1995), and Safa (1995). Such policies have directly resulted in economic crises that often combine with regional conflicts to push poor women into sex work at least in part because of the demand for prostitutes created by military bases and economies dominated by tourism (Enloe 1990; Mullings 1999; O'Connell Davidson and Sanchez Taylor 1999). Migration can no longer be clearly classified as a male phenomenon, and numerous authors have discussed women's mobility as part of individual economic survival strategies. See in particular Ehrenrich and Hochschild's (2004) general analysis of neoliberalism and female labor migration, Gamburd (2000) on Sri Lankan women housemaids in affluent Gulf states, Keough (2006) on migrant mothers in Eastern Europe, Mills (1999) on rural Thai women in urban garment factories, Constable (1997) and Chang (2000) on Filipina migrants, Salzinger (2003) on gender and factory labor in Mexico, and Hondagneu-Sotelo (2001) and Parrenas (2001) on female migrant domestic workers.

These texts have sparked a number of debates and questions about the position of women of all nationalities, and such questions are by no means confined to Women's Studies or women's interests. From the use of the term *Mother India* by extremist Hindu politicians to mobilize anti-Muslim sentiment in India to the practice of rape as a tool of war by Serb nationalist soldiers in Bosnia-Herzegovina, femininity is a locus within which the tense dynamics of nationalism and identity are routinely questioned and reaffirmed. Despite the universality of this phenomenon, the term *victimization* remains extremely controversial in both policy and feminist circles, because it suggests a lack of agency and implies the need for rescue and redemption. I have deliberately chosen to use this word in reference to women who sell sex because they have no other means of economic support. Yet this is not because I have failed to observe their self-improvement strategies in my fieldwork, but rather because of the elaborate social and institutional processes that combine to undermine their efforts to exercise autonomy.

My experiences with such women have encouraged me to characterize many of their behaviors as psychological coping mechanisms that can indeed be construed as agency if the term is simply defined as the human ability to act. Examples of such self-preserving behaviors that I have encountered among women who have sold sex under the extreme duress defined as trafficking by most organizations include the refusal to cooperate in prosecution or other counter-trafficking efforts, aggressive behavior toward assistance workers, and counting clients in order to calculate the profits others earn from the abuse of their labor. The case studies presented in this book demonstrate that these behaviors are often the direct result of fears of retribution by traffickers and pimps, post-traumatic stress disorder, and a desire to maintain sanity in an abusive and psychologically destabilizing environment. It must be acknowledged that although it is problematic to imply that women forced for whatever reason to engage in sex work do not make choices designed to improve their lives, it is even more dangerous to argue that they are free agents who are not coerced by poverty, a lack of other opportunities, and often a history of abuse. Women who work as prostitutes because they choose to should be respected out of the conviction that feminism is about choices, and yet the telling reality is that most who argue that prostitution is a form of work have not chosen to engage in it themselves as a form of long-term economic support. As the founder of the Belgian counter-trafficking NGO Payoke succinctly put it, "we need to face it that prostitution is not number one on the list of jobs university graduates would like to have."

This book will demonstrate how victimization has been formalized, codified, and institutionalized in regard to sex trafficking at least in part because of the stigma associated with prostitution. Sanchez describes prostitutes as "sexual outlaws" (1998, 543) who are denied full citizenship and thus occupy a position that simultaneously renders them invisible and likely targets for violence unworthy of state protection. Prostitutes are positioned in a social category that by default defines them as deserving poor treatment because of their choice (however coerced) to sell sex for money. Yet just as it is virtually impossible to separate prostitution from trafficking, it is equally difficult to distinguish the way most women experience sex work from "abuse, poverty, poor working conditions, inexperience or despair" (Pheterson 1993, 40).

It is not helpful to be constrained by arguments about whether prostitution is a choice that should be defined as work or an inherently dehumanizing set of behaviors that "no woman would voluntarily choose" (Hughes 2002). Doezema's use of the phrase *forced to choose* (1998) in her article of the same name, which discusses the blurry boundaries between prostitution and sex trafficking, may be the telling description that most accurately describes the lives of women featured in the case studies of this book. And it is sobering to recognize that the kinds of binary distinctions between "agency" and "victimization" that are so important to policymakers and feminists alike often have very little meaning for the vast majority of women who sell sex in order to survive.

Findings from my previous research at Diamond Dolls, a topless dancing bar in New York, revealed that women who perform erotic labor do in fact clearly demonstrate their agency by privately mocking the men who patronize their establishment as lonely, pathetic creatures who are easy to exploit for money. The discourse in the backstage area where women prepare for their performances onstage was often redolent with references to the power of female sexuality to make men part with their money, and dancers took pride in claiming that they earned hundreds of dollars per night despite never finishing high school. I was initially very impressed with what seemed to be a clear demonstration of women's economic empowerment in a space I had assumed to be extremely masculinist and threatening. Yet after awhile, cracks began to appear in the image most dancers portrayed of themselves as seductresses who turned men into helpless fools who handed over large sums of cash in exchange for a brief view of a bare breast or thigh, especially as I learned that almost all of the women either had been, or were still in, abusive relationships and that almost none had employment skills with which to support themselves and their children.

Over time, dancers who had initially spoken with pride about their ability to earn hundreds of dollars in tips for just a few hours of provocative undulating around a metal pole explained how they had developed addictions from their use of alcohol and drugs as a form of nightly self-medication before starting work. Others characterized the money they earned as "dirty" and described how they lived in fear of the day their children would be old enough to need an explanation of the kind of work they did. None of the women described their occupation as a career choice, and nearly all of them were adamant that they hoped to find another way to earn an income that would place them above the poverty line. For most of the dancers, such cracks in the dominant discourse backstage revealed that the social stigma and abusive labor practices that are inseparable from their work made it clear that the agency they evinced as seductresses and self-described "hustlers" was an example of the "weapons of the weak" (Scott 1985). It is these cracks and slippages that I am particularly interested in exploring and on which I will focus to provide an understanding of how the exchange of sex for money between men and women, in all its various forms, is understood both by the women who engage in this practice and by the agencies and institutions that seek to assist them.

This relates to the book's key concept of institutionalizing victimization, because one of the most bizarre results of national and international legislation on sex trafficking is that whether a woman is characterized as a victim or as a prostitute depends on the country in which she sells sex. Even though the woman in question may simply see herself as choosing what she believes is the best option from a limited menu of life choices in order to survive, the way institutions and the individuals who staff them respond to her has everything to do with social and institutional forces. And these often do not acknowledge that women who perform sex work rarely share a monolithic set of circumstances or experiences.

Some women are abused in ways that mirror the stories of sadistic exploitation presented by radical anti-prostitution activists, whereas others migrate of their own volition and then find that their marginal status compels them to enter numerous exploitive situations, including prostitution. It is precisely because of the complicated question of agency and the bifurcated nature of the debate that we must examine interactions between victims of trafficking and the institutions that specifically seek to assist them. One of the key conclusions of this examination of three very different societies is that numerous elements in a society need to be complicit in order for the trade in women's bodies to continue.

Any discussion of female sexuality as a commodity available for male consumption in the global marketplace runs the risk of replicating broader discourses on male power and female oppression. Studies on the subject sometimes reinforce preexisting norms and inequalities by using the bodies of poor women who work in the sex industry as theoretical spaces in which to conduct academic exercises, thus implicitly legitimizing the social stigma attached to sex work. I have often had my research on trafficking described as "sexy" by academics—a shocking and sad reality that reflects both the idea of topical trends in academia and the failure of educated people to be sensitive to the ways in which women survive poverty and marginalization. It is true that some academics may simply mean that the subject is of great public interest, and yet the consistent decision to use such an eroticized adjective as *sexy* is telling. The underlying message is clearly that interest in women's bodies as commodities is nothing more than a trend of momentary interest.

Sex work in any form is hardly a metaphor; rather, it is a reality to which women are subjected as a result of life in a world cross-cut by gross socio-economic and gender inequalities. This book is a call for more responsible scholarship on the sex industry, for research which will consider not only the sociocultural meanings of the objectification of women's bodies, but also the views and everyday living conditions of the women who are the real authorities on the subject of how they can best be assisted. Just as academics are guilty of perpetuating stereotypes about the lives of women who sell sex, policymakers at both the international and governmental levels have also advanced their own political agendas through their engagement with the subject of trafficking.

The fact that international organizations and governments, NGOs, and individuals alike in many countries recognize sex trafficking as a significant problem that should be dealt with through legislation, donor-funding initiatives, and moral outrage raises profound questions about the contemporary state of the world. Yet the various categories of groups and individuals involved in counter-trafficking activities have such different motivations, ranging from humanitarian idealism to xenophobic concerns about unwanted immigration, that it is imperative to explore how this single social problem has been defined and addressed by so many social actors. The choice of these groups to engage with an enduring problem encourages us to ask deeply human questions that transcend what some perceive to be the narrow scope of feminist concern and to embrace new ways of thinking about poverty, gender, sexuality and, above all, what it means to be a human being in a time of unprecedented migration.

INTRODUCTION TO THE CASE STUDIES:
ARMENIA, BOSNIA-HERZEGOVINA, AND INDIA

The three countries discussed in Chapters 3, 4, and 5 could easily be addressed in several books of their own because of the complex way that sex trafficking, state policy, and donor aid uniquely affect each of them. My intention in analyzing all three in the scope of a single book is not only to demonstrate that the traffic in women is a phenomenon of international concern, but also to highlight the specific sociocultural realities which surround the problem in very different geographic locations. The causes of trafficking are generally perceived as poverty, social instability, gender inequality, and the normalization of migration, and my research supports this understanding. But in order to understand how this transnational phenomenon operates around the world, it is equally important to describe how these somewhat abstract causes manifest themselves in highly localized contexts.

It is to be expected that each country has its own set of difficulties to overcome in combating this problem, and these include economic instability, poverty, institutional corruption, the lack of legislation or inability to enforce existing legislation, and the fact that the society itself may still be in the early stages of adjustment to major changes in the civil and political order. Armenia, for example, has a law that specifically forbids trafficking, and this law has not done any more to reduce the number of poor women who accept offers for illegal work abroad than the complete lack of such legislation has done in Bosnia-Herzegovina. Both Armenia and Bosnia-Herzegovina are still attempting to consolidate the roles of governments, international organizations, and NGOs in what effectively remain new societies two decades after the collapse of the Berlin Wall and the conflicts that ensued in each country. Yet India is a stable democracy with very clearly defined roles for international organizations, government agencies, and civil society, and the country still struggles with a significant trafficking problem.

These three case studies reveal that it would be irresponsible to point to a discrete set of causes for the traffic in women, just as it is impossible to conclude that violence against women has a single identifiable source. The head of the International Organization for Migration counter-trafficking unit at the time of my research in Sarajevo raised the important point that trafficking also exists in affluent nations with high levels of border security, such as the United States; clearly, poverty and conflict are not the sole causes of the problem. She was quick to note that lax border control and rampant corruption are indeed conducive to criminal behavior, and she cited the example of the obvious choice a thief would make in deciding whether to break into an alarmed car or an unlocked car parked next to it. "But to the really skilled thief who is organized and has planned out how to do it," she added, "it does-n't make a difference whether there's an alarm there or not, and that's why you...have trafficking to the United States; it's just more organized than in Bosnia. It helps to have tighter borders, but if there is a will there is a way."

Generalizations are always dangerous in their tendency to reduce the com-plexities of a nuanced social issue to a reductive set of causes and behaviors, but the combined experience of international organizations, governments, and NGOs in dealing with trafficking does allow for a synoptic introduction to the patterns it follows. Approaches to the issue usually divide countries into the three categories of origin, transit, and destination as a means of describing the migration trends that are characteristic of them. Countries of origin tend to have the weak economies, high unemployment, social instability, war, and other problems that push individuals to make the decision to migrate; these are that countries that the majority of migrants come from.

Armenia

Armenia is considered a country of origin because its economy is not able to provide jobs to all of its citizens, and this makes migration the only option many people have if they want to support themselves and their families. Coun-tries of transit are those that migrants pass through en route to a country of destination where they hope to find work, and these transit nations often have either unclear or loosely enforced borders. Bosnia-Herzegovina's borders were completely redrawn after the war in the early 1990s, and the low salaries earned by border police encourage them to take bribes in order to earn a living wage. A significant number of migrants pass through the country on their way to European Union countries of destination characterized by stronger and more diversified economies.

Armenia is a small nation nestled in the Caucasus Mountains and sur-rounded by Iran, Georgia, Azerbaijan, and Turkey. With the latter two, it has a particularly bitter history of conflict. Armenia is one of the oldest countries in the world, with origins dating to the first century BCE, and yet prior to 1991 it had experienced only a few years of independence from powerful empires. It was subject to conquests by Romans and Byzantine Greeks, but the most unfortunate chapter in Armenian history opened when it became part of the Ottoman Empire in the early 1500s. Muslim Ottoman rulers were particularly oppressive to their minority Armenian Christian constituents, and four hundred years of discriminatory policies culminated in the genocidal murders of an estimated 1.5 million Armenians by Ottoman Turks at the turn of the century, as part of a horrific solution to what Ottoman Turkish nation-alists called "the Armenian question."

After a scant few years of independence from Ottoman rule, Armenia was forced to become part of the Soviet Union and remained so until its dissolution in the early 1990s. The nationalist movement that eventually led to Armenia's independence began in the late 1980s over concerns about environmental degradation, political corruption, and a territorial dispute between Armenia and Azerbaijan. These issues were abruptly complicated when a disastrous earthquake in the north took 25,000 lives, completely destroying the city of Spitak and heavily damaging Gyumri and Vanadzor. Forty-three percent of Armenian territory and approximately one million people (25 percent of the population) were directly affected by the earthquake. More than 150,000 individuals were evacuated from the disaster zone to other Soviet republics and an additional 400,000 to regions of Armenia that had suffered less damage (Frelick 1994). The grimmest aspect is that the earthquake would not have caused so many deaths if Soviet architects had designed apartment and office buildings better, in light of their knowledge that Armenia is part of a broad seismic zone stretching from Turkey to the Arabian Sea. Because they did not, these ill-constructed edifices collapsed as soon as the earthquake struck, immediately crushing their inhabitants.

From September 1989 until 1994, neighboring Azerbaijan and Turkey imposed a blockade of Armenian fuel and supply lines in a dispute over Azerbaijan's claim to the Armenian territory of Nagorno-Karabakh, a decision that was particularly devastating in the wake of the 1988 earthquake. The blockade meant that most Armenians had electricity and heat for less than two hours a day for three consecutive winters until the government restored a Soviet-built nuclear power plant to fully functioning capacity to provide its citizens with these essential services. Simultaneously, the two-year war between Armenia and Azerbaijan created hundreds of thousands of Armenian and Azeri refugees and internally displaced persons in both countries (Frelick 1994).

These conditions laid the groundwork for the massive emigration that ensued when Armenia's borders were opened after independence in 1991. Approximately 10 percent of the population of four million people left the country at the peak of mass departure in 1993, and roughly 2 percent of Armenians continue to migrate every year, primarily in search of economic opportunities in relatively more affluent Russia. Although the official statistics on migration are estimated to reflect only 10 to 15 percent of the much greater number of people who leave each year without proper work authorizations, Armenian government statistics reveal that 53 percent of documented migrants go to Russia, 17 percent to Azerbaijan, 8 percent to Ukraine, and the remainder to Germany, Greece, Israel, and the United States. The Armenian Diaspora now totals nearly 5.5 million people, which is approximately one and a half times the current population of Armenia, and since

1991 a total of 25 percent of the country's Soviet-era population has emigrated (Republic of Armenia 2005).

Armenia's numerous sociopolitical and economic crises have created a situation in which it has become relatively easy for traffickers to exploit both preexisting gender inequalities and contemporary weaknesses in a destabilized social structure. Families are fragile compositions in times of prolonged national stress and conflict, and the resulting high rates of divorce have had a particularly negative impact on Armenian women who do not have specialized education or employment skills and must support their children alone.

Single women who do not have children are presented with a different set of hardships by a declining male-to-female ratio caused by male emigration, and the result is that a significant number of women will never be able to marry in a society that offers even fewer opportunities for economic self-sufficiency to women than it does to men. Soviet-era social welfare institutions such as state-sponsored daycare, universal employment, and free education, which formerly served as social safety nets, are no longer in place in an independent Armenia, and contemporary privatization initiatives have by and large ignored women.

A new Armenian criminal code that became effective in 2003 recognizes trafficking as a criminal offense defined as the use of force, fraud, or coercion to profit from the sexual exploitation of others. Trafficking in Armenia is punishable by a fine ranging from $6,900 to $11,500 (three to five hundred times the monthly minimum wage), up to one year of correctional labor, or one to four years in prison. The maximum sentence is eight years in prison, which may be imposed if the crime is committed by an organized group, makes use of life-threatening violence or the threat of it, involves a minor, or results in the death of the victim. Other important offenses related to trafficking and covered by the criminal code include abuse of office, passive and active bribery, official fraud, and official negligence.

Armenian women who have been assisted as victims of trafficking most frequently report being coerced into prostitution in Turkey and the United Arab Emirates. Occasionally, women are informed that they will be working as prostitutes but can still be considered victims of trafficking because of the exploitive nature of their treatment and the harsh working conditions they face. Victims of trafficking in Armenia tend to be in their mid-twenties and even early thirties, and a significant number of them are divorced single mothers. A reliable source on trafficking in Armenia is a report based on an IOM study establishing that there is widespread trafficking of women and children from Armenia. Fifty-nine women and children were identified and interviewed by the IOM research team, and the majority of the interviewees were recognized by the group as victims. A pimp in detention told the IOM research team that for two years, she had been transporting at least five women per week (about 500 women a year) to the United Arab Emirates. Armenian Airlines officials have reported the presence of at least two Armenian female deportees on each of the biweekly return flights to Yerevan from Dubai, which indicates that at least 200 women a year are deported from one of the main destinations for trafficking from Armenia (IOM 2001).

Bosnia-Herzegovina

Bosnia-Herzegovina (which I will follow general practice and abbreviate to "Bosnia") has long been a cultural crossroads, and it is difficult for historians and anthropologists to concisely describe a predominantly Muslim country in Eastern Europe that is also home to numerous Orthodox and Catholic churches. Bosnia's historically tenuous position on the frontiers of Europe began to take shape in the sixth century when Slavs from Poland and Ukraine migrated to the region and divided themselves into two groups with allegiances to either the Orthodox Byzantine Empire or the Catholic Holy Roman Empire, which were then the most influential powers in the region. The medieval ancestors of these two contemporary groups lived in two entities under the protection of their respective religious empires: Serbia, populated by Orthodox Christians, and Croatia, predominantly Catholic. Neither of these states would have been able to function without the support of their respective religious empires, and this put Bosnia in an unprotected position until the conquest of the region by the Muslim Ottoman Empire in the late 1300s. Regional dynamics changed forever when Bosnians converted to Islam in order to receive Ottoman protection from the powerful politico-religious groups that supported Serbia and Croatia.

The entire Western Balkan region was administered as a single Ottoman zone until the empire collapsed at the end of World War I, but Serb and Croat nationalists led numerous unsuccessful revolts and rebellions that remain the focus of contemporary nationalist rhetoric in both countries. Serb and Croat nationalist leaders agitated for independent states with the help of new and powerful actors in the region, which led to the formation of the Nazi-allied Ustashe in Croatia and independent Serb guerrilla units who called themselves Chetniks. A three-sided civil war ensued when Tito and his anti-Ustashe, anti-Chetnik soldiers known as the Partisans sought to defeat nationalism in the region and create a country free of ethnic divisions.

Tito's efforts led to the post-World War II creation of socialist Yugoslavia, a federation that included Bosnia, Croatia, Montenegro, Serbia, Slovenia, and part of Macedonia. However, Tito's death in 1980 allowed Croat and Serb opportunist politicians to employ nationalism to win popular support at least in part because of the growing economic crises faced by socialist and communist countries throughout Eastern Europe. Croatian and Serbian presidents Franjo Tudjman and Slobodan Milosević had begun to meet secretly, prior to the outbreak of violence, to discuss how they would partition Muslim Bosnia, and elections in Slovenia and Croatia soon pointed toward the national independence of both entities. It seemed clear by the early 1990s that Yugoslavia was destined for collapse, and the results of the first Bosnian multiparty elections revealed that individuals voted almost exclusively along ethnic and religious lines. All political parties that did not support a particular religious or ethnic agenda suffered total defeat.

The increased likelihood of independence meant that Bosnia found itself in an unprotected position that encouraged the escalation of tensions by Bosnian citizens of Serbian descent with the support of the Serbian state, and in September 1991, Bosnian Serb extremists formed Republika Srpska, an autonomous Serbian region within Bosnia. Extremely worried by this development, the European Union asked Bosnian authorities to hold a referendum in which all Bosnians could vote on the question of the state's independence; the vast majority of voters indicated that they supported an independent and multiethnic Bosnia.

Bosnia was internationally recognized as an independent state on April 6, 1992, the same day the Bosnian Serb nationalist leader Radovan Karadzić proclaimed that the Republika Srpska had expanded to Pale, an area located in the mountains above Sarajevo that had hosted the Winter Olympics in the 1980s. Serb paramilitary units shelled Sarajevo for three and a half years as part of a genocidal campaign to destroy the Bosnian Muslim population, and non-Serb cemeteries and places of worship throughout the former Yugoslavia were destroyed by Serb nationalist troops. Serb soldiers constructed internment camps that housed thousands of Bosnian Muslims and directly contributed to the deaths of approximately 100,000 people from a pre-war Bosnian population of just four million (Burg and Shoup 1999, 48).

Unsuccessful proposals for resolution of the conflict began to be made in Western Europe in 1992, followed by a second set in 1993 that was rejected by Bosnian Serb, Serbian, and Croatian leaders. These efforts coincided with the deployment of United Nations Protection Forces (UNPROFOR) troops who were paradoxically forbidden to engage in combat or to discharge their weapons, a fact that made them a source of ridicule by Serb paramilitary groups. The presence of these soldiers in Bosnia is widely believed to have directly contributed to an enormous increase in the number of prostitutes in cities and larger towns, many of whom were victims of trafficking both from Bosnia and from the former Soviet republics.

The Dayton Accords that formally ended the war in Bosnia were signed in mid-December of 1995 and divided Bosnia into thirteen administrative units (including the Republika Srpska), which currently find it almost impossible to cooperate with one another as a consequence of technical problems, political differences, and significant residual conflict. The United Nations International Criminal Tribunal for the former Yugoslavia (ICTY) has failed to locate or prosecute many of the war criminals who were responsible for atrocities and human rights abuses, and such individuals continue to exert influence in Bosnia, in Republika Srpska, and in neighboring Serbia. Government corruption is rampant and regularly undermines the ability of NGOs and international organizations to implement counter-trafficking and other social justice projects. "The politicians are not running the state," one Bosnian man explained to me before rhetorically asking, "so who do you think is really in charge?"

Bosnia has no specific laws that forbid trafficking, although a number of articles in its criminal code have been successfully used to prosecute the crime. The transportation of foreign women to Bosnia for the purposes of sexual exploitation may be addressed by articles on smuggling of human beings, organized crime, document forgery, or pimping in relation to fraud. All of these have been used to bring criminal charges against Bosnian citizens and foreign nationals for the traffic in women, and yet legislative counter-trafficking measures often exclude women who are coerced into prostitution without leaving their country of citizenship.

The Bosnian Council of Ministers is currently in the process of adopting a set of standards referred to as a "draft decision," which notably does not constitute legislation, to deal with Bosnian victims of trafficking. The most significant aspect of government discussions on this set of standards is that they have consistently contradicted the experiences of NGOs that work directly with prostitutes and Bosnian victims of trafficking, as the government continues to insist that there are not enough domestic cases to necessitate the passage of a separate law. The intention of the draft decision, then, was not to create legislation but rather to set standards for the protection of Bosnian women who are coerced into prostitution in their own country. The draft decision explicitly states that all organizations and institutions in Bosnia are required to exchange information in order to protect and assist victims of trafficking and must make use of standardized victim identification procedures. Further, measures for the protection of both victims and witnesses include legal assistance, education, medical treatment for addiction, and additional procedures specific to children. The draft decision acknowledges that education and sensitization of the general public are necessary to prevent the problem, and it recommends the inspection of businesses that could be used as fronts for trafficking rings, such as hotels and modeling, marriage, and travel agencies.

Numerous logistic and infrastructural factors complicate counter-trafficking efforts and law enforcement in Bosnia, but the most significant is the division of the country into three parts based on the underlying premise of the Dayton Accords that separation between Bosnian Muslims and Bosnian ethnic Serbs was essential to the sustainability of peace in the region. These parts are the Federation of Bosnia-Herzegovina (Bosnia), Republika Srpska, and the District of Brčko. The Federation of Bosnia-Herzegovina (Bosnia) is further subdivided into ten "cantons," each with its own Ministry of Interior, which means that there are a total of thirteen such ministries for a population of just under four million people. Each canton is governed by separate administrative and police bodies, and cooperation between cantons is discouraged by differences in investigative procedures and systems.

The United Nations International Police Task Force (IPTF) was the primary law enforcement body in Bosnia between 1999 and 2002, when it ceased operation and transferred its authority to the local police. This transfer was facilitated by training provided by the European Union Police Mission, which has far fewer officers than the IPTF did and is thus not able to organize or conduct raids in the bars and other locales where victims of trafficking are likely to be found. On paper, the post-IPTF period has resulted in a significant reduction in the number of trafficking cases, but this decrease simply reflects the cessation of police raids on brothels because of a lack of resources and personnel following the departure of the IPTF. These cutbacks mean that the vast majority of women who are held against their will in such locations now remain undetected and thus cannot be assisted.

Organized criminal groups have used these postwar divisions and gaps in legislation and law enforcement capacity to their advantage in order to obtain travel documents, residence and work permits, visas, and adoption documents that can be used to mask the traffic in women and girls. Widespread corruption and the low salaries of border police make it very difficult to ensure the security of land borders with Albania, Croatia, and Serbia, but travelers who enter Bosnia by air also may not be adequately screened or documented. When I entered the country through the Sarajevo airport, for example, my passport was only cursorily examined by the immigration officer and was not stamped with my date of entry or with any other indication that I had been in Bosnia. This is significant because it reveals how simple it is for a young woman to enter Bosnia through formal channels with no documentation of her arrival and testifies to the ease with which women can be trafficked into the country.

The majority of women who have been assisted as victims of trafficking by IOM and its partner NGOs in Bosnia have come from the former Soviet republics of Moldova, Romania, and Ukraine, with a smaller number from Russia and the former Yugoslav states of Serbia and Montenegro. Victims tend to be quite young, compared with those in Armenia, and average between eighteen and twenty-four years of age, with 10 percent of all victims being under the age of eighteen. Many women report having been sold several times both in Bosnia and between different Balkan countries, and many had lived in Bosnia in a situation of forced sexual servitude for more than two years. There has been a general decrease in the education levels of assisted women in the past few years, because members of the generation who grew up after the end of the Yugoslav and Soviet periods of free university education are now in their twenties.

Bosnia's porous borders encourage its use as a transit point from countries further east to destinations in the European Union, especially Greece and Italy. Italian police have recorded statements from Nigerian women who were forced into sex work in private apartments in Sarajevo and later transported to Italy to work as street prostitutes. As a completely borderless space, the Internet is also a venue for the sexual exploitation of victims of trafficking in Bosnia (and elsewhere) who have reported being held captive in private homes to perform for the streaming video that can be paid for online and easily located anywhere in the world through an Internet search. The anonymity of the Internet makes the discovery and prosecution of such activities nearly impossible and clearly demonstrates how traffickers have seized upon the growth of technology to adopt increasingly sophisticated methods.

India

India has not suffered the same types of traumas that have wreaked havoc in Eastern Europe in the past two decades, but the legacy of its former British colonial status endures in the form of a large bureaucracy that is ill-equipped to address the needs of a large population of rural and urban poor. Indian history predates its encounter with European imperialism by thousands of years, and prior to colonization the country was ruled by independent and regional kingdoms that the British manipulated to their advantage by engaging in the politics of divide and rule. India became a unified state in the Western European sense in the mid-nineteenth century and suffered from the extremely unfair trade arrangements through which the British profited singularly (and enormously) from South Asian raw materials such as cotton and tea. The Indian independence movement is famous for its Gandhian strategies of passive resistance, and in 1947 the country became a self-governing state with seventeen official languages and countless cultures and regional dialects that many Indians half-jokingly insist change every five miles.

India's first prime minister, Jawaharlal Nehru, placed a heavy emphasis on the development of Indian industries, especially in the fields of science and engineering, and his daughter, Prime Minister Indira Gandhi, became a strong ally of Soviet socialism prior to her assassination in 1984. Her son, Prime Minister Rajiv Gandhi, prompted a major shift following his election in 1984 by strengthening ties with the United States and taking steps toward the establishment of a free-market economy. Rajiv Gandhi's legacy of economic reform ensured that the Indian economy was more or less open to foreign investment by 1991, when structural adjustment policies were implemented by the International Monetary Fund (IMF) in response to India's balance-of-payments crisis. India is by no means unique in that such policies dramatically increased the divisions between social classes.

Structural adjustment programs have been introduced in over seventy countries around the world, which have incurred significant debt to the International Monetary Fund. The IMF was formed in 1944 to establish a framework for economic cooperation and development, and it provides policy advice, technical assistance, and short-term loans to remedy balance-of-payments crises. Structural adjustment consists of two phases, both of which are aimed at reducing account deficits: short-term macroeconomic stabilization and the implementation of structural reforms deemed necessary by the IMF. In India these reforms included devaluation of the national currency by 23 percent, introduction of a new industrial policy more conducive to foreign investment, government disinvestment in potentially profitable public sector areas, the closure of unproductive public sector units, the introduction of private banks, a liberalized import/export policy, cuts in social welfare spending, and legal amendments to support all of these reforms. These policies deeply disadvantaged the poor, most notably in the closure of cloth mills and other sources of employment that the IMF deemed unproductive state ventures.

Following a pattern exhibited in most countries that have undergone structural adjustment, the poor were also victimized by deteriorating public health care and a general government shift away from social services. Those who have benefited the most from structural adjustment are corporate investors who have ties to multinational corporations involved in foreign direct investment; many of them are from the same powerful families who profited from the economic restructuring that occurred following independence in 1947. Despite its status as the world's largest democracy, India has a number of social problems, many of which stem from endemic poverty, extreme social stratification, and the fact that most citizens of the country live at a subsistence level. Easily preventable diseases and conditions are still major causes of death, a large percentage of the population does not have access to health care, and diarrhea-related dehydration remains a significant killer of children.

Structural adjustment policies have only exacerbated such problems by deepening the divisions between social classes. Neoliberal trade policies have made it possible for a wealthy woman to buy a $1,000 purse at the Louis Vuitton boutique in Bombay, but following her purchase of such a luxurious item, she is quite likely to encounter a person debilitated by malnutrition begging on the street outside. These socioeconomic inequalities have had a disproportionately negative impact on women because of the almost universal desire for sons throughout India. The widespread practice of dowry, in which a substantial amount of money is given to the family into which a daughter marries, contributes to this preference for sons in the same way as the cultural norm that male offspring support their parents in old age. The expression "a daughter is a guest in the house" is found in many Indian languages. It refers to the cultural practice in most Indian communities that encourages a newly married woman to live with the family of her new husband. The structural marginality implicit in this move underscores how some girls and women find themselves at a distinct gender disadvantage, which, of course, is further amplified by the effects of poverty.

The Constitution of India prohibits trafficking in persons and forced labor and is complemented by the Immoral Traffic (Prevention) Act (PITA), which deals more explicitly with the traffic in women. PITA specifies punishments for pimping, forcible detention in a brothel, allowing premises to be used as a brothel, and living on the earnings of prostitution. Prostitution is illegal in India but remains largely tolerated by the police and the government, although frequent police raids on brothels do remand a significant number of underage girls into government care. The majority of the traffic in women occurs within India's borders, but a substantial number of girls and women from Nepal are coerced into prostitution in India every year, and a lesser number are pushed into sex work following their migration as housemaids and nannies to the affluent Gulf States. Victims of trafficking who have been assisted by IOM and NGOs in India commonly report being pressured to sell sex by someone they know, including family members, or being sold to a brothel owner through false marriage. As is the case in Armenia and Bosnia, women report that both genders are equally engaged in the recruitment and exploitation of victims of trafficking.

Indian and Nepali victims of trafficking are often very young, with approximately one-third below the age of sixteen and more than half under eighteen. The growing incidence of HIV in South Asia greatly influences the types of women whom prostitute users seek out, because the popular perception is that younger sex workers are likely to have had fewer sexual partners than older women. While this may be true, the medical reality is that because the bodies of minor girls are often unable to produce adequate lubrication for sex, so their delicate vaginal tissues are much more likely to tear and allow the introduction of HIV directly into the bloodstream. Cultural constructions of fair skin as beautiful and exotic encourage the traffic in light-skinned girls and young women from rural Nepal to urban brothels in Bombay, Calcutta, and Delhi. This preference has also resulted in a less common but more lucrative trade in women from post-Soviet states such as Russia and Ukraine to more clandestine houses of prostitution frequented by higher-status men in the same cities and in the tourism-centered state of Goa.

IMPORTANT QUESTIONS AND CLARIFICATIONS

This book presents an introduction to the traffic in women and raises important questions about contemporary responses to, and definitions of, the problem at the international and local levels. No other universal social issue has prompted such a sensationalized response, and many discussions of it employ hyperbolic language such as *sex slave* and *human commodity*, which may be accurate in description but are also diminishing in their effect. After all, it is difficult to think of ways to solve a problem that is characterized by perhaps the only case of linguistic similarities between (some) feminist discourse and certain niche genres of pornography. What should be a fundamental debate about migration and human rights is obscured by such language and by the gendered principles that underlie it, so a few points of clarification are necessary to dispel popular misconceptions about a very real and pressing phenomenon that occurs every day, all over the world.

The lives of women who have been assisted by the employees of the numerous international organizations, governments, NGOs, and shelters I spoke to as part of research for this book are characterized by a number of trends that contradict many popular perceptions of sex trafficking. For example, it is often believed that traffickers are male, and yet all of the women I spoke to or was told about reported that they had been forced into prostitution by people of both genders in equal numbers. It is clear that although the traffic in women has deep roots in gender inequality and sexism, it is not a crime committed exclusively by men, as some depictions of the problem would have us believe. My research also revealed that many women who leave situations of forced prostitution can do so because of sympathetic male clients who want to help them, and sometimes even marry them, which underscores how trafficking is not a simple case of the male oppression of women. Equally important is recognition that the problem is not caused by some sort of global conspiracy by organized crime to kidnap women from their homes and lock them in brothels. Indeed, the sad fact is that there is no shortage of women who do not have the economic or social resources to refuse an abusive or unhealthy situation even when it is in their best interests to do so. This is why many cases of trafficking are committed by people who are known to the victim and whose exploitation follows patterns at work in the abuse of trust that characterizes most forms of violence against women, particularly sexual assault and domestic violence.

The question remains: Why is the traffic in women a universal phenomenon that has proved intractable despite numerous efforts to end it? It has long been known that sexual exploitation follows a path that begins in situations of poverty, desperation, and the limited or nonexistent life choices created by war, socioeconomic collapse, and endemic inequality. Above all, however, the traffic in women presents a compelling case of a single social issue present in every country in the world and exposes points of tension surrounding gender, power, and the role of institutions in individual lives.

Methodology and Background on the International Organization for Migration

Conducting research for this book was the most difficult thing I have ever done. Nothing raises deeper questions about the inequalities inherent in the human condition than prostitution and trafficking, and my experiences educating others about them, both in and outside the classroom, have taught me that concerns about the kinds of violence that both practices inflict on humanity transcend gender, race, and social class. My experiences as a researcher over several years of ethnographic work in Armenia, Bosnia, and India taught me more than I ever could have imagined about the human capacity to hurt and the capacity of individuals to survive the violence of war, poverty, and social injustice.

I am forever indebted to the people who opened their hearts and their workplaces to me with no expectations and very few questions about the final form this book would take. It would have been far too easy to write a singularly negative critique of the institutional responses to the traffic in women that I found in all three countries, but it also would have been irresponsible to do so after having witnessed firsthand the difficulties encountered by some extremely dedicated individuals who engage in counter-trafficking efforts. I have tried my best to accurately document the struggles faced by workers at international and nongovernmental organizations in their efforts to assist victims of trafficking, but it is my sincerest wish also to offer them recommendations about possibilities for improvement. A disturbingly large literature documents the inability of international organizations (particularly the United Nations) to reach their admirable goals of a more peaceful and stable world, and I do not want my book to join their ranks. I have a deep and abiding respect for the work of the International Organization for Migration, and this book was not written to malign its inspiring efforts to make the world a better place for the most marginalized and invisible communities.

A Personal Journey

The research for this book forced me to undergo a deeply personal journey that almost immediately assumed the form of a pilgrimage that frightened me in its emotional intensity. Work for this book coincided with major changes in my own life and socioeconomic status—changes that were impossible for me to separate from my examinations of the lives of poor women and from efforts by relatively privileged individuals to assist them. I spent most of my early life in poor rural communities in West Virginia and parts of New York called "the rust belt" because of the regional economic devastation that followed the closure of factories as corporations sought out cheaper labor in the global South. I deeply identify with women throughout the world who have been pushed into the sex industry because of poverty and a dearth of other choices. I worry that to hide behind my PhD and my credentials (however modest they may be) as a feminist anthropologist would obscure the unique set of life experiences that helped me more than any amount of education or work experience ever could have in researching and writing this book. My own life has made me understand how poverty and violence shape women's lives and self-perceptions, and this is why I felt I should add my voice to the burgeoning literature on the traffic in women.

Self-Perceptions of the Stigmatized

Attempts to compare erotic labor across cultures are dangerous in that they threaten to obscure the distinct sociocultural context that frames them. I was especially conscious of this fact throughout the portions of my research that brought me into direct contact with women in their workplaces, including the time I spent at Heera, an erotic dancing bar in Bombay, India. In their conversations with me, women at Heera were quick to distinguish themselves from prostitutes, and women throughout the world who perform erotic dances for money expressed just such a sentiment. The belief that dancers are nothing more than glorified prostitutes exists in the United States as well, and my research at a topless dancing establishment in New York revealed that female performers were quite conscious of this perception and actively fought against it. All of my interviews with dancers in the United States included at least one completely unsolicited reference to prostitution, usually some variation of, "I'm not a whore." That so many women felt the need to clarify this point, despite my continued insistence that they were skilled performers, speaks volumes about the power society has to influence self-perception among stigmatized groups.

When I asked US dancers why they felt it was so important to make such a clear distinction between the two forms of erotic labor, they insisted that doing so was of critical importance. "There are some lines that once you cross them," one nineteen-year-old performer said in a serious tone, "you can't go back." This statement underscores how dancers themselves employ broader social constructs about gender and appropriate female sexual behavior in their understandings of life and work, especially in reference to the hierarchy of descriptions performers use in reference to themselves. *Exotic dancer*, for example, has an entirely different meaning to women who self-identify with this term than the behaviors and traits they ascribe to the morally loaded word *whore*, which dancers frequently apply to distinguish themselves from women who actually sell sex, rather than its simulation onstage.

Unlike at establishments in the United States, women who dance at Heera are not considered what most strip clubs call "independent contractors," a term that means they are individually responsible for earning their entire salary from tips solicited from male customers. Dancers at Heera perform in groups of at least ten women, and the money given by men is distributed evenly among them at the end of the night—a strategy designed to discourage competition among the dancers. However, my initial impressions of a work environment far superior to most comparable establishments in the United States were quickly dispelled by dancers who explained that although they helped each other, there was no sense of sisterhood at Heera. Dancers privately explained how they resented having to receive all of their income from collections of tips divided evenly at the end of the night and complained that the system would be much more equitable if they were able to take money directly from male patrons. Conversely, US dancers were vociferous in their condemnation of the prevailing system in which women are entirely responsible for earning their income from tips (and sometimes have to pay for the right to perform as well, an exploitive labor practice called a "stage fee").

What did remain constant in my conversations with women in three very different cultural areas, however, was women's insistence that their decision to engage in any form of sex work was part of a temporary strategy designed to improve their lives. Very few women used the language of victimization so often found in books on the subject, although it is equally important to note that almost none of them expressed a sense of pride in their socially stigmatized occupations. My confusion about this seemingly contradictory set of beliefs—the different ways in which sex workers themselves and those who write about their lives regard sex work and the traffic in women held by sex workers—led me to a rather unusual field site that enabled me to examine how these contradictions affect both policy formation and the lives of women who engage in the sale of sex for money.

The International Organization for Migration

My ethnographic fieldwork on international responses to sex trafficking was conducted in my capacity as an unpaid Consultant on Gender and Counter-Trafficking to the International Organization for Migration in Yerevan, Armenia (2004) and Sarajevo, Bosnia (2007), where I spent several months as an active participant and full-time voluntary worker on each office's counter-trafficking activities. Research for the chapter on India was carried out in tandem with my work on gender and structural adjustment over eighteen months between 2001 and 2003 and on gendered violence in 2004. These three countries were chosen for their unique socioeconomic circumstances as a means to document responses to the trade in women in three very different contexts: Armenia remains a post-Soviet power vacuum with a weak civil society; Bosnia is a country still recovering from the effects of war and geno-cide; and India is home to the world's largest democracy, a vibrant NGO culture, and endemic poverty that is not at all comparable to the challenges faced in Eastern Europe.

Many international organizations materialized from the chaos of World War II and were thus dedicated to the goal of a more peaceful and stable world. IOM was created in 1951 as an agency to assist European governments in the monumental task of resettling millions of refugees who had been displaced by conflict. It remains the sole international organization dedicated specifically to serving the needs of migrants and displaced persons throughout the world, and it has assisted in numerous late-twentieth-century humanitarian crises of displacement, including 1956 Hungary, 1968 Czechoslovakia, 1973 Chile, 1975 Vietnam, 1990 Kuwait, and 1999 Kosovo and Timor, as well as the crises caused by natural disasters in 2004–2005 in South Asia.

IOM has 118 member states with 5,400 staff members in over 100 countries and divides itself into four main fields as part of a comprehensive approach that recognizes that globalization has resulted in the unprecedented flow of humans and capital across borders. IOM understands that it is impossible to address just one facet of the numerous complex processes involved in different types of migration, so it also deals with issues related to economic development, the facilitation and regulation of migration, and solutions to forced migration. IOM is organized around the central belief that "humane and orderly migration benefits migrants and society," and in keeping with this holistic approach to migration, IOM approaches the traffic in women by carrying out information campaigns, conducting research, facilitating the safe return and reintegration of victims, and strengthening the capabilities of governments to combat trafficking through legislative and technical reform.

IOM is situated at the center of debates and controversies on trafficking because of its focus on migration, and it serves as a dynamic single location from which to examine and interact with victims of trafficking, bureaucrats, policymakers, NGOs, and activists alike. IOM is a particularly interesting field site because of the numerous and often insurmountable hurdles its staff members face in dealing with victims of trafficking. These include low overall resources, frustration with limited impact, problems in interacting with socially stigmatized groups, and the burden of determining the "eligibility" of women for assistance programs. This is further complicated by the gravity of the life-changing (and, indeed, potentially life-destroying) decisions that staff members must make for women as part of the sometimes conflicting set of obligations they face, while simultaneously trying to assist victims, cooperate with governments and law enforcement officers, and work within legal and financial restrictions. One IOM Armenia staff member described the difficulties inherent in the job as follows: "You have to think like a cop and act like a humanitarian, all in your second language," a statement that exposes just one of the numerous paradoxes arising from the dominance of international organizations in Eastern Europe by Western European interests, languages, and staff members in high positions.

The "Global and the Local"

The reports of international organizations, governments, activists, and scholars on sex trafficking often begin with a somewhat apologetic note about how difficult it is to obtain accurate statistics on a clandestine phenomenon that is vastly underreported and rarely prosecuted. The hundreds of reports I have read from international organizations, governments, and NGOs cite, without mentioning their sources, such wildly variant statistics on the traffic in women that decided to leave out such estimates for the simple reason that there is no consensus on the numbers of victims. The underground nature of the crime is compounded by the variations in definitions and the difficulties inherent in separating it from prostitution.

No matter how many international experts and activists I asked, no one was ever able to clearly separate the categories of "prostitute" and "victim of trafficking" for me beyond some vague description that always involved the adjectives *force*, *fraud*, and *coercion*, which will be discussed later in reference to the Palermo Protocol. It is almost universally accepted that figures for domestic violence and sexual assault reflect only a fraction of the number of actual cases because of the shame and stigma associated with reporting such crimes. And because this book is not a policy document or an application for donor aid, I see no real need to add my own conjectures to the voluminous statistics on the traffic in women, which range from the US Department of State estimate that 1.5 million women are victimized each year to the insistence of some governments that the problem does not exist at all.

There were many moments throughout the course of this research when I wondered how any sort of progress could be made toward ending a problem that is both universal and highly localized. This striking degree of overlap between what anthropologists sometimes call "the global and the local" is evident in the fact that most countries in the world now fit all three of the categories of origin, transit, and destination for victims of trafficking. Although the assignment of various countries to these categories earlier in this chapter is relatively accurate, it would be irresponsible to suggest that sex workers from affluent nations in North America and Western Europe cannot be found in Asia or the Middle East, or to ignore that such migration also occurs within countries classified in one of the three categories.

Labor migration is a phenomenon as complicated as the human lives it shapes, and yet the most consistent impetus in all decisions to move to another country in search of work is the individual's desire for a better future. All cultures in the world place a strong emphasis on providing for one's children and attempting to improve one's position in society; how this is done varies from place to place, but this such local differences are almost secondary to the universal impulse underlying such individual hopes and dreams. What is similarly self-evident is that migration affects all of us and is thus a focus of extremely contentious debates at both the personal and the policy level.

As I sat listening, I often felt a deep sense of concern that debates among representatives of international organizations, governments, and NGOs, many of which led to policy formation, were taking place in a vacuum, far from the realities of the lives of women who would be most affected by their outcomes. I sometimes wondered whether it was unethical to write a book that criticized the efforts being made to end the traffic in women at the policy level, as I considered the possibility that perhaps any amount of attention given to the problem could be a positive step toward ending it.

Yet the longer I listened and the more I learned about the political motivations that underlie many counter-trafficking initiatives and about the lack of clarity at the policy level regarding what circumstances constitute coercion into sexual exploitation, the more I felt a deep sense of betrayal both as a human being and as a feminist. When these policy debates went on for hours, I would often find myself distracted as I recalled stories I had been told by semi-nude bar dancers about the insurmountable debt, violence, and abuse that informed nearly all of their decisions. I sometimes sat in meetings silently remembering the fourteen-year-old single mothers I had lived next-door to in West Virginia, who were forced to make the impossible choice between living alone with their young children in absolute poverty and living in slightly less marginal circumstances with an abusive and often much older man. Where were they, I wondered, when these decisions were being made about the realities of their lives?

2

From "White Slavery" to National Security

Historians are in agreement that what was known in the nineteenth and early twentieth centuries as "the white slave trade" was the product of mass hysteria regarding immigration and what was then an unprecedented mobility of poor white women in search of employment in Western European (Walkowitz 1996; 1980) and American (Donovan 2006) cities. Discourses of gender and power are inseparable from both governmental and popular cultural responses to sex trafficking, because the trade in women's bodies has often been used as a cultural symbol for a changing world with social norms in a state of flux. This is due at least in part to the fact that female sexuality constitutes a point of tension in every culture because of the complex associations of women with motherhood, morality, and the family.

The first international response to the early-twentieth-century socioeconomic changes that were perceived to be conducive to what is today known as sex trafficking was titled "The International Agreement for the Suppression of the White Slave Traffic" and was signed in 1904 by fifteen Western European powers, many of whom tellingly reserved the right to apply it in their colonies on a case-by-case basis. Although the extremely problematic category of "white" was removed from subsequent international conventions and protocols in 1921, 1933, 1950, and 2000, the majority of donor and media attention paid to sex trafficking has continued until relatively recently to be focused on countries where the victims are white—specifically, countries of post-communist and post-socialist Eastern Europe. The reasons for this extend far beyond simple racism, and the Chief of Mission at IOM Sarajevo was quick to point out that the Eurocentric nature of most funding initiatives has much more to do with the fact that powerful nations and organizations in the West "tend to more immediately target the countries of origin which come on their soil."

Sex trafficking first became a topic of popular interest in the United States at the turn of the century when the urban anonymity and sense of rapid social

change created by the massive growth of technologies, information generation, and cities was especially conducive to the creation of moral panics.
Chicago prosecutor and founding member of the American Bureau of Moral
Education Clifford Roe, whose work has been extensively documented by historian Brian Donovan, authored half a dozen texts on the subject, with titles
ranging from the ominous *The Girl Who Disappeared* (1914) to the quasi-
militant *The Great War on White Slavery* (1915). Roe's language was indicative of the kind of entrenched racism that informed turn-of-the-century
thought about sex trafficking. "The white slave of Chicago is a slave as much
as the Negro was before the Civil War," he wrote in *Panders and Their White
Slaves* (1910, 26), and, he added, "that is the condition of hundreds, yes, of
thousands, of white girls in Chicago at present." Roe draws a very clear distinction in this statement between enslaved African Americans of the pre-
Emancipation American South and the "white slaves" of the urban Midwest,
which suggests that he believed the women's race should prove a point of particular moral outrage to his readers.

These references to slavery in the antebellum American South continue to
be employed in counter-trafficking discourse used by activists and members of
Congress alike. Representative Cynthia McKinney of Georgia began a hearing
before the House Subcommittee on International Relations regarding the
alleged involvement of UN peacekeepers in the traffic in women in Bosnia by
asking, "Who would have thought that in the year 2002, almost 200 years
after Denmark became the first of the world's nations to outlaw slavery, we
would still be here fighting the hideous practice of buying, selling and trafficking human beings?" (US Congress 2002, 6). She immediately went on to add
that "probably no one group in this country [better] understands the horror
and cruelty involved in these practices than the grandsons and granddaughters
of African slaves" (2002, 6). McKinney's use of the slavery trope in reference
to Bosnia is exceptionally notable in that almost nothing of substance in the
past fifteen years of the congressional record has explicitly addressed the traffic in African women in the same ways in which women from Eastern Europe,
and to some extent Southeast Asia, have been discussed.

Representative Christopher Smith of New Jersey extended the analogy
of sex trafficking as a form of slavery by graphically relating to Congress
the conditions described to him by a prominent American anti-trafficking
activist:

> ...the deprivations of food, the beatings with electrical wires, metal rods
> and leather straps, the cigarette burns, and the brutal rapes are conducted
> in the hidden rooms and upper floors where, if you can get to them, you
> can find women and children locked in literal cages (US Congress 2002,
> 10).

This sort of language almost identically mirrors the moral panic surrounding the "white slavery" trope, which revolved around a number of themes that Doezema (2000, 24) describes as "innocence, established as youth and sexual purity, helplessness, degradation and death." The mobilization of moral crusaders such as Roe in the nineteenth and early twentieth centuries are indeed far removed from the somewhat more racially inclusive approaches taken by international organizations today, and yet they are important because they present a fascinating parallel to the contemporary debates on sex trafficking. A comparison between the two demonstrates why definitions are so contentious and just how much they reveal about the social and historical context in which they are conceived.

As Doezema has documented in her discussion of similarities between language used to describe "white slavery" and current abolitionist rhetoric on prostitution and sex trafficking, these two points in history have both been marked by disagreements about definitions of victimization, have occurred in periods of increased female migration for work in times of economic crisis, prompted a response that increased state control over poor women's freedom of movement, rely on sensationalism to advance their claims, distinguish "innocent" victims of trafficking from "ordinary" prostitutes, and are characterized by xenophobia and a fear of mysterious "foreign criminal gangs" (usually characterized as Asian or Russian) that take advantage of "naïve" women in periods of increased economic stress (Doezema 2000, 24–38). All of these depictions draw on established and unfortunately enduring stereotypes about race, nationality, and gender in the predominantly white, affluent nations of the European Union and the United States, but they are certainly not limited to these regions. Dekić (2003), for example, has noted how the Serbian media consistently characterize traffickers as ethnic Albanians, thus engaging in a process of ethnic othering that scapegoats a regionally maligned Balkan group as responsible for the traffic in women.

COUNTER-TRAFFICKING DISCOURSE AND IDIOMS

Counter-trafficking discourses cannot be separated from their cultural and historical context regardless of whether they use the term *white slavery* or *sex trafficking*. And just as "white slavery" cannot be discussed in any depth without reference to concerns about female mobility and migration, current counter-trafficking policies enacted and advocated by international, national, and activist organizations are inseparable from concerns about borders and national security. The comparison of "white slave crusades" to contemporary counter-trafficking efforts highlights how much definitions of the trade in women (and the institutions and organizations that advance those definitions) reveal about the context in which they are framed.

Sharma positions the counter-trafficking rhetoric adopted by governments and international organizations as a conspiracy to limit migration through protectionist policies that not only "view women solely as victims forced or duped into migrating for the sole benefit of the predatory trafficker" (2005, 90), but also seek to limit the number of unwanted migrants through heightened border security. Kempadoo concurs by arguing that the current UN counter-trafficking framework, which is discussed below, "supports the neoliberal economic interests of corporations, multilateral aid agencies, policy experts, and national governments" (2005, 36) rather than women who are pushed into selling sex as a survival strategy. Such contemporary critiques are strikingly similar to more critical historical analyses of "white slavery," and although it is not particularly useful to extend the scope of the discussion on parallels between the two historical periods, it is important to note that current approaches to, and perceptions of, trafficking are not as novel as some authors and activists claim.

Much of the contemporary work published on the traffic in women is unfortunately not all that different from books written during the "white slavery" panics of Roe's generation in its use of unsubstantiated statistics and highly emotional language that sometimes blurs the focus of the debate. This is particularly worrying given the relatively low stature of Women's Studies vis-à-vis other academic disciplines and, of course, the persistent cross-cultural marginalization of women. It is indeed very difficult to gather reliable statistics on a clandestine phenomenon perpetrated by individuals ranging from members of organized criminal groups to desperate family members. It may even be nearly impossible to ascertain the actual numbers of women who are forced into prostitution each year. This difficulty arises both from the underground nature of the problem and from the varying definitions of what constitutes victimization, as is discussed later in this chapter.

The research for this book was designed after careful consideration of the gaps in existing literature and with extreme wariness of what Ortega (2006) calls "loving, knowing ignorance" in reference to the propensity of white middle-class feminists to "speak for" less-privileged women. Sociologist Ronald Weitzer's alarming article, "Flawed Theory and Method in Studies of Prostitution" (2005) analyzes texts ranging from book-length works to short articles posted online and concludes that "few of radical feminism's claims about prostitution are amenable to verification or falsification. . . . How would one ever test the platitudes that customers are predators, that prostitution is paid rape" (2005, 936). Anthropologist Gayle Rubin (1993) has also discussed the tendency of feminist activist literature on the sex industry as a whole to make use of sensational examples and unsubstantiated statistics. It is crucial to conduct research that is both feminist and activist in nature, but to abandon the principles of social science and the need for empirical evidence to support one's claims not only is inexcusable but also serves to undermine and further marginalize Women's Studies as a discipline and, by extension, women's interests.

It is not surprising that popular cultural discourse that addresses the trade in women is not much better than, or much different from, some of the other work available on the subject by academics or policymakers. Increased contemporary awareness about sex trafficking has spawned an entire literature in popular culture that ranges from the salacious to the bizarre and often revolves around the experiences (both real and imagined) of white women. This trend is certainly not without historical precedent, but it reemerged with particular force following the dissolution of the Soviet Union and the subsequent socio-economic changes that overwhelmed Eastern Europe and Central Asia.

Popular discourse surrounding sex trafficking from the countries of the former Soviet bloc often seems to follow a single plot line: An innocent young woman eager to escape grinding poverty answers a job advertisement in a newspaper, only to become trapped in a vicious cycle of sexual exploitation. Popular literature on the topic underscores this depiction of victims of trafficking as helpless women devoid of human agency and thus in desperate need of rescue. One text written for popular consumption (*The Natashas: Inside the New Global Sex Trade*) wholly embraces the rhetoric of the helpless woman victimized by circumstance with characteristically patronizing language bemoaning that "despite the barrage of warnings on radio and TV, in newspapers and on billboards, desperate women continue to line up with their naïveté and applications in hand, hoping that, this time, they might just be in luck . . . [and get] a chance at a new start (Malarek 2004, 26).

This genre of popular literature closely mirrors a cultural fixation with the plight of victims of trafficking who are, as this passage illustrates, "naïve," "desperate," and hoping for "a chance at a new start." Some work in this category capitalizes on these gender stereotypes to embrace quasi-pornographic typologies of power and domination that often contain subnarratives of economic and national exploitation by beginning with a tale of innocence wrenched from a bucolic Eastern European life. With a title that could easily belong to Clifford Roe's generation, the titillating *Commodity Trading: A Story of the White Slave Trade* (Mainor 1999) exemplifies this type of writing. The first page opens with the idyllic: "spring always took my village by surprise . . . for then we knew that the days of fruit tree blossoms were not far away" (1999, 1) but rapidly shifts to a sadistic tone just pages later when the young female protagonist is "utterly alone, captive and naked in total darkness"

(1999, 7). Such popular literature may quickly be dismissed as pulp fiction not worthy of comment, and yet the similarities to contemporary discourses in all fields that address the traffic in women, as well as similarities to the language that characterized turn-of-the-century moral panics about "white slavery," are unmistakable.

Discussions of trafficking have even found their way into science fiction in the form of a series of captivity narratives that evince a sense of alienation from the state and depict life in a liminal space, namely the US–Mexico border. The same themes of women's bodies pushed into dangerous and marginal spaces against their wills are employed in this category of writing, though in an extreme form that almost parodies some discussions of sex trafficking. One such book, titled *Slave Trade: Abducted by Aliens, Forced into Bondage!* (2003) narrates the journey of the captive protagonist as she is "bound for the far reaches of space and compelled to cater to the depraved desires of her new alien masters" (Wright 2003, 35). It is particularly revealing that the author's use of borders, "aliens," and sexual exploitation all reflect the same kinds of anxieties about migration that underlie much of the policy debates on the traffic in women.

Sex trafficking has definitely developed its own idiom that describes a sometimes very literal sense of alienation in a world in which rapid socioeconomic changes, ranging from the fall of the Berlin Wall to the implementation of structural adjustment policies, have resulted in dramatic alterations to everyday life. In the process of making sense of these changes, who "counts" as a victim continues to be construed as a matter of class and geography, with some groups distinguished as "more" violated than others. Indeed, the increased amount of concern demonstrated by wealthier and more powerful nations about the predominantly white countries of Eastern Europe, which has driven major donor efforts in the post-communist/post-socialist period, has a great deal to do with concerns about border security, organized crime, and, above all, unwanted migrants.

INTERNATIONAL EFFORTS AND PROTOCOLS

Renewed concern on the part of governments, international organizations, and activist groups on the subject of the traffic in women began to take shape in the mid-1980s (Chew 2005), a period also marked by the inception of a number of global changes, such as the implementation of economically devastating structural adjustment programs in countries indebted to the International Monetary Fund, the collapse of the Soviet Union, and policy discussions about policing the external borders of the European Union. As the conditions of dire economic crisis that inevitably encourage labor migration were being created in Asia and Eastern Europe, governments of the more powerful nations of Western Europe and North America sought to tighten their borders against unwanted outsiders. There has been an enormous amount of institutional and organizational attention directed toward trafficking in the past two decades, and the following discussion will illustrate that there is no shortage of international agreements, laws, and activist energy devoted to the subject. The question remains, however, whether any of them are actually able to assist the impoverished women who suffer the most from the crimes these policy documents are designed to prevent.

Palermo Protocol

The most important international declaration of the world's commitment to address trafficking in persons of either gender for the purposes of labor or sexual exploitation is the Palermo Protocol of 2000, the full title of which is the United Nations Protocol to Prevent, Suppress and Punish Trafficking in Persons, Especially Women and Children, Supplementing the United Nations Convention Against Transnational Organized Crime. The Palermo Protocol holds that

> Trafficking in human beings shall mean the recruitment, transportation, transfer, harboring or receipt of persons, by means of threat or use of force or other forms of coercion, of abduction, of fraud, of deception, of the abuse of power or of a position of vulnerability, of the giving or receiving of payments or benefits to achieve the consent of a person or of having control over another person for the purpose of exploitation. Exploitation shall include, at a minimum, the exploitation of the prostitution of others or other forms of sexual exploitation, forced labor or services, slavery or practices similar to slavery, servitude or the removal of organs (United Nations 2000).

The Palermo Protocol is especially significant because it is the first globally binding instrument to explicitly and comprehensively address the traffic in women. Its uniqueness in this respect resulted in its use as the basis of national legislation in many countries, which theoretically could lead to increased international cooperation in combating an international problem. Despite these strengths, the Palermo Protocol also has a number of weaknesses that raise doubts about whether it can truly be an effective counter-trafficking instrument. The most significant of these flaws is the fact that it must be read and construed together with its parent convention, which was designed as an instrument for the control of international crime and is not specifically related to the traffic in women. This means that the convention applies only to the prevention, investigation, and prosecution of crimes that involve more than one country, so it does not encompass cases which take place within a single nation.

As is the case with all UN protocols and conventions, the burden of implementation falls on the states that are party to it, which leaves the interpretation of critical terms such as *force, coercion,* and *threat* up to the discretion of individual UN member states. This chapter's section on definitions of consent and choice will clearly demonstrate that how these words are defined makes an enormous difference in how prostitutes and victims of trafficking are treated. If we consider poverty and lack of education to be coercive and threatening forces, then the vast majority of women who sell sex are victims of trafficking, whereas if we follow the more rigid definitions of these terms used by most governments, very few prostitutes are victims of trafficking because most have not been subjected to the extreme forms of violence that are generally construed to constitute "force." Just as the Palermo Protocol does not make a clear effort to define these crucial terms, Sharma observes that it similarly "fails to acknowledge the current worldwide crisis of displacement" (2003, 54) and thus ignores the reality that high levels of labor migration and increased economic inequality may necessitate a reexamination of the concept of "choice."

UN Universal Declaration of Human Rights

Given these problems with the Palermo Protocol, it is useful to examine other international instruments that may provide additional mechanisms to address trafficking from a human rights perspective. Under the UN Universal Declaration of Human Rights (UDHR) states are obligated to abolish slavery and servitude and to prohibit degrading treatment. UDHR recognizes the individual right to life, liberty, security, freedom of movement, free choice of employment, just and favorable conditions of work, equal pay for equal work, and an adequate standard of living, all of which are compromised in cases of trafficking. Although UDHR is widely recognized as the most authoritative interpretation of human rights obligations contained in the UN Charter, and thus binding on all UN member states, it can still be argued that UDHR is a declaration with no true binding force, because the UN has virtually no power to ensure its implementation. All three of the countries discussed in the case studies in this book have ratified other binding United Nations documents that include an explicit reference to the traffic in women: The Convention Against the Elimination of All Forms of Discrimination Against Women (CEDAW) and The UN Declaration on the Elimination of Violence Against Women (DEVAW), both of which assert that trafficking is a form of violence against women that states are obligated to combat.

European Union Policies

The definition of trafficking contained in the Palermo Protocol informed the 2002 European Union Framework Decision on Combating Trafficking in Human Beings. However, this decision also contains an addendum that specifically addresses sex trafficking as a threat and an external problem located outside the borders of the European Union—one that can best be controlled through increased border surveillance, document security, initiatives to combat organized crime, and what is euphemistically termed *migration management*. As a result, the European Union is now a major donor to counter-trafficking initiatives in Eastern Europe; the mechanics of this aid will be discussed at length in Chapter 4. This is a positive step in the sense that it ideally facilitates cooperation in counter-trafficking activities between EU and non-EU member states and recognizes that the existence of the problem is inseparable from poverty and corruption. However, there are also problems with the EU stance on trafficking, and Peterson (2001) has documented how much of the Western European discourse on the subject is based on tensions between EU and non-EU member states in that it focuses on sex trafficking primarily as a matter of migration and border control. The resulting friction is compounded by the lack of a united stance on prostitution in EU countries and conflicting state policies on state regulation, complete illegality, and state tolerance of the sex industry.

EU policy on sex trafficking has a complex history that is inseparable from the development of the supranational organization itself. Former Swedish EU commissioner Gradin described her role as part of 1993 Maastricht Treaty's third pillar, which focused on migration, refugee policy, and international organized crime. She was adamant that such issues needed to be dealt with internationally and noted that "a united approach had to be taken to tackle issues such as illegal migration and trafficking in human beings. It was equally clear that we had to make sure that legal migrants who had lived on EU territory for a long time should be given rights comparable to those of EU citizens" (Gradin 2007). The EU position on the traffic in women was thus specifically focused on migration from its inception, which points to a curious separation of the issue from prostitution in favor of positioning it as a matter of national security.

The first EU conference on the traffic in women was held in Vienna in 1996, not long after the formation of the supranational organization itself. This meeting resulted in a Plan of Action recommended by the Council of Ministers and the European Parliament to EU member countries and explicitly stating that trafficking should be regarded and punished as a criminal offense. This was followed in 1997 by the Ministerial Hague Declaration on

European guidelines for effective measures to prevent and combat trafficking in women for the purposes of sexual exploitation. The Framework Decision that followed in 2003 resulted in the creation of a group of experts on trafficking that called for increased cooperation between agencies and greater information exchange with the European police agency Europol. This group maintained that counter-trafficking strategies must be coordinated with plans to combat poverty and corruption, and it called for the elimination of all forms of sexual exploitation (Gradin 2007). However, the EU is certainly not the only powerful organization invested in the subject of the traffic in women.

US Legislation and Policy Frameworks

The Victims of Trafficking and Violence Prevention Act of 2000 (TVPA) is the most significant piece of US legislation on the traffic in humans. It defines this activity as "the recruitment, harboring, transportation, provision or obtaining of a person for the purpose of a commercial sex act" and additionally defines "severe forms of trafficking in persons" that take two forms:

> [1] sex trafficking in which a commercial sex act is induced by force, fraud or coercion, or in which the person induced to perform such act has not attained 18 years of age, or [2] the recruitment, harboring, transportation, provision or obtaining [of] a person for labor or services, through the use of force, fraud, [or] coercion for the purpose of subjection to involuntary servitude, peonage, debt bondage or slavery (US Congress 2000).

The TVPA mandated the creation of the US government's Interagency Task Force to Monitor and Combat Trafficking, as well as a threefold plan to provide economic alternatives to sex work, including micro-credit lending programs that provide small-business loans to poor women, initiatives to keep girls and young women in school, and grants to NGOs that work on counter-trafficking issues. An Office to Monitor and Combat Trafficking was also established as part of this legislation and charged with assisting the Task Force and writing an annual Trafficking in Persons (TIP) Report. This TIP report describes the nature of trafficking and efforts to combat it in almost every country and is compiled in conjunction with US embassies around the world.

TIP reports divide countries into four "tiers" in accordance with the US government's estimate of how effectively each national government fights the traffic in humans, and assignments to one of the four tiers is based on how good a given government is at meeting US minimum standards for prevention. These standards consist of a checklist of nine criteria that assess government involvement in trafficking, agencies designed to prevent it, steps taken to deter officials from engaging in trafficking, punishment of traffickers, assistance to victims, cooperation with extradition and international investigations, recognition of victim rights, and prevention of double victimization by the legal system (US Congress 2000).

Placement in the lowest category of tier 3 indicates that a country has failed to take "significant actions to bring itself into compliance with the minimum standards for the elimination of trafficking in persons." The next level up is the tier 2 watch list, which indicates that even though a country has taken some steps to combat an especially significant trafficking problem, it is still far from taking "reasonable steps" against trafficking. Placement in tier 2 indicates that a country is making "significant efforts" to bring itself into compliance with US minimum standards. And tier 1, the category that reflects "full compliance" is the highest placement a country can receive. Tier status is not without consequences. Assignment to tier 3 could prompt the suspension of US nonhumanitarian assistance in the form of donor aid for much-needed infrastructural projects (US Department of State 2004). In 2006 a total of twenty-five countries held tier 1 status (US Department of State 2006). The vast majority of them were in Western Europe and had close diplomatic and trade ties to the United States, a fact which indicates that the tier system may not be so equitable as it initially appears.

The reductive set of extremely clear-cut criteria that make up the tier system is ineffective, simply because the mere fact that a country meets the terms defined by the United States does not mean that trafficking is being effectively dealt with by that country's government. An underlying premise of the minimum standards for prevention is that the checks and balances of civil society exist everywhere, that the respective justice systems function equally well, that citizens feel free to express their concerns about institutional corruption without fear of repercussions or loss of position, and that prosecution is the answer to ending trafficking—in essence, that all countries operate exactly like the United States. Despite its reductive nature, however, the tier system also depicts trafficking as an abstract problem by lumping countries with extremely different socioeconomic and cultural systems together with little consideration of the way the individual justice systems and gender norms of each country function.

Thirty-two countries were assigned tier 2 watch list status in 2006, including nations as culturally disparate and geographically distant as Armenia, Brazil, Cambodia, and South Africa (US Department of State 2006). The question is whether such broad categories can provide a meaningful picture of the extent and scope of trafficking or, whether the current system of ranking countries needs complete restructuring because it contributes to an institutional culture that insists on compliance with US minimum standards as a condition for the receipt of US donor aid. This would be an extremely dangerous flaw, because the ability of individual countries to devise much more effective priorities could be undermined by the need to embrace US standards that might not be as useful. Chapter 3 will clearly demonstrate how the implementation of these US standards can in fact be extraordinarily harmful to women who sell sex.

Nonetheless, the post-9/11 Bush administration has committed more funds to counter-trafficking than any other government or international organization in history, including its authorization of $200 million for that purpose in 2003 alone. Countries that do not meet US minimum standards not only risk losing US donor funds but may find it more difficult to obtain assistance from international financial institutions such as the International Monetary Fund and development organizations such as the World Bank (US Dept. of State 2004, 28). This potential for coercion has fueled the argument that the US commitment does not demonstrate concern for the welfare of poor women who sell sex but, rather, paranoia about migration and national security. The theoretical strength of the TVPA is that it reflects a commitment to ending the traffic in persons and simultaneously commits large sums of donor funds for that purpose. But as Chapter 3 will show, the assumption that prosecution is the answer has, in at least one instance, indirectly encouraged a national government to pursue a false trafficking conviction for the sole purpose of continuing to receive US foreign aid.

South Asian Policies

The traffic in women has also received attention at the South Asian policy level through the South Asian Association for Regional Cooperation (SAARC), an organization composed of eight member states that facilitates security and cooperation in South Asia and, in 2002, issued the Convention on Preventing and Combating Trafficking in Women and Children for Prostitution. It defined the crime as "the moving, selling or buying of women and children for prostitution within and outside a country for monetary or other considerations with or without the consent of the person subjected to trafficking" (SAARC 2002). The convention provides recommendations for assistance to investigators and prosecutors, sensitization of police and judiciary, the establishment of a regional task force to oversee the convention's implementation, bilateral mechanisms for cooperation and implementation, information exchange, supervision of employment agencies, prevention and development efforts in known "source" areas, awareness raising, and the care for, and repatriation of, victims. This is promising in that it allows for inter-South Asian cooperation and does not limit the definition of sex trafficking to cases where an international border has been crossed. However, the convention does not address trafficking from a general perspective that includes an understanding of how poverty and corruption facilitate the trade in women, and its provisions have unfortunately been used to justify restrictions placed on women's mobility through the introduction of bans on voluntary female migration to the affluent Gulf states (Huda 2006, 380).

THE EASTERN EUROPEAN BIAS

The relatively low levels of per capita funds and the limited institutional attention devoted to the traffic in women in South Asia reveal much about the Western concerns that underlie the issue. After all, if international organizations and powerful governments such as the United States are truly interested in ending the problem, it seems that South Asia would be a high-priority area, given that the number of girls and women who are sold there far exceeds the number in Eastern Europe by virtue of an enormous population and greater poverty. Yet these groups have not addressed the problem in Asia until relatively recently. Donor aid and popular perceptions of the traffic in women continue to be concentrated on white women in the former socialist and communist states of Eastern Europe.

Several factors result in the privileging of Eastern European victims at the expense of those in South Asia, and geography is paramount among them. Unlike the non-EU member states of Eastern Europe, South Asia obviously does not share any borders with the EU, so the possibilities of overland migration are significantly limited. From the American perspective, Eastern Europe is granted higher priority because of the complex adversarial relationships that characterized the Cold War. The region is composed primarily of what continue to be termed *transition states*, and the United States has a vested interest in cultivating positive relationships with these countries in the interest of creating spheres of influence. Although Chapters 3 and 4 make it clear that certain Eastern European governments are complicit in the traffic in women, the topic nonetheless presents a unique opportunity for the United States and the European Union not only to engage directly with state policy formation in Eastern Europe but also to do so by prioritizing a topic that few people would publicly criticize as agenda-based. After all, who would publicly make the argument that the traffic in women is a good idea?

The most insidious principle underlying the comparative lack, until quite recently, of US and EU funding initiatives outside Eastern Europe is racism and the assumption that there is broad acceptance, in other regions, of unequal gender relations as enduring cultural forms that are somehow distinct from the European context. This way of thinking uncomfortably mirrors colonial perceptions of Asian and African women as oppressed, suffering beings devoid of individuality and rights. Eastern European staff members at international organizations that work on counter-trafficking initiatives were often adamant that the key difference between the situation in their region and the rest of the world was that this phenomenon was fundamentally not a part of what they viewed as a pan-European conception of gender and family relations. One woman in her early thirties commented that international organizations were more inclined to fund Eastern European counter-trafficking initiatives because "in Asia and Africa parents sell their young girls because it is part of their culture, so they need much more work, funds, and support than the international organizations could ever provide."

Such a point of view positions Asia and Africa as a part of a neocolonialist discourse that depicts non-European regions of the world as inherently misogynistic, and the speaker's use of the phrase *more work* also implicitly places Eastern Europe closer to the West on a continuum of development and civilization. Eastern Europeans often drew parallels among Asians, Africans, and the marginalized Roma population that was much more familiar to them as a point of reference when I raised the question of why trafficking in Eastern Europe received more donor attention. One woman was convinced that the Roma were essentially similar to Asian populations because "it is their culture to do this, the Indian and the Roma population, they buy and sell wives, push their children to beg on the street. This is how they live, so what can you do?"

Eastern European workers at international organizations who had spent significant periods of their lives in Western Europe often presented more critical analyses of the donor focus on their region of the world. Tellingly, they responded to my questions about discrimination in global counter-trafficking efforts by positioning themselves as lower on a hierarchy led by Western Europe and the United States. This was particularly salient in Sarajevo, where one young woman presented a sad assessment of what she termed the *worth* of different groups of people:

> If you take the example of the refugees in Bosnia, we were given so much more money per day than Rwanda or Sudan because we are white. They don't say it out loud, but that's the way it works in governments. There is racism based on where you come from and it determines how much you are worth. You see it with the way our refugees were better treated, and it's the same when it comes to trafficking. It's just like how we accept trafficking more here if it happens to Roma than if it happens to Bosnians.

These issues will be discussed in greater depth in Chapter 5 via case studies of Indian and Nepali women who work in the sex industry and whose lives complicate the definitions of sex trafficking and the responses to it detailed throughout the rest of the book.

ANTI-TRAFFICKING ORGANIZATIONS

Anti-trafficking activist Lin Lap Chew notes that groups dedicated specifically to the eradication of the trade in women that began to emerge in the mid-1980s were almost immediately split between activists in support of prostitutes' rights and those who were vehemently opposed to prostitution (2005, 66). Unfortunately, this split continues to exist today and characterizes the groups that have emerged since trafficking became a topic of both feminist and popular concern. Dozens of international human rights and women's groups include sex trafficking in their portfolio of activities, including Amnesty International, Anti-Slavery International, the Gabriela Network, and Human Rights Watch. Because it would be impossible to discuss all of them in any meaningful detail, I will deal only with those that directly address the traffic in women as their main activity.

The Foundation Against the Traffic in Women (STV) was founded in 1987 to support legislation and awareness about the problem in the Netherlands and was instrumental in changing Dutch law to define trafficking and support the rights of trafficked women. STV provides victims of trafficking with shelter and legal assistance and regularly undertakes information dissemination campaigns to raise awareness about the problem. STV makes a clear distinction between forced prostitution (which it defines as trafficking) and prostitution as a choice. This differs significantly from the Coalition Against the Traffic in Women (CATW), which was founded in 1988 at least in part because of disagreements about the legalization of prostitution. CATW also has consultative status with the UN Economic and Social Council, and it helped to develop the Palermo Protocol despite having been sharply criticized by both activists for prostitutes' rights and anti-trafficking feminist organizations such as the Global Alliance Against the Traffic in Women. These criticisms stem from CATW's depiction of both traffickers and victims "as part of negatively racialized groups" (Sharma 2005, 102) and its positioning of women who sell sex as "helpless victims in need of rescue" (Doezema 2001, 16).

The Global Alliance Against the Traffic in Women (GAATW) was formed in 1994 in Thailand when a group of women activists and scholars decided that governments and international organizations had created a system that relies on unfair labor practices that uniquely discriminate against women. GAATW differs from other organizations that deal with sex trafficking because it was founded by women from what is often referred to as "the global south" who recognized that it was essential (1) to understand the problem in the broader context of migration and (2) to accept that the idea of "global sisterhood" neglects to acknowledge the hierarchies of race, nationality, and class present in the outside world. GAATW supports women's choice to migrate and to engage in prostitution.

The International La Strada Association was founded in 1995 in the Czech Republic and currently consists of a network of nine independent human rights NGOs (in Belarus, Bosnia, Bulgaria, the Czech Republic, Macedonia, Moldova, the Netherlands, Poland, and Ukraine). Like STV and GAATW, La Strada respects the right of women to choose to engage in prostitution and distinguishes it from trafficking. La Strada believes in building networks throughout Central and Eastern Europe to raise awareness about the problem, provide advocacy/assistance to victims, and sensitize police and border officials. This distinguishes it from Captive Daughters, an organization founded in 1997 that argues that prostitution is one of the root causes of sex trafficking and advocates against its legalization. The organization believes that economic alternatives must be offered to women in order to eradicate both prostitution and sex trafficking. It also maintains that US and EU governments should more aggressively punish sex tour operators that visit Asia and Latin America.

DEBATES ON AGENCY, CONSENT, AND CHOICE

Many feminists argue that prostitution is itself a violent act both in its intention of placing intimacy in the marketplace and in its consequence of making women's bodies into marketable commodities. Such violence necessitates that women who sell sex develop dissociative coping mechanisms that separate their physical and emotional selves as a form of psychological self-protection. The use of such mechanisms as a survival strategy can also transfer into other spheres of emotional life, including family relationships, such that prostitutes must constantly struggle to maintain the bifurcation of sex for sale and genuine intimacy shared out of love.

Intense emotional processes of separation and rationalization are necessary for women who engage in sex work because of the stigmatized nature of prostitution in almost every society in the world. Women who sell sex in societies such as Armenia, Bosnia, or India, all of which place a particularly high value on motherhood and devotion to family, find themselves categorized as especially immoral, socially degenerate beings who violate social norms and codes that mandate female chastity in the face of assumed male promiscuity. Women who are pushed to the margins of society in this way are more likely to suffer low self-esteem and, as a result, are less likely be able to engage in loving relationships of equality because of the numbing and socially stigmatized behavior they are forced to engage in on a regular basis. Many "normal" family behaviors are situated in a moral economy of emotions that are predicated on assumptions of altruism and the capacity of mothers (and other relatives) to pour all of their love and energy into their children. The fractured self that prostitution necessitates may also explain the frequency with which women who have been forced into sex work recruit younger women, including their own daughters, into the profession in order to profit secondarily from their bodies. Throughout Eastern Europe, such women are called Mama Rosas and are considered particularly effective traffickers because of their ability to insist that if they can survive what they often depict as a "temporary" psychological and physical ordeal, other women can as well. What they neglect to mention, of course, is that although the behavior itself may be temporary, the emotional consequences may last a lifetime.

Prostitution entails a process of psychological violence that necessitates a different understanding of the body, money, and perceptions of life choices, and the failure to recognize this renders many counter-trafficking programs ineffective. However, the fact remains that anti-trafficking institutions and activist groups are sharply divided into two camps that disagree profoundly about the nature of prostitution. The first camp is made up of a curious assortment of entities discussed above (including the US government and activist organizations), which unequivocally believe that prostitution is a form of violence against women. The strong religious stance and focus on Republican "family values" evinced by the former must be distinguished from the kind of support that activists and feminists have for the criminalization of prostitution as a violation of human rights. Activists maintain this point of view at least in part because of their domination by a generation that adheres to the first-wave and second-wave brands of feminism that were concerned primarily with equal socioeconomic and legal rights for women as part of the initial stages of the US and Western European women's movements in the 1960s and 1970s. First- and second-wave feminisms were the product of a social environment that necessitated an extremist stance in order to advance the basic civil rights of women, and both thus tend to be characterized by a rather uncomplicated view of women as universally subjugated by men. This way of thinking leads proponents of these feminist schools to maintain that prostitution is a manifestation of unequal gender relations writ large, in the sense that sex work can function as an easy metaphor for male economic power and female submission.

The fact that two groups with otherwise divergent political opinions agree that prostitution is detrimental to women and to society is significant and demonstrates the pressing nature of the traffic in women as a deeply human issue that transcends what are normally static political boundaries. However, the approach of the first camp is also very naïve, because it implies that the criminalization of prostitution will stop relatively wealthier men from exchanging money with less-privileged women for sex. Visits to almost any city in the world where prostitution is illegal quickly reveal that legislation serves only to push the sex industry further underground and thus make it less visible to those who have a voice in society. This invisibility in turn puts prostitutes at greater risk of violence and abuse by both clients and the police because of their status as criminals and members of a socially stigmatized group.

It is crucial to remember that even though it may be against the law to buy sex in many countries, prostitution is often tolerated in certain areas that the police ignore as a consequence of several factors: low levels of concern with the problem, a lack of regard for the safety and well-being of sex workers, the need for law enforcement to urgently respond to other crime scenes, and the tacit understanding on the part of officers that the arrest, release, and re-arrest of prostitutes is a wasteful, cyclical process. Experienced police officers often believe that prostitution is a relatively victimless crime in the sense that women who sell sex are at least theoretically making a choice to do so and thus must accept the consequences of their actions. In many countries, the stance that prostitution is morally and legally offensive results in the sex trade being concentrated in low-income neighborhoods that have been abandoned by businesses, middle-class families, and other indicators of social and civic well-being.

The US government maintains toward prostitution a "zero tolerance policy" so extreme that it refuses to fund any international initiatives that provide services to sex workers. This policy is quite paradoxical, given that many women who become victims of *trafficking* according to most definitions of the term have previously sold sex as a survival strategy and thus could potentially be targeted by the numerous US-funded counter-trafficking projects through existing local agencies and NGOs that have experience assisting prostitutes. The EU and SAARC policies discussed earlier reflect more conflict than those of the US government, largely because of the varying degrees of legality and tolerance for prostitution in each of their individual member states. This lack of consensus among governments and organizations means that many of the meetings held by these groups on the traffic in women quickly become discussions of various countries' policies and of the need for cooperation, rather than providing a true forum for the information sharing that leads to concrete decision making and action. Despite this indecisiveness, none of these organizations suggests that prostitution is a desirable profession that should be promoted, and all agree that its effects are deleterious to women and to society at large.

More radical members of the first camp believe that *consent* and *choice* are loaded words when used in conjunction with sex work. Kathleen Barry (1996) has argued that prostitution cannot legitimately be considered a choice, because it is meant to benefit men rather than women. She uses the persuasive example of how the system remains oriented toward male consumers even in countries such as the Netherlands, that register sex workers with the government in efforts to monitor the sex trade. She contends that if such regulatory systems were indeed meant to assist women workers, their male clients would also be tested for sexually transmitted diseases, which is of course not the case. MacKinnon (1990) uses characteristically forthright language to argue that consent "is not a meaningful concept... when fear and despair produce acquiescence and acquiescence is taken to mean consent." Farley (2004) concurs, comparing the consent of prostitutes to the "consent" of battered women who are sometimes mistakenly believed to accept their abusive situation, when in truth they simply feel they have no choice but to remain with their partner.

This notion of choice is one of the most contentious points surrounding debates on the differences between prostitution and sex trafficking, and many adherents to the first camp contend that consent is rendered irrelevant when women's bodies are for sale in a male-dominated market. Jeffreys is heavily critical of the "pro-prostitution lobby," a term she uses to describe the second camp, which maintains that women have the right to choose to sell sex and that their decisions should be respected rather than criminalized. She insists that this position "distorts the language of women's right to sexual choice and orientation" in order to promote "the right to choose to be used as the raw material in a massive capitalist sex industry" (1998, 10). Her language reveals the kind of naïveté that underlies the argument against the legalization of prostitution, because it does not accurately reflect the life circumstances of most women who sell sex; rather choosing "to be used," as Jeffrey's description would have it, most are simply choosing to survive.

The second camp adopts a more analytic framework and seeks to redefine the debate to include new conceptions that move beyond the somewhat simplistic descriptions of abused women and predatory men presented by the first camp. Proponents of this school of thought believe that such bifurcated labels obscure counter-trafficking efforts by effectively ignoring the realities of women's lives. This camp is composed primarily of feminists who support prostitutes' rights and who must be distinguished from what Jeffreys mislabels "the pro-prostitution lobby." Women who sell sex are seen by this group as agents and actors—a view that helps scholars and activists of the second camp to avoid the kind of highly emotionalized language that characterizes the work of those who believe prostitution should be illegal and undermines many of their claims by leading them into the trap of reinforcing sexist stereotypes of men as abusers and women as victims. The less-nuanced approach of the first camp is unhelpful in explaining many of the ground realities of sex trafficking, such as why and how female traffickers are able to operate so successfully throughout the world, a common phenomenon that will be discussed in depth in the case studies in Chapters 3, 4, and 5.

Dutch Social Democrat and Member of Parliament Hans Spekman (2007) speaks to the dilemma faced by policymakers in regard to the debates on trafficking in countries, such as the Netherlands, in which prostitution is legal and subject to government regulation. He echoes the stance taken by the Dutch government in acknowledging the substantial difference between what he calls a "would-be society" and the messy realities of everyday human existence. Spekman attended a European Forum conference at which he described how unregulated street prostitution that was effectively ignored in the Dutch city of Utrecht directly benefited traffickers because their exploitation of women became invisible to society. By outlawing and ignoring prostitution, Spekman argued, politicians and policymakers are easily able to credit themselves for not becoming involved in taboo issues, but women continue to be exploited. The social invisibility of prostitution in many countries where it is illegal exposes sex workers to violence and simultaneously makes them afraid to approach the police. The counterpoint to this argument, of course, is that government regulation of prostitution may also be construed as state complicity in what many believe to be an essentially sexist and violent act.

These debates are of critical importance, because the way a society thinks about prostitution and sex trafficking directly affects the social services that are provided to women who sell sex. According to O'Connor and Healy (2006), the view of prostitution as a form of violence against women leads to service provision outcomes that recognize that the commoditization of sexuality is inherently misogynistic and labels clients as abusers. Unfortunately, this position comes very close to embracing the idea of what Spekman characterized as the "would-be society" that exposes sex workers to increased violence, because simply to label all men who pay for sex as abusers obscures the complex ways of thinking about gender and power that inform their decision to do so. Conversely, O'Connor and Healy (2006) argue that viewing prostitution of a form of work can result in a lack of social incentives for governments and organizations to assist prostitutes, because it is contrued as a career choice. The authors contend that when sexuality is seen as part of a market exchange, government regulation often simply protects the health and anonymity of male clients by screening prostitutes for sexually transmitted diseases and designating certain areas of cities for prostitution.

Female sexuality is a subject of tension and a matter of enormous concern in every culture in the world, so it is no surprise that ideas about agency, consent, and choice are so hotly debated in regard to prostitution. Both schools of thought on the subject expose the gendered power inequalities that provide much of the debate's structure and substance and, in turn, influence the way sex workers are treated. In studies of prostitution, there is significant danger of such debates obscuring the fact that a real population is being discussed; after all, if the subject of gender relations has a somewhat abstract quality, prostitution constitutes an extremely concrete set of actions and behaviors. As a result, it is crucial to analyze how popular culture makes sense of the traffic in women and how counter-trafficking organizations use the media to influence popular cultural perceptions of both trafficking and prostitution.

Sex Trafficking in Popular Culture: *Lilya 4-Ever*

Perhaps it is self-evident that the individuals of both genders who profit from the traffic in women are people who manipulate a complex set of tragic historical and political events to their economic advantage, but it is a bit less obvious that the women who suffer from their actions are doubly victimized by popular culture. Unfortunately, there is a tendency in the Western Europe and American media to emphasize the explicitly sexual nature of trafficking through graphic descriptions of abuse and a focus on victimization that positions women as in need of rescue. Popular culture often depicts women who have been trafficked as nothing more than victims of trickery and deceit, and although this certainly is an accurate way to describe what some women experience, it is essential to explore the associated cultural meanings that lie beneath such understandings of the problem. This is especially true because many traffickers are themselves women and because many victims of trafficking have been prostitutes before.

The much-lauded film *Lilya 4-Ever* (2003) tells the story of a teenaged girl abandoned by her mother "somewhere in the former Soviet Union" (Moodysson 2003), a choice by Swedish filmmaker Lukas Moodysson that serves to underscore what many Western Europeans and North Americans perceive to be the locus of the problem in Eastern Europe. Indeed, offices of the International Organization for Migration in several former Soviet republics have used public screenings of the film as a way to foster dialogue about trafficking. The film opens with a conversation in which Lilya's mother informs her that she is leaving for the United States with a man she has agreed to marry and will send for her daughter later. Lilya is understandably distraught by this abandonment, and the plot rapidly takes a further turn for the worse when her mother's sister claims ownership of Lilya's former home.

Lilya takes up residence in an abandoned and decrepit apartment and soon learns about the way prostitution works in her town from her friend Natasha, who occasionally sells sex at a local nightclub and saves the money she earns underneath her mattress. When Natasha's father discovers this money and angrily accuses her of engaging in prostitution, a frightened Natasha lies to her father and most of the community, claiming that she was only holding the money for Lilya as a favor. Lilya is raped by a gang of neighborhood adolescents who see her as an easy and deserving target after this "information" gets around, and she becomes even further isolated from the community in which she lives. Lilya finds a friend in her young neighbor Volodya, who is repeatedly thrown out of his house by his abusive father, and the two pass their time by sniffing glue in an abandoned former Soviet military base and talking about the cruel ironies of life.

When Lilya learns from the social welfare board that she has been disowned by her mother and that there is no state support available to assist her, she realizes that she has no choice but to go to a local nightclub and make herself available as a prostitute. In the scene immediately after her first paid sexual encounter with a much older man, we see Lilya vomiting in a dark alley, followed by a cut to a scene of Lilya buying groceries with the money the man has given her. A bruised Lilya is on her way home one night when she meets Andrei, a young man driving an expensive red car who spends several days showering her with love and attention. When he suggests that they move to Sweden together, she is delighted and agrees without hesitation. Lilya accepts the passport with a false name and age that Andrei gives her, as well as his promise that he will join her later.

Once in Sweden, however, Lilya is locked in a room and forced into prostitution by the Swedish man who has "bought" her from Andrei. Lilya's linguistic and physical isolation in Sweden is compounded by the physical and sexual abuse that she undergoes, and she rapidly slips into a fantasy world in which she and Volodya talk about angels as she hides under a table like a child. Lilya eventually escapes by jumping to her death, and the shot of Swedish paramedics attempting to revive her transitions to a final scene of alternative possibilities in which a better-informed Lilya refuses Andrei's offer with the indignant line "I'm no fool."

The ending of the film seems to imply that Lilya's life would have been infinitely better if she had never left home, and yet the fundamental question raised by the film's ending remains unanswered: How was Lilya to support herself in a fundamentally destabilized socioeconomic system, if not through prostitution? Reviews of the film vacillate between understandable pity for Lilya's situation and an almost titillating description of her suffering. Critics describe "Lilya's innocence being systematically and repeatedly exploited at the hands of Swedish customers and their Russian suppliers" or the process by which her "dreams of a glamorous Western existence, safe under the blanket of consumerism and popular culture, are proven very quickly to be unattainable and stained with lies" (Huggins 2004). Lilya is thus envisioned as a young woman abandoned in a post-Soviet landscape in which she has nothing left to expect but degradation and death.

Other reviews are less innocuous, and in these we read of a Lilya "cut completely adrift from any safety measures" in a "pathetic existence" (Lundegaard 2003). The backdrop of the film is clearly designed to be one of desperation, yet these reviews focus on the suffering of the characters without considering its context, through their descriptions of people who exist "in cold and broken down buildings, filthy living conditions, a palpable stench of decay in the air of a world broken first by economy and then by barbarism" (Huggins 2004). Such reviews illustrate the disturbing tendency of popular culture to focus on the eroticized darkness of the subject and the exploitation of young women like Lilya who have no other choices in life. By focusing on the victimization of women and the utter hopelessness of the situation, such depictions mirror sadomasochistic pornography in an extremely unsettling way. One critic, for example, described the film as replete with "humiliating sex and violence that is not all gratuitous, but more of a comment on the matter-of-fact reality of survival on the edge of a world that's left you for dead" (Shoquist 2003). This graphic language focuses directly on how Lilya suffers, before going on to ask the telling question "What's left to live for if everyone has discarded you and used you up until there's nothing left?" (Lundegaard 2003).

It is interesting to note that some members of the Armenian audiences who watched the film as part of an IOM awareness-raising campaign were adamant in their insistence that the circumstances depicted in *Lilya 4-Ever* did not apply to Armenia. Several women stood up following screenings in the capital city of Yerevan to observe, of Lilya's abandonment, something along the lines of "Only a Russian mother would do such a thing." This statement must be viewed in the context of Armenia's former position as a Russian satellite state subjugated in numerous ways by Soviet policy, but it also reveals how graphic horror can distance viewers from what should be a discussion of how trafficking works.

IOM EFFORTS TO PROVIDE MORE SENSITIVE IMAGES OF SEX TRAFFICKING

Unfortunately, other sites in popular culture offer more salacious descriptions of the suffering women experience as part of the trafficking process. Articles have appeared in the Western European and American press with titles such as "Janie's Secret" and "Trafficker's New Cargo: Naïve Slavic Women," and the same true in Armenia, where journalists have published pieces titled "Return from Hell," "The Crafty Head of Village and his Poor Victims" and (even more bizarre) "Victims of Trafficking Were Guarded by Bears." Such language borders on the titillating and serves to doubly victimize the women whose traumas the articles purport to document. This rhetoric of victimhood also infantilizes women and obscures the realities of sex trafficking behind prevailing—but faulty—cultural assumptions about the nature of sex work.

IOM has made notable efforts to sensitize journalists throughout Eastern Europe to appropriate ways to cover stories on the traffic in women, and it also been extremely active in producing its own awareness-raising literature on the subject for public distribution. In Bosnia these efforts usually take the form of a pamphlet, and in Armenia they are generally confined to a postcard-size piece of paper with a striking image of a young and very attractive woman being led into an exploitive situation by a much older man. These generally have a caption that reads something like "You are not for sale," "Know about risk," or "Don't trade your life" in the local language. Many of the pamphlets and postcards are quite provocative and feature semi-nude professional models or actresses in poses that suggest extreme domination and abuse; several feature a completely naked woman cowering in a dark corner with her hands covering her head as if in defense from a beating. Notably, these pamphlets and postcards are conspicuously absent in India, not only because of their cultural inappropriateness for South Asia but also because much less donor funding is available for the purposes of raising awareness.

IOM staff members who had either designed or approved these images in both Armenia and Bosnia responded in a variety of ways to my questions about such depictions of women, which in my opinion very closely resembled the kind of pornography sold in specialty shops and on websites catering to sadists and bondage fetishists. A senior IOM staff member responded to my question of why such beautiful women were used by exclaiming, "But this is the reality! Traffickers are not looking for ugly women. They are looking for young, beautiful women. What woman hasn't imagined walking down the street and being discovered by someone who says, 'You are the character for my next film; you are so beautiful!' Many women think they are so beautiful and they want to be a model, so this catches their attention and it makes them look." Other IOM staff members who self-identified as Eastern European in background and identity, despite having spent significant amounts of time in Western Europe, were more critical. One such young woman looked at a particularly violent image of a woman covered in bruises and curled in the fetal position with a caption that read "Don't trade your life" and said, "This definitely does not speak to me as a woman." When I asked her to elaborate, she shrugged and said, "Young women who think they know everything aren't going to look at this woman who obviously had something horrible happen to her and think, 'that could be me,' because it's too terrible to imagine."

These graphic images were the subject of an hour-long discussion I had with a Bosnian woman who was nine years old during the war and who was adamant that several years of conflict had dramatically altered the ability of individuals to be shocked or affected by violence. "A girl who has grown up here is different because she has grown up during the war," she said. "I grew up with images of massacred bodies, and I feel that a girl needs to see this kind of violence to make her read it." Yet this does not explain why Armenia, a country that has not experienced the same degree of war and upheaval as Bosnia, distributes the same kinds of materials. The American chief of Party at the international news agency Internews in Armenia, maintained that these images of beautiful women being brutalized were ironically less a function of their intended effect than the result of an economy that could not provide jobs to all its citizens. "It's obvious" he smirked, "that they're all made in a new market economy by men who would much rather work in advertising."

Two particularly striking Bosnian pamphlets produced by IOM were titled "Ne Trguj Svojim Životom," or "Don't Trade Your Life"; notably, the Bosnian verb *trguj* has various connotations and, depending on the context, can mean "trade" or "sell," which made it a particularly effective word choice. The first pamphlet was printed in vibrant red and blue tones and featured a bruised young woman seated on a bed with her knees pressed against her chest. Its four pages were designed in a cartoon format and told the story of a bilingual college graduate who answered an advertisement in a newspaper for a job on the coast in an unspecified location. In the Bosnian context, this could be Croatia, Greece, or Italy, all of which are major countries of destination for victims of trafficking from the Western Balkans. Everything about the position seemed ideal until one night she was locked in a room and sold with three other women, and they were all forced to engage in prostitution.

The images in the pamphlet rapidly change after the frame in which an insidious-looking older man smoking a cigarette takes her passport and closes the door behind him with an ominous *klik*. The next image is fragmented by what looks like broken glass into three images of rape and violence, followed soon after by a scene in which the bruised and vulnerable protagonist explains her situation to a client in a fatherly sleeveless sweater, who immediately takes her to the hospital. The pamphlet ends with an image of the same girl, now a confident and professionally dressed young women walking purposefully down an urban street past a travel agency, with a caption that reads "It is now five years later, but every time I walk past a travel agent, I remember the terrifying sound of the door opening to let in another man." A small thought balloon to the left of this image of the confident young woman shows a terrified girl shaking in fright at the *klik* of the door opening.

A second pamphlet with the title "Don't Trade Your Life" features darker colors, includes much more graphic images of violence and rape, and tells a story of betrayal by a loved one that is reported by many Bosnian victims of trafficking. The cover shows a slim, attractively proportioned young woman standing in a dark corner dressed in a thin cotton dress, with her head lowered toward the ground, her long, dyed blond hair obscuring her face. Her hands are clutched in an expression of anxiety where her dress ends just below her hips, and she stands with one foot perched protectively over the other. "It looks like a horror movie because you can't see her face; she's not a real human," one young Bosnian woman to whom I showed the two pamphlets said. "I like the other one much better because you can see that she's a person."

The pamphlet's story begins with a cartoon image of a family photo album in which a high school student poses with her happy family. She soon meets and falls in love with a young man who proposes to take her on a weekend vacation to Croatia, only to beat her, rape her, and sell her to a trafficker who locks her in an isolated and dark house deep in the countryside. The next four scenes show the girl in an identical position of terror and attempted self-protection on a bed in a corner, as four different men, including a soldier in uniform, stand facing her with their backs to the reader, as though they have just entered her room. The pamphlet's final scenes show the girl escaping through an unlocked door and running through the woods until she finds a police car. "I realized that I was in that hell for 8 months," reads the caption underneath the final cartoon image of a photograph in a family album featuring an unsmiling girl with bruises on her face.

The central theme contained in both pamphlets is the idea that such young women can definitely go on to live a normal life and yet will never be the same. Although both end with images of women who have survived their terrible ordeal, they are changed and altered in an irreparable and negative way. Both are accurate in that they were compiled on the basis of real-life experiences and thus can potentially serve as effective warnings to young women. However, the images themselves are strikingly similar to narratives of sexual exploitation featured in pornography and directed toward certain niche male audiences. Thus it is essential to contextualize them in the broader framework of institutional responses to the traffic in women, all of which speak to cultural norms about sexuality, reflect ambivalence toward prostitution, and raise profound questions about the state of the world we live in today.

3

Armenia: Institutionalized Indifference, Reliance on Donor Aid, and Local Disempowerment

Liana lit a cigarette as we sat listening to the sounds of homeless children playing in an abandoned building next door to the small IOM mission where I worked in Yerevan, Armenia. She was a twice-divorced and chronically unemployed mother of four who, like many women in the depressed economies of the former Soviet Union, believed that short-term emigration for work was the only way she could continue to support her children alone. When a woman approached her with an offer of assistance in obtaining work in the affluent Middle Eastern nation of Dubai in return for a percentage of her future earnings, Liana sent her children to live at her mother's house, with the understanding that she would return in six months with substantial savings to reclaim them. It was only when Liana arrived in Dubai that the woman who had offered help in finding a job revealed herself to be a trafficker who insisted that Liana owed her an exorbitant sum of money for travel and other expenses—money that she would have to repay with interest by working as a prostitute. Liana's hands shook slightly as she explained her dire situation to me. She had just escaped from months of forced prostitution in a foreign country, was in fear of retribution from her trafficker, and desperately hoped that the counter-trafficking program at the IOM mission in Yerevan could help her regain custody of her children from her mother, who had rejected Liana as a prostitute after learning of her ordeal in Dubai.

Liana was by no means a naïve young girl; she was in her mid-thirties and had occasionally worked as a prostitute before embarking on her journey to Dubai. What the sad facts of her life reveal, however, are not flaws in her character but rather the realities of life for many women like her who do not have the education, skills, or social connections required for survival in the weakened economies of most former Soviet republics. Her case underscores

57

both the suffering and the attempts at resiliency of women who are forced to choose from an extremely limited number of life options in order to survive. Liana and I sat behind the small IOM mission smoking for quite some time before she inhaled deeply on her cigarette, crushed it on the cold cement steps, and waved goodbye. As I watched her disappear into the crowd milling about in Republic Square, I wondered whether I would ever see her again.

Around the time that Liana left Armenia for Dubai with hopes of earning money to provide a better life for her children, eight women from the Central Asian republic of Uzbekistan arrived in Armenia under the assumption that they would work as waitresses in a café. All eight women were like Liana in that they were unemployed and unskilled and had left their home country with an individual who promised to find them work in exchange for a per-centage-based fee to be paid at a later date. Once they arrived in Armenia, however, they were told not to leave the apartment in which they were housed and were forced to work as prostitutes until each had earned several thousand dollars for the trafficker who had promised to help them. All nine women had been victimized as part of the international trade in women's bodies, which is estimated by many law enforcement professionals to be more lucrative than the multi-billion-dollar traffic in narcotics.

The experiences of Liana and the eight Uzbek women with counter-trafficking professionals at the International Organization for Migration reveal much about how international conceptions of, and donor responses to, sex traf-ficking in Armenia expose points of tension surrounding gender, social class, and nationality. This chapter addresses these points of tension by considering how victims of trafficking often have very few life choices even before they are recruited for employment abroad and how they are sometimes doubly victimized via institutionalized indifference and well-intentioned donor aid programs.

It is not difficult to imagine how Armenia's socioeconomic difficulties and the normalization of emigration as an economic survival strategy contributed to Liana's decision to travel to Dubai for work. Less immediately apparent are the international and institutional forces at work, including US counter-traf-ficking legislation and policy formulated in Washington, D.C., which failed Liana so miserably in Armenia. Sex trafficking cannot exist without signifi-cant institutional corruption, which facilitates the issuance of fraudulent doc-uments that the women need to cross borders and pass immigration control, undermines the prosecution of traffickers, and denies adequate assistance to victims. Corruption in the nations of the former Soviet Union, including Armenia and Uzbekistan, has become institutionalized to the extent that sig-nificant portions of foreign aid, World Bank loans, and International Mone-tary Fund financial transfers are reported to have been diverted from their intended destinations to privately held offshore accounts (Shelley 2003). Donor aid that does reach its intended recipients has had a number of unintentionally negative consequences, not least of which is the mushrooming of NGOs set up for the sole purpose of obtaining international funds (Wedel 1998). This competition for funding has led to fractious relationships between many NGOs, which, in turn, effectively hamper even the best-designed counter-trafficking initiatives.

A related issue is the lack of political will from government officials in many former Soviet republics who demonstrate little or no interest in addressing sex trafficking, This attitude reduces counter-trafficking efforts to mere window dressing in order to avoid domestic criticism and foreign pressures and thus undermines prevention and protection efforts, as well as denying assistance to victims. Governments of some former Soviet republics have made significant progress by criminalizing trafficking, yet laws are of little use if the elements of the crime are not defined clearly enough to facilitate effective prosecution. Maximum sentences for those convicted of trafficking are often extremely low and do not recognize the offense as a serious crime; in Armenia, the maximum punishment for trafficking resulting in the death of the victim is eight years of imprisonment. Counter-trafficking legislation also does not call for the confiscation of traffickers' assets, which allows better-organized syndicates to continue their activities even if a few of their members are imprisoned. Further, no workable mechanisms are in place for the protection of victims who choose to testify against their traffickers, which leaves them vulnerable to violence, intimidation, threats, and even murder.

The undermining of counter-trafficking laws and initiatives demonstrates both the inadequacies of these policies and the enormous obstacles faced by institutions involved in attempts to end the trade in women's bodies. One of the major issues in dealing with the traffic in women is that although the problem itself is hardly new, its scope reached massive proportions in many former Soviet republics following independence in the early 1990s. The international response to the problem thus dates to the mid-1990s and presents a fascinating case of how a very old human issue is framed and politicized by the international community, including IOM.

Fragile economies, institutionalized corruption, and lack of political will all hinder counter-trafficking efforts, but the fact remains that sex trafficking could not exist if not for highly stigmatized and gendered social structures such as prostitution itself. This reality sets a precedent for the disconnections that can occur between US foreign policy and its implementation in Armenia as part of the elaborate webs of power that position numerous actors in elaborate hierarchies designed to combat sex trafficking. All of the intricate machinations surrounding counter-trafficking mechanisms in Armenia abruptly collided when Liana, who had hoped to save money for her children by working in Dubai, approached IOM for assistance in regaining custody of her children from her mother after escaping the horrific ordeal of forced prostitution in a foreign country.

Liana clearly demonstrated all of the defining characteristics of a victim of trafficking: she had not known that she would be performing sex work when she agreed to leave Armenia, she had not been paid for her work, and her life was being threatened by an angry trafficker who insisted that Liana still owed her money. Her case was fraught from the very beginning with misunderstandings and skewed perceptions that drew upon Armenian cultural stereotypes of prostitutes as immoral and socially degenerate women.

Much research documents the perception of trafficked women as victimized sex objects rather than real human beings (Doezema 2000; Haynes 2004; Kempadoo 2005; Peach 2005; Sharma 2005), and scholarship has addressed the difficulties inherent in communicating between positions of relative privilege and marginalization to effect positive social change (Bruno 1998; Fisher 1997; Tzvetkova 2002). The highly educated professionals who staff most international organizations are sometimes unable to overcome their misconceptions about prostitution, which results in the increased incidence of miscommunication and moral judgment. For example, some IOM staff members criticized Liana as "irresponsible" and "unreliable" because she would often not answer her phone, a particularly contentious issue because IOM had given her money specifically to pay her phone bill. Liana was also evasive about certain details of her life story and reluctant to reveal why she had made particular decisions, so although it was clear that she had originally agreed to travel to Dubai with a woman who later turned out to be a trafficker, the details of her relationship with her estranged husband and others remained fuzzy. Liana returned to Armenia via Moscow after escaping from Dubai with another victim of trafficking named Karine, and some IOM staff members who were supportive of their close friendship were also extremely critical of her decision to pay nearly $600 for a second-trimester abortion that Karine had after conceiving at work. For some, the fact that Liana had spent nearly all of the money with which she had escaped from Dubai to help her friend Karine was simply further evidence of her irresponsible and frivolous nature.

Liana's complicated life reveals much about the circumstances of women who become victims of trafficking and the social stigma they face if they choose to reveal their stories. From Liana's point of view, not answering the phone was the only way to avoid receiving threats from her trafficker (and possibly her estranged husband), but some IOM staff members interpreted her lack of communication as irresponsibility and laziness. And when Liana explained that she had no money after spending it all on a costly second-trimester abortion for her friend because Karine was desperate and would have done the same for Liana if the situation were reversed, some IOM staff members criticized her as improvident.

There were several exceptions in the IOM office to the rather low esteem in which some staff members held Liana's handling of her own life situation. This palpable disregard was matched in equal measure by the enthusiasm of an IOM employee who returned from a year of studying law at Georgetown University on a US Embassy scholarship shortly after my arrival in Armenia. I remember noticing Armine visiting Hans Muller's office with copies of the lengthy reports she had written on the traffic in women during her time at Georgetown. Muller privately commented to me on several occasions that her analyses contained "nothing new," and I remembered feeling a distinct sense of pity for Armine after my first meeting with her, in which she described her deep sense of commitment to counter-trafficking efforts in her country.

Muller eventually decided to present Armine with the offer of a one-year contract to work on counter-trafficking issues, which was extremely important given that the overstretched and underfunded office did not have anyone devoted specifically to that activity. Armine enthusiastically began her job as a liaison between the main Yerevan shelter for victims of trafficking and the IOM office and as the IOM representative at all meetings on trafficking held by the government of Armenia, international organizations, and NGOs. She became my closest colleague during the time I spent in Armenia, and we were often mistaken for one another by many workers at international organizations and NGOs because of our similarities in age and diminutive stature and because we were always together. Armine generously interpreted for me at meetings held in Armenian, became my close friend, and even convinced my Armenian landlady to install a washing machine in my apartment.

Armine was exceptionally reflective about her work and the elaborate networks of government ministries, NGOs, international organizations and donor governments involved in counter-trafficking activities in Armenia, at least in part because her year away in the United States had given her a new perspective. Yet she also found herself forced to confront a number of issues upon her return that she did not face when she had been alone in the United States, including the responsibilities she had as a working mother of a very young child. She found it difficult to maintain a healthy body weight because of the stress her work placed her under, and she looked perpetually fatigued from the late nights she spent helping her husband with his part-time work designing websites for a US-based company. Although he was a skilled computer programmer, there were no jobs for him in Armenia, and his lack of regular employment was a constant source of tension in their marriage.

Armine was by no means alone in her position as the main source of income for her family; in fact, many Armenian women who worked for donor-funded organizations described their conflicted sense of pride and guilt regarding their work. A woman named Lola who worked for a shelter that provided her with a steady salary as part of a three-year grant it had received from a Western European development agency described how she felt that her husband did not understand that her fluency in English and professional associations with relatively privileged Western Europeans did not mean that she was treated as an equal in the workplace. "What my husband doesn't see," she explained to me in tears one day after her German supervisor had made some particularly insulting comments about Armenians, "is that my salary comes at the price of my self-respect because Westerners come here and they feel they can treat people like me however they wish."

Armine often shared similar sentiments with me as we sat drinking tiny cups of Armenian coffee on weekends, when her mother-in-law cared for her young child. I would light the burner of my red East German stove and boil three spoonfuls of Armenian coffee powder in a water-filled *jazzve*, a small pot used to make the beverage that is so essential to any Armenian social encounter. I would then pour it into small cups as Armine and I each placed a sugar cube between our teeth and sipped the strong brew through it to infuse it with sweetness, as most Armenians do. Both of us were emotionally and physically exhausted by the long hours we had been working on an issue that was of great importance to us but often seemed to be little more than a means of generating donor funds to many of our peers. Armine complained about her responsibilities at home and her husband's demands on her time, while I lamented my then-single status and loneliness.

"But you can spend all of your time on trafficking" she said as she turned her cup upside down onto its saucer to allow the coffee sediment to form a shape that is supposed to reveal what the future will bring. "I wish I could work all the time, too." I shook my head and told her how my nightmares about the trafficking stories we heard everyday at work were beginning to frighten me during the day as well. I was not proud of that fact and worried that my internalization of other women's real lived experiences made me an ineffective anthropologist, or perhaps just a weak and self-absorbed person. Armine nodded and then said something rather perplexing about her somewhat conflicted identity as a professional woman and an activist who often found herself disregarded as a "local" worker and a mother and wife in a conservative society. "Oh well, just give me a couple of months, and then I'll be jaded like everyone else at work, and maybe I'll think that victims of trafficking are all a bunch of useless prostitutes too," she said. "Then my husband and baby can have me all to themselves."

As Armine indicated, there is often quite a difference in worldview between many employees of organizations that deal with the traffic in women and the women they ostensibly seek to assist. This point was made exceptionally clear when Liana returned to Armenia from forced prostitution in Dubai and sought out IOM's assistance in regaining custody of her children. Armine and I were both extremely invested in her case and took great care to ensure that she received as much assistance as possible from our agency. Our roles were significantly limited by budgetary constraints and our junior status in the organization, and we could not intervene when Chief of Mission Hans Muller decided that Liana could receive only free legal support to help her regain custody of her four children in exchange for her participation in an IOM project. Our business cards both read "Consultant on Gender and Counter-Trafficking" and this was reflective of our responsibilities, for although we could make suggestions, neither of us could direct the course of action taken with women who approached IOM for help.

How anthropologists are received by those they interact with in the course of their ethnographic fieldwork is always influenced by a number of factors, gender and age being foremost among them. My voluntary consulting work at IOM Armenia directly affected my research in a number of ways that I suspect were informed by both my age and my gender, and how I positioned myself during Muller's first meeting with Liana had everything to do with my previous interactions with him as a woman. I contacted Muller via e-mail before my arrival in Armenia and explained that I was writing a book on the traffic in women in several countries and hoped to offer my consulting services free of charge to IOM in order to facilitate useful contacts with donor agencies and governments. Muller agreed to schedule a meeting with me on my first day in Yerevan. He took me to dinner at an outdoor café and walked around downtown Yerevan with me. During this time, he discussed his previous relationships with women, despite my repeated attempts to steer the conversation back to the traffic in women.

I was distinctly uncomfortable with what felt much more like a date than my first meeting with someone who was effectively able to curtail my research in the country by refusing to allow me access to IOM, and yet the experience taught me a great deal about the nature of gender and power as exercised by some Western Europeans in an Eastern European context. Meeting Muller made me realize how lonely and isolated Western Europeans in positions of Eastern European power can become. Such Westerners are in an awkward position because their local employees earn far less than they do; in the words of one Armenian IOM staff member, "Hans's salary equals ten of our salaries." This distancing is compounded by the fact that they often do not speak the local language and the fact that single Western men are often propositioned by much younger and more attractive Eastern European women who want to emigrate.

This combination of extreme social isolation and overly solicitous behavior breeds distrust in people who already feel lonely, and thus they may assume an indifferent air such as the one Muller evidenced with Liana or may adopt the age- and status-inappropriate behavior he exhibited with me and many other women in their twenties. For a jaded individual such as Hans, Liana was no longer a person but rather a part of his work that needed to be dealt with before he left for a new posting—and what he hoped would be a happier life—in Moldova. "I can't wait to get out of this Mickey Mouse country!" Muller exclaimed during a meeting I attended with Armenian staff members one afternoon, leaving little doubt in anyone's mind that he had little invest- ment in their country's future. No one said a word in response, and when I asked several of those who had been in attendance about this lack of surprise, most responded with some variation of a sarcastic "Isn't that how Western Europeans behave?"

This office tyranny was in some ways offset by Muller's desire to incorpo- rate Liana into the IOM counter-trafficking strategy in the form of her partic- ipation as a speaker about trafficking at Armenian performances of a play on the subject. IOM had contracted a playwright to script a drama on trafficking that would tour towns and smaller cities throughout Armenia. Titled "Tomor- row without Today," it told the fictional story of an Armenian woman traf- ficked to Turkey and was designed to inform audiences about the risks of accepting offers to work abroad. Muller proposed that Liana travel through- out the country as a spokesperson on trafficking once the play was staged. Muller's asking her directly was fairly unusual; employees of international organizations in positions such as his often leave most of the interaction with victims of trafficking to NGOs and rarely meet with such women.

Muller sat behind his desk typing e-mails throughout his first meeting with Liana, punctuating particularly salient points in her narrative with neutral interjections such as "yes, yes, very interesting" and neither making eye contact nor setting aside his work. A law enforcement professional before he began working with IOM, Muller may have regarded his lack of eye contact and unobtrusive presence as a technique designed to instill a sense of trust and safety in Liana. Victims of trafficking often have difficulty relating socially to men after they have escaped bondage because of the sexual abuse they have suffered and their recent isolation from any nonviolent social or sexual encounters with the opposite sex, and Muller may have been sensitive to this and tailored his behavior accordingly. In an excellent example of the kinds of miscommunica- tion that can occur between those who have specialized knowledge about vic- tims of trafficking and those who have actually been victimized by trafficking,

Liana read Muller's behavior in quite a different way, and she revealed less and less of her story the longer he feigned distraction from her telling of it.

While Muller sat typing e-mails at his computer, I sat opposite Liana at the long table that occupied the other half of his office. It seemed that even the arrangement of the room itself was not conducive to real dialogue; Muller's desk sat in the far right corner surrounded by filing cabinets that almost gave the impression of a protective barricade. Liana and I sat at a table that had been pushed as close to the wall as possible on the left side of the room. I listened to the tone of Liana's voice grow increasingly faint as it became clear that Muller was not really listening, and I felt distinctly embarrassed. I saw that the cavernous space of his large office resembled my first Armenian courtroom, in which the accused were cornered in a room that was completely overwhelmed by the massive chair on which the judge was seated behind his imposing heavy wooden bench.

It was only when Liana stopped talking that he discontinued his work to propose her participation in the IOM project related to the counter-trafficking play, in exchange for free legal assistance in her custody battle with her mother. Making eye contact with her for the first time in the course of their meeting, Muller explained to Liana that the opinion of his Armenian colleagues was that audiences "would not accept" a sex worker as a speaker regardless of her life circumstances, and so it had been decided that Liana should present herself not as a victim, but as a woman who had gone to help a friend who had been trafficked to Dubai. In effect, Liana was to remain something of an innocent bystander to her own life story.

Liana shook her head and told Muller that she could not agree to his terms. Muller was understandably disappointed by her refusal to participate in what he had seen as an excellent opportunity to present a human witness to the traffic in women for Armenian audiences. "We've helped you so much in this office" he shook his head, "and you can't do this one thing that we need you to do?" Liana showed no emotion and simply repeated that she would not travel with the play. "I can't" she said, "because it isn't possible." Muller emphatically shrugged his shoulders and went back to answering e-mails in what effectively signaled the end of the conversation. I was deeply confused by the dynamics of their conversation, in which the balance of power between Muller and Liana had shifted in an unclear direction.

Did Muller give up in frustration simply because he felt that Liana owed a debt to IOM for having helped her in her time of greatest need, or because he knew he was on his way to a new posting in Moldova and no longer considered Liana's case a priority? Had Liana exercised agency by refusing to participate in a series of events for which IOM needed her, or was she simply afraid to associate herself with prostitution in any public capacity? Most important, why did Muller fail to ask Liana why she did not want to participate? I am aware that these questions are to some degree unanswerable because they speak to the intricate interpersonal dilemmas faced by unique individuals whose inner thoughts can never really be known, and yet they were on my mind as I watched Liana walk out of the office and sit down on the steps outside.

I went outside and sat next to her, both of us smoking and staring into space for a few moments before I told her something that had been foremost in my mind during my first few months of counter-trafficking work in Armenia. This was not an ethnographic strategy but rather an outgrowth of my sense that she needed to talk and of my own need to communicate with another woman who might understand me. "Do you ever have nightmares?" I asked her. She nodded emphatically and widened her eyes for dramatic effect. "Sometimes my nightmares are so real," I said as I fumbled in my bag for my cigarettes, "that they frighten me during the day." I immediately felt self-absorbed and callous as I realized the circumstances under which I had said these words; sitting next to a woman whose life was in a very real state of chaos, I had no right to talk about my own stories.

Yet instead of feeling affronted, Liana lit a second cigarette and passed it to me before I could locate my own. "Nightmares are very bad," she said in the English she had learned in Dubai, "because they are the only way that people can hurt you over and over again." I nodded and inhaled deeply on my cigarette, suddenly feeling the need to support her decision not to participate in the play. "I think you did the right thing," I said cautiously, "even if it was difficult." Because of the deep social stigma attached to prostitution in Armenia, Liana was clearly uncomfortable with the idea of being displayed in an extremely public forum as someone who had personal experience with sex trafficking in any capacity, and she also had a legitimate fear for her safety as a result of the threatening phone calls she continued to receive from her trafficker. From Muller's perspective, Liana had nothing to lose by being part of the traveling play; after all, he had privately explained to me, she would not have to identify herself as a former prostitute, she would receive free legal assistance, and she would be fulfilling what IOM viewed as a moral obligation to warn others about the dangers of accepting offers to work abroad. Liana saw the situation in a very different light. She had to take into account the manifold risks she would incur via public involvement with IOM when her trafficker was already threatening to harm her, she was reluctant to inflict stigma and shame on her family by publicly associating herself with prostitution in any capacity, and she did not agree that she was personally responsible to help other women avoid the situation she had just escaped. After all, she thought, why should she place the potential of helping a stranger above the pressing and cruel consequences for her own life?

"They think I have to do what they say just because they gave me some help" she sighed, "but I'm not their toy to play with." Liana's linguistic usage struck me as extremely notable when she went on to explain that she had to think of her future. Almost everything she said directly contradicted the notion that victims of trafficking do not exercise choice and agency in planning their life strategies. I felt deeply disappointed that a woman who had survived such difficult circumstances in life was treated with a combination of disdain and disregard by an institution that exists at least in part to help individuals in situations like hers. Liana and I went on talking about our nightmares for a few minutes, but it was impossible to avoid the fact that because of her decision not to participate in the counter-trafficking play, she would no longer have access to legal assistance. "Sometimes," she said before extinguishing her cigarette and standing up to leave, "I also think nightmares are the way our heart teaches us how not to treat other people."

Liana's talk of nightmares was clearly not the worst aspect of her double victimization at least in part by the organization that was meant to help her. Within weeks of approaching IOM for assistance, Liana was arrested and prosecuted by the government of Armenia as the leader of a trafficking ring. Her trafficker had raised enough funds to bribe the Prosecutor's Office, which was desperate to convict someone of sex trafficking in order to demonstrate compliance with US minimum standards and to avoid jeopardizing future donor aid through a reduction in tier status. At that point, the IOM office was in a state of transition as Muller prepared to leave for his new posting in Moldova, and the incoming chief of mission was still bound by his responsibilities to IOM Georgia, Armenia's northern neighbor. The confusion that ensued over responsibilities and roles combined with the broader social and institutional disregard for women like Liana to ensure that although the Armenian IOM staff members knew that Liana was innocent, they were powerless to do much in the absence of a strong (and, some argued, Western) central figure to organize support for her.

In a private e-mail exchange I had following my return to the United States, an Armenian IOM staff member wrote, "of course Liana is innocent, but what can I do since I'm just a local?"—a statement that highlights the disempowerment that some Armenians feel vis-à-vis the Western Europeans and Americans who hold positions of power in international organizations and embassies based in their country. In a bitter irony, the false prosecution of Liana at least partially ensured the continuation of US donor aid to Armenia, because her conviction presumably helped to convince the US Embassy officials responsible for compiling the information on counter-trafficking efforts that makes up the TIP report that Armenia was indeed making progress. As was discussed in Chapter Two, the abstract qualities of the tier system at least partially obscure the realities of sex trafficking as it affects individual women such as Liana by reducing the complexities of their lives into a dangerously neat categories and criteria that deal solely with actions at the state level without taking the implications of those actions into account. Liana was given a prison sentence of seven years, which means that she is still incarcerated as you read this book.

The sobering reality that those who formulate and enact policies that have deep impacts on women's bodies and lives may not always understand crucial structural issues about sex work compounds the invisibility of victims by rendering many counter-trafficking initiatives ineffective from the beginning. Trafficked women run the risk of being victimized again by organizations that ostensibly exist to assist them, and this example of how counter-trafficking efforts in Armenia are hindered by institutionalized corruption and unfair legislation reveals the use of women's bodies as political tools. Liana was exploited not only by the Mama Rosa who trafficked her and the men who paid a third party to have sex with her in Dubai, but also by the corrupt Armenian justice system under pressure from government authorities to meet US minimum standards by obtaining a trafficking conviction, by at least one international organization that sought to maintain high levels of donor aid by documenting its support of a victim, and, more indirectly, by the US government, whose views on trafficking are far too simplistic and broad to to take the complex realities of Liana's life into account.

Many activists and policymakers alike with whom I spoke in the course of my research argued that because of its especially egregious and morally objectionable nature, sex trafficking should be seen as a human rights violation rather than as a criminal act akin to the trade in narcotics. This issue was raised at the Conference on the National Action Plan for the Advancement of Women in Armenia on October 5, 2004, by senior Organization for Security and Cooperation in Europe (OSCE) representative Helga Konrad. Konrad began her speech, which was delivered before US Embassy Chargé d'Affaires Anthony Godfrey was scheduled to address the audience, by emphatically arguing, "human trafficking must not be seen as a fight for national security and against organized crime. It is first and foremost a human rights issue. What is needed is the political will to put theory into practice." Godfrey politely applauded what could be construed as an observation on how US counter-trafficking policies treat the problem in a manner akin to the illegal trade in arms and narcotics and then began his speech with "my government takes these issues very seriously" before proceeding to detail the approximate amounts of money that the US Department of State had allocated to Armenia to fight sex trafficking.

In the course of an interview in which I inquired about US Embassy rhetoric employed in the funding of counter-trafficking activities that Godfrey described in his speech, an officer of the Bureau of International Narcotics and Law Enforcement explained that the US Department of State provides approximately one billion dollars in donor aid to Eastern Europe and Central Asia as part of the Freedom Support Act, a piece of legislation that provides donor assistance to former Soviet republics to help ensure peace and stability in the region. He named a former chargé d'affaires as the source of the immense amount of attention paid to sex trafficking in Armenia, and he mentioned that the $392,000 in "performance funds" provided for the IOM production of "Tomorrow without Today," combined with the quarter-million-dollar budget earmarked specifically for counter-trafficking activities might not have been terribly effective. An officer spoke about the difficulties inherent in trying to coordinate activities among the vast number of international organizations and NGOs working on trafficking-related subjects. He cited the US Embassy's request that the local representative of the OSCE perform a legislative gap analysis to determine how Armenian law could better address trafficking, only to discover weeks later that the United Nations Development Program was already well into research on the same topic. He shook his head and said, "we're having trouble coordinating the big organizations, let alone the small NGOs. It's a real mess here, but we're trying. There's a real culture of dependency on the US here now."

Sadly, an officer's acknowledgment of "a real mess" regarding counter-trafficking activities in Armenia was an understatement. This is particularly well illustrated by the case of a US-funded study by the Armenian Sociological Association (ASA) that was ostensibly designed as a means to gauge how many victims of trafficking actually exist in Armenia. In response to a previous IOM study documenting the existence of sixty-five victims of trafficking, an officer noted that "we're doing the study to determine if trafficking is a problem and now we're wondering if it even is, because the IOM study only came up with sixty-five women. The ASA is planning to sample 2,500 women, so let's see what they come up with because we need at least one hundred to continue funding these initiatives." I left my interview with an officer at the US Embassy, eager to relate this information to my Armenian colleagues at IOM, one of whom smirked especially wryly and whispered, "if the Embassy requires one hundred victims, the study will produce three hundred. That's just the way the system works here. They'll print their thousands of forms and fill them out themselves, without even speaking to a single woman. That's how it works here." Similar sentiments about "how it works here" were unanimously expressed by Armenian workers at both international and nongovernmental organizations, all of whom privately insisted that the sample of 2,500 was probably designed as a way to make the study less focused and obtain more donor funds. As the example of the whispered comment "That's how it works here" illustrates, even the relatively privileged IOM staff members were somewhat marginalized because of their reliance on donor aid to fund their counter-trafficking projects and initiatives and, perhaps above all, their salaries.

The first trial involving alleged violations of Armenian counter-trafficking legislation was held in October 2004. An Uzbek woman and her adult son and daughter with all charged with trafficking eight women from the Central Asian republic of Uzbekistan into sexual slavery in Armenia. Because the trafficked women had chosen to return to Uzbekistan, the court was forced to rely on the deposition the women had provided to police rather than on actual in-court testimony, which would have been far more relevant. It is not surprising that the defendants used their absence to highlight what they perceived to be a hollow case. "Who is accusing us?" the son stood up and shouted angrily, "Where are they?" The literal invisibility of the victims was compounded by the lack of precedent in prosecuting a trafficking case and by an almost tangible sense of apathy that filled the nearly empty courtroom. IOM had maintained regular contact with the Uzbek trafficking victims via e-mail and had learned that the family's trafficking ring was threatening the safety of the accusers, making this a case in which the victims were literally not even safe in their own homes. However, perhaps the most striking feature of the three traffickers was their utter normality: as a family encircled by the wooden enclosure of the defendant's box, their ordinary appearance was difficult to reconcile with the crimes they had committed.

This banality was matched by the courtroom itself, which was located in an unmarked, dilapidated apartment and office building in a suburban Yerevan alley. The floorboards looked as though they had been made of hewn tree trunks and were punctuated by inch-wide gaps between slats that held yellowed cigarette butts of indeterminable age. A single guard stood just outside the courtroom dressed in the Soviet uniform that, because of a lack of state funds, is still in use in Armenia two decades after independence. Despite the fact that this was the first case of sex trafficking to be tried in Armenia, there were no journalists in attendance, a fact that an Armenian colleague attributed to lack of public interest and continued mistrust of news sources. I shared the single shaky, rough bench in the back of the room with a man wearing ill-fitting combat fatigues, his grease-stained hands nervously fumbling with a half-empty pack of West cigarettes.

The brother and sister entered a guilty plea, while their mother, who had previously been charged with trafficking in Uzbekistan, professed her innocence. All three had refused the services of a lawyer by claiming they had no real hope for a fair trial and insisted that although they did bring the eight Uzbek women to Armenia to engage in sex work, they should not be charged with trafficking because the women had gone willingly with full knowledge that they would work as prostitutes upon their arrival. The defendants, who did not speak Armenian, presented their closing statement in mutually intelligible Russian to the judge and insisted that they should be sent back to Uzbekistan because they had already been in prison for nine months. The judges sentenced the brother, mother, and sister to four, four and a half, and two years in prison, respectively.

The tone of the post-trial IOM staff meeting was one of resignation rather than happiness at the conviction, with Chief of Mission Muller pausing briefly after lighting a cigarette to announce, "Yes, they'll bribe someone and be back in Uzbekistan by the end of the year." The consensus was that no real victory had been won and that only a tiny fraction of a broader trafficking network linking Tbilisi (Georgia), Baku (Azerbaijan), and Dubai had actually been exposed in the courtroom. Muller's acknowledgment of the ability of trafficking rings to regroup quickly and take on different forms doubtless contributed to this sense of defeat despite the judge's sentence. This was especially salient given the direct involvement that IOM had in the outcome of what was referred to in the office as "The Uzbek Returns," an event that marked the first time Armenia was recognized as a country of destination, rather than origin, for victims of trafficking. Eight women had been brought to Armenia from Namangan, a region located approximately 150 miles from Tashkent near Uzbekistan's border with Kyrgyzstan. The case of "The Uzbek Returns" reveals many of the complex hierarchies and disjunctures at work in Armenian counter-trafficking activities, as well as the capacity of disparate groups' differing political agendas to affect individual women's lives.

The case began when eight Uzbek women who had been held for approximately one month in Armenia as victims of trafficking reported their situation to the Armenian police, who promptly notified the Prosecutor's Office. All eight of the women were temporarily housed in donor-funded shelters, and the mechanics of the counter-trafficking system in Armenia were set in motion for the first time. An enormous controversy immediately arose between the US Embassy and IOM, the two main suppliers of financial support to the women, regarding the pregnancy of one of the women, who had conceived as a result of a paid sexual encounter with a client. Two key pieces of American legislation prohibit the use of US donor funds to pay for abortions: the 1973 Helms Amendment to the Foreign Assistance Act of 1961, which states that "no foreign assistance may be used to pay for the performance of abortion as a method of family planning," and the 2001 Mexico City Policy, which requires international NGOs to certify that "they will not perform or actively promote abortion as a method of family planning as a condition of receiving... assistance" (United States Agency for International Development 2007). Thanks to the influence of religious conservatives on the formation of international policy, American law does not allow abortion to be financed in any way in other countries by government agencies, and the US Embassy was adamant that the woman could not have an abortion with American financial support. IOM eventually acted independently to help the woman obtain an abortion in the interests of her rights and emotional stability, but the question of the controversial termination of her pregnancy remains extremely relevant in this case. Herein lies the irony of state support for counter-trafficking projects: policies designed with a specific political agenda in mind may have extremely deleterious effects when actually applied at the local level.

The next major hurdle in handling "The Uzbek Returns" began when logistical questions of support arose between the IOM offices in Armenia and Kazakhstan (no equivalent office existed in Uzbekistan). A flurry of e-mails between the chief of mission in Armenia and the counter-trafficking program coordinator in Kazakhstan documented the intricacies of organizing the return of eight women and underscored how difficult it is to facilitate the safe reintegration of victims of trafficking into their home environment. In some ways, it also revealed the vast networks of customs officials, border guards and immigration authorities that traffickers have to bypass or co-opt into their world in order to sustain their operations. The return of the Uzbek women was paid for by a multilateral aid-funded project titled "Combating Trafficking in Central Asia," which covered Kazakhstan, Tajikistan, and Uzbekistan and had a set amount of funds reserved for the voluntary return of victims of trafficking. The total cost for all eight of the women to be returned to their homes in Namangan was approximately seven thousand US dollars and included airfare, temporary housing in Tashkent, and spending money. IOM officials in Kazakhstan recommended that the one hundred and fifty US dollars the women would be provided with to facilitate their safe journey home be given to them by an escort only after their arrival in Tashkent to ensure that law enforcement authorities would not steal it at the airport. Of course, the abuse of sex workers by the police is by no means limited to the countries of Eastern Europe and Central Asia, but victims of trafficking often tell about having all of their money and possessions stolen by the very people who are supposed to assist them.

A smaller point of contention then arose regarding which language the women should use to complete a series of questionnaires about their experiences as victims of trafficking. The IOM mission in Armenia felt that what they called the "international language" of English should be used, but IOM authorities in Kazakhstan argued that Uzbek or Russian, a second language common to all, should be substituted to ensure clarity. IOM Armenia eventually compromised by using forms filled out in English translated from conversations conducted in Russian with the Uzbek women by IOM staff members in Armenia. This approach was chosen because the forms had already been printed in English and many staff members felt that budgetary constraints demanded that they not be wasted. This underscores the complexities of the situation as well as the disturbing propensity of international organizations to focus an enormous amount of energy on matters of little importance relative to the gravity of the problems facing the women they are tying to help. Discussions about the women's reintegration into Uzbek life centered on the assumption that they would immediately be identifiable to airport authorities and to those in their home region as victims of trafficking and would consequently be stigmatized as prostitutes. This was a matter of major concern to both Armenian and Kazakh IOM staff members, who wanted to maximize the women's chances of completing a safe reintegration into their former lives. The unspoken theory on both sides of the return coordination effort was that the women's provocative clothing, status as travelers in a small, all-female group between two post-Soviet countries, and behavioral cues would enable strangers to identify them as easy to exploit. In other words, they were assumed to be somehow "marked" as sex workers.

The idea of the Uzbek women being "marked" reveals a set of assumptions that the relatively privileged staff members at international and nongovernmental organizations sometimes share: the idea that sex workers are somehow culturally distinct from other women. The word *prostitute* is often seen as an identity and a permanent professional category, rather than as a noun that describes a woman who has engaged in the exchange of sex for something of value as part of a temporary role she has taken on as a survival strategy. This conflation of sex work with immorality and marginalization highlights the gendered reality that even though the Uzbek (and other) women may wear less provocative clothing, additional factors also work against their efforts. Corrupt border guards and other law enforcement officials may assume that women with little education, no professional experience, and no place of employment have no reason to be traveling internationally, so discrimination against such women becomes not so much a matter of "what she was wearing" as of "what she was doing."

Knowledge of outsiders' assumptions about their behavior and moral character definitely informed the behavior and choice of language that the eight women employed with IOM staff members—to the extent that it became almost impossible to determine how much the women really knew about the type of work they would do in Armenia prior to their arrival. Victims of trafficking are well aware of the stigma that marks them as sex workers and may be ashamed of the choices they have been forced to make because of their unstable economic circumstances and social marginalization. Only one of the Uzbek women stated that she knew she was coming to Armenia to perform sex work; the other seven insisted they had been promised jobs as waitresses in a café. It seems highly unlikely that eight women traveling together outside of their country for the first time would not have discussed the type of work they were going to do once they arrived. This by no means implies that all victims of trafficking know the conditions they will be working in when they reach their country of destination, but the difference in opinion among the Uzbek women does suggest that there are profound gaps in education and authority between workers at international and nongovernmental organizations and the trafficked women themselves. These disparities can serve to silence victimized women in a very real way.

The result of such gaps is that in some (but by no means all) cases, job titles such as "waitress," "dancer," and "entertainer" may serve as code words that mask the women's awareness that they will have to sell sex upon their arrival in a new country. Such code functions to preserve cultural notions of morality in the presence of outsiders, especially the relatively privileged individuals who staff most organizations designed to assist victims of trafficking. By tailoring the reality of their situation to fit the neatly circumscribed typologies that most international and nongovernmental organizations have for victims of trafficking, women are able not only to preserve some degree of dignity in what has the potential to be an extremely humiliating situation, but also to exercise agency in a space where very little room exists to do so otherwise. Yet the agency exhibited by the Uzbek women closely resembles Scott's (1985) "weapons of the weak" in their decision not to testify in the court case or their use of linguistic code to preserve cultural notions of female propriety.

Advance knowledge of the circumstances women find themselves in once they reach the country to which they have been trafficked is of course tempered by the reality that desperate and impoverished people who are offered what they perceive as their only chance to earn money for themselves and their families are not likely to ask many questions about the conditions under which they will have to work. The discourses of naïveté and trickery presented in many analyses of sex trafficking thus may not be entirely representative of the way in which women's anxieties about their futures and very real lack of choices temper their ability to inquire about what circumstances await them in a new country or even to effectively seek help from organizations designed to assist them.

FAMILY VIOLENCE AS AN INDICATOR OF RISK

The choices that women perceive themselves to have as adults are often shaped by the broader socialization processes they undergo as children and adolescents. Victims of sex trafficking in Armenia have almost universally been physically or sexually abused by family members or other trusted individuals long before they are recruited into prostitution, which reveals that the problem has roots far deeper than the post-Soviet socioeconomic crisis that continues to shape life for many Armenians. My visit to an orphanage in the northwestern city of Gyumri underscored how early many of the risk factors for trafficking are introduced into the lives of women with fractured family histories of violence, prostitution, and economic instability. Sadly, sex trafficking increasingly affects multiple generations of families as part of a vicious cycle of victimization, learned helplessness, and perceptions about lack of choices so deeply entrenched that women occasionally make the seemingly illogical decision to engage in prostitution rather than taking much lower paid but considerably lower-risk job.

Chief of Mission Hans Muller and I traveled to Gyumri from Yerevan with Armen, an Armenian IOM staff member well-known for his proficiency in writing successful grants to international aid agencies, in order to attempt to persuade Sister Hasmik, of a local orphanage, to attend the opening night of IOM's counter-trafficking play "Tomorrow without Today." Gyumri is the second-largest city in Armenia and had been chosen as the opening location for the play because of IOM's concern that its counter-trafficking efforts had become too centralized in Yerevan. In many ways, Gyumri can be seen as a geographic metaphor for Armenia's reliance on donor aid; buildings in a striking variety of architectural styles had been erected by aid agencies that provided infrastructural support in the wake of the devastating 1988 earthquake. Sobering reminders of this destruction were also evident in the hundreds of tombstones that read "1988" in the unusually large cemeteries surrounding the city, as well as in the temporary structures that still house displaced families almost twenty years after the earthquake.

A cloudless gray sky hung over Gyumri as we entered the city. It was a cold day and the streets were deserted, giving the empty, reconstructed city an eerie feel that hung like a specter in the air. We had come to Gyumri to invite Sister Hasmik to the performance of "Tomorrow without Today" specifically because girls and young women from abusive, fragmented, or otherwise dysfunctional homes have a greater risk of victimization by traffickers. Orphans in particular are targets because they are part of a population of women who are largely invisible in a strongly family-oriented society. This effectively makes them disposable people who are not of great interest to government or law enforcement authorities because of the fragile and tenuous ties they have to Armenian society at large. We entered the orphanage with the disturbing knowledge that the girls and young women we saw all around us had an increased likelihood of eventually being forced into prostitution because of the lack of infrastructural support systems in place to help them once they attained majority status—and, for some, the damaged self-esteem that results from physical and sexual abuse by family members or other trusted individuals.

Sister Hasmik was an extremely forthright and efficient communicator as a result of her fourteen years as director of an orphanage in a post-Soviet country, and she was surprisingly adamant that the increase in sex trafficking cases from Gyumri had very little to do with the lack of employment opportunities for women. She started our conversation by emphatically stating, "This is not a problem of economics, because bad economic conditions are the easiest way to explain behavior. The real problem is with a social system which is not fully functioning." Sister Hasmik had seen far too many of the girls who grew up in her orphanage become prostitutes in Gyumri itself and victims of trafficking in Dubai and Turkey, and thus she had a very different perspective from that of policymakers and international organization staff members in Yerevan. She was exceptionally candid in her description of the role that trust had played in the cases of trafficking she had been secondarily witness to, and she felt it was extremely unlikely that strangers could persuade young women to travel abroad for unskilled work as effectively as family members and friends are able to.

Not unlike the strategies employed by pedophiles to trap young children in a cycle of sexual abuse and guilt, family members can play an important role not only in determining a young woman's likelihood of entering prostitution but also in instilling the perception that she has no other choice. Sister Hasmik described the story of a fourteen-year-old girl who had been abandoned to an uncle soon after her father died in the 1988 earthquake because her mother was no longer able to support her. The girl's extended family already had a daughter who worked as a prostitute in Dubai and sent home, via monthly bank transfers, money that was used to pay most of the family's expenses. Although there is no way to know whether the young woman in Dubai actually fit one of the various legal criteria for victims of trafficking or had chosen prostitution as her only option for income generation, it is clear that her family situation was especially conducive to exploitation as a consequence of its poverty, its fragmentation and, to some degree, its willingness to accept the sale of a daughter's body as a suitable means of support. Sister Hasmik insisted that there was more to the family's situation than was immediately apparent and that the fourteen-year-old girl had been subject to a kind of psychological violence that was far more damaging than physical abuse:

> At fourteen, she was a very well-developed child, and her family said, "It's time now that you repay us because we raised you. It's your debt and your obligation." I took her away and she stayed with us for three years, and her family would come see her for an hour every Sunday, and we made the

mistake of not supervising this, which is why today this girl is also a prostitute in Dubai. They actually convinced her that she is paying them back for
raising her.

There are a number of issues at work in this situation that problematize the
general belief that sex trafficking is an offense perpetrated by strangers and
also indicate that family violence is a predictor of vulnerability. Once the individual lives of women who have become victims are more carefully examined,
it becomes clear that there are numerous factors at work that uniquely disadvantage particular groups of women, including family violence and economic
insecurity. This is crucial because it indicates that contemporary approaches
insisting that almost any woman is at risk obscure the existence of especially
marginalized groups of women who could be more effectively targeted by
counter-trafficking initiatives. It remains something of a mystery in many
organizations, for example, why married women whose husbands live with
them in poverty and young women from families with both parents in the
home and no history of physical or sexual abuse are very rarely represented in
shelters or in police cases that deal with trafficking, and yet this absence itself
reveals much about the effectiveness of social support systems in preventing
the problem, even in times of severe socioeconomic stress.

In Sister Hasmik's example of the abandoned fourteen-year-old girl who
was pressured into sex work by her relatives, the techniques used by her
family members were essentially the same as those that would have been
employed by a trafficker who was a stranger to her. Of course, this process
was compounded by the added emotional weight of the complexities of family
relationships, the especially traumatic loss of her parents at a young age, and
the "normalization" of sex work in the family itself. Sadly, Sister Hasmik's
intervention seems to have merely forestalled what may have been almost
inevitable for a young woman who had so much working against her from a
very early age, as her family's acceptance of their own daughter's body as a
means of economic support was further used to rationalize the obligation that
the adopted niece had to "repay" the family for raising her. This abuse of trust
and instillation of guilt were matched by an insistence on the young woman's
indebtedness to the family, thus meeting the legal definition of sex trafficking
in both Armenia and the United States.

Sister Hasmik described forced prostitution almost as one would describe a
congenital disease, in terms of its predictability and devastating impact on
families:

> We have seven children whose mothers are prostitutes. Our greatest fear is
> that when the girls reach thirteen or fourteen the mothers will take them
> and put them into prostitution, because that is what their mothers did
> to them. Children who are not from normal homes are already wounded

children, and the potential is much greater for them to fall through the cracks of society.

Individuals who are emotionally and sexually abused as children or adolescents often become abusers themselves later in life, a sad reality that helps to explain the seemingly incomprehensible choice mothers who work as prostitutes sometimes make in forcing their daughters to enter the profession as well. Sister Hasmik acknowledged that sex work is indeed far more lucrative than the other options available to most of the young women who leave her orphanage when they attain majority status. She recalled walking down the main street in Gyumri and recognizing one of her former charges who had recently turned eighteen and become a single mother leaning against a corner dressed in provocative clothing. "Isn't it a shame that you are doing the same thing your mother did?" Sister Hasmik asked her, to which the young woman replied, "If you can pay me a hundred dollars a night, then I won't go. Otherwise I have to." Sister Hasmik then described how a Mercedes with Iranian license plates pulled up to the corner and the teenager got inside without saying goodbye.

The young woman's assertion that she would hypothetically not engage in prostitution if she had other options just as lucrative requires some further analysis. My previous research on topless dancers in the United States revealed that when speaking to outsiders, women who perform erotic labor often inflate the amount of money they earn as part of a process of self-empowerment and justification. Even so, there is more to the statement made by the teenager soliciting on the corner of Gyumri's main street than a desire to seem in some way economically justified in her behavior. Her flippant offer to stop selling sex in exchange for work that would pay one hundred dollars a night (an exorbitant sum of money in Armenia that equals the monthly salaries of some low-income workers) also reveals a deep sense of hopelessness and perceived lack of life choices. Young women like her are socialized very early in life through a process of abuse and marginalization that destroys their self-esteem and makes them believe that the only way they can earn wages above subsistence level is to sell sex. In other words, the abusive childhood and adolescence experienced by the girl from Gyumri combined with poverty, a lack of job opportunities, and the consistent life lesson that she is unwelcome in mainstream Armenian society.

Nonetheless, it is essential to stress the agency that such girls and young women demonstrate despite their perception that sex work is the only option for income generation open to them. I met approximately a dozen teenagers who fit most of the definitions of *victim of trafficking* discussed in Chapter 2, and yet none of these young women described themselves as victims. Instead, they called the males whom policymakers would describe as traffickers "my boyfriend" or, in the case of women traffickers, "my friend who helped me." Such terms are much more than euphemisms or expressions of shame about engaging in sex work. Rather, the teenagers who had been prostitutes before their placement in the orphanage were simply explaining their version of the world and their position as actors within it. They often rationalized abuse they experienced as part of what they viewed as "normal" human relationships, in which people beat and hurt each other when they are angry, trade sex for money and other necessary commodities, and (somewhat paradoxically) draw self-esteem and a sense of self-worth from the fact that men are willing to pay them for sex.

Young women in particular often voiced conflicted notions of pride and shame about prostitution, such as the fourteen-year-old who privately told me, "It [being paid for sex by much older men] makes me feel like I am valuable, but I also feel ashamed to say this. I could never make this much money doing anything else." This conflicted sense reflects the fact that in addition to living in desperate economic circumstances, many young prostitutes have never received unconditional love, and it combines with the extreme social stigmatization of sex work to send them a number of contradictory messages. Nonprostitutes may face similar issues. An example is the Armenian university student familiar with my research on trafficking who approached me to describe a time when she felt she could have been recruited into sex work without her knowledge. She was fluent in English, Russian, and her mother tongue of Armenian, and she often earned extra money by translating for groups of businessmen who came to Yerevan for work. After describing how well she had gotten along with three Turkish men she had worked for as a translator, she detailed the offer they had made her of a job in Istanbul at a salary four times what she earned in Armenia. "They told me, 'A pretty girl like you can earn so much money, you are wasted here in your country.' I felt so beautiful, like a film star who had been discovered! Later, when I talked to my mother, I realized that this was just straight trafficking, and there probably was no job in Istanbul. Those men wanted to make me into a prostitute." The university student's description of realizing, after talking to her mother, that she might have been forced into sex work in a foreign country raises important questions about what happens to young women who do not have a support network to assist them in similar ways.

The similarities between the orphaned teenage prostitute and the relatively privileged university student in ways of framing the offer of money for youth and beauty underscore how the human desire to feel valuable and have a better life frame many women's seemingly irrational decisions to enter into risky situations that involve prostitution. It is notable that neither of the statements employs the language of victimization, and yet many non-sex workers who deal with the traffic in women tend to view prostitutes as objects of pity and targets of assistance. However, it would be irresponsible to ignore the equally human reality that no one wants to self-identify with the pathetic word *victim* and its connotations of helplessness and failure.

Perhaps no one will ever know what happened to the young woman from Gyumri who got into the Mercedes with Iranian license plates without bidding Sister Hasmik goodbye (or the many others like her in the orphanage), and this testifies to the blurry lines that distinguish prostitution from sex trafficking. Armenian counter-trafficking legislation is heavily informed by the Palermo Protocol, which states that force, fraud, or coercion must be employed by an outside party in order for a woman to be considered a victim of this crime. When one considers the lives of women who are victimized, however, the meaning of these terms becomes increasingly unclear, and the central question remains: What actions constitute "force" when men are the ones who have the money to pay for the use of the bodies of women who have no other means of income generation? In a social system in which poverty and a lack of hope for the future inhibit women's abilities to ask informed questions about the conditions under which they will work in another country, "fraud" is a similarly relative concept. The definition of "coercion" is also vague when used in reference to impoverished women who have no family or social support system, have no place to stay, and see prostitution or emigration on someone else's terms as their only option for survival. All three of the criteria—force, fraud, and coercion—are met on different levels by many women who sell sex, and yet laws in every country are careful to distinguish between prostitution and sex trafficking. The young woman on the street corner in Gyumri, for example, was not a victim of trafficking so long as she continued to sell sex in her home country in order to support herself and her baby. She she would meet the Palermo Protocol's criteria (and those of the numerous pieces of national legislation inspired by it) only if the Iranian Mercedes took her to Tehran to perform the same actions.

It was in the context of such personal experiences that Sister Hasmik explained to us that she could not attend the performance of "Tomorrow without Today" as a result of the stigma attached to prostitution and, by default, sex trafficking. Her worry was that the girls and young women in her orphanage already faced so much discrimination as abandoned people in a strongly family-oriented society that she did not want to risk increasing such negative perceptions in the community. She contextualized her decision with telling references to the temporality of aid agencies, police corruption, and Armenian perceptions of women who engage in prostitution as inherently immoral:

> I feel bad when aid organizations come here and then pull out because they think nothing can be done, but I have sixty-five girls in my orphanage, and for the sake of them I cannot participate. I know the mentality here, and what people would deduce. I have to save my girls. IOM can talk about trafficking, USAID [United States Agency for International Development] can talk about trafficking because you are all here temporarily, but I live here. We are still not at the point as a society where the authorities can associate you with prostitution and leave you alone.

Sister Hasmik's connections between the seemingly disparate elements of donor aid, morally loaded suspicion of young women without families, and abuse of power by the police underscores the complex social world in which sex trafficking operates in Armenia. Her insistence that donor agencies are free to address culturally taboo issues because they are "all here temporarily" is particularly troubling in its implication that their efforts do not always operate in a manner that takes into account local sensitivities and fears.

Sister Hasmik went on to make disturbingly clear connections to other particularly devastating events in Armenian history, and to the contemporary exploitation of vulnerable women, in a way that reflected how her religious perspective framed her understanding of the past:

> What Armenians went through after the genocide is comparable to what our people are going through today, but then no one thought about prostitution as an option. A girl who went to the police to report that her mother's boyfriend wanted to sexually abuse her was raped by the police in Gyumri. By the police. In what kind of society can that happen? Communism destroyed the humanity in people as a whole, and our leadership today is still Soviet-trained; that's why they have this apathy. In every area there are people who care on an individual level, but the fair and just operation of our institutional systems and laws is not where it needs to be.

Armen, the IOM staff member known for his success in obtaining grants from foreign aid agencies, took umbrage at Sister Hasmik's assignment of blame to a system he felt had some intrinsic merits. "You can't blame communism for all of this!" he snapped. "If communism was so bad, why didn't we have a problem with trafficking in Soviet times? Trafficking only exists in this country because today money solves everything." From Sister Hasmik's Catholic perspective, communism had oppressive antireligious and therefore soul-destroying qualities, whereas Armen still had faith in communism's potential for creating socioeconomic equality. Sister Hasmik pressed her point further by insisting, "Armenians have always had a very high self-pride and communism made us lose that." "That wasn't communism," Armen said in what effectively ended our meeting at the orphanage. "You could just as easily say that about foreign aid."

An uneasy silence immediately descended on the unheated room following Armen's controversial statement. Although Armenians often privately lament the culture of dependency that Armenia has developed upon Western European and North American governments and compare it to the Soviet system in which their autonomy was subjugated to Moscow-based interests, such statements are generally not part of discussions related to policy implementation. Armen's association of foreign aid with oppressive Soviet-era practices had exposed the tense fault lines between ways of thinking about the traffic in women that each of us in the room harbored, and the awkward silence reflected how the political or religious perspective used to frame the traffic in women drastically changes what are seen as appropriate solutions to the issue.

Sister Hasmik was the first to speak after Armen's response to her statement about the loss of humanity under communism. "That's fine for you to say" she began, "because you are obviously not a religious person. Trafficking is a moral issue for me, and the best way for me to address it is to provide a stable environment for my girls, where I can protect them from these influences that will lead them astray." Hans was watching the debate between Armen and Sister Hasmik with rapt attention, leaning forward to listen more closely to what seemed to be a debate between two unique Armenian cultural systems, and I was silently wondering whether I should intervene before their differences escalated to a level that would make an enemy of Sister Hasmik and potentially jeopardize future efforts to establish connections with her orphanage.

"All the care and protection in the world cannot make up for poverty," Armen began in response. "If you don't address the reasons why women become prostitutes, how can you come up with a solution?" Sister Hasmik pursed her lips slightly and shook her head, remarking that she did not have the power to change society before adding, "Didn't the failure of communism in this country teach us what these supposedly idealistic efforts can do to people? How do you propose to improve my girls' futures?" Hans spoke up at this point to describe the numerous microenterprise development projects financed by international donors who aimed to assist young women and concluded by adding that the Armenian economy could never improve until effective anticorruption laws were implemented and enforced by the government.

I could no longer stay silent and simply listen. "Isn't this really all about gender inequality and the fact that it is still acceptable for men to buy sex from women?" I asked. Armen, Hans, and Sister Hasmik all looked at me and emphatically disagreed. "That's the easiest way to look at it," Hans said dismissively, "because there is absolutely no way to come up with concrete policy solutions when you take that approach." Sister Hasmik cited the unique disadvantages men faced in poverty, and Armen explained that isolating sexism as the central cause was about as useful as saying world hunger is caused by a lack of food to eat. Suitably chastised, I suddenly realized how narrow my own approach to the issue was, when just moments before I spoke I had thought of myself as the sole individual in the room who was genuinely enlightened about the traffic in women. And I immediately realized that everyone else felt exactly the same way.

It is true that such extreme differences in opinion can function to obscure the importance of combating the traffic in women, yet even more significantly, they show how institutional norms begin to take on their own momentum. Even though I had initially believed that my gendered perspective was the most comprehensive and inclusive in the room, I quickly found myself taken to task by the equally extreme points of view presented by the unreconstructed communist, the policymaker, and the religious figure. All four of us were simultaneously informed and bound by our professional obligations and limited social roles, just as institutions such as IOM are limited by the roles they are allowed to play in governments and international organizations.

Armen's comment had sparked a revealing debate among the four of us, and yet he was hardly alone in his sentiments. Like Armen, both victims of trafficking and ordinary Armenians sometimes evince a clear nostalgia for their Soviet past in the face of an insecure present and even more uncertain future. A number of positive meanings and symbols are summed up in the phrase "in Soviet times this never happened"—a sentiment commonly voiced by many Armenians in reference both to sex trafficking and to the vast array of socioeconomic and political crises that accompanied Armenian independence.

"IN SOVIET TIMES THIS NEVER HAPPENED": THE POLITICS OF NOSTALGIA AND MEMORY

I spent a weekend with Armen driving through the mountains to the southern town of Meghri to pay the salaries of workers who had participated in a project funded by the USAID to restore an ancient system of underground waterways called *chaheriz* that had been abandoned during Stalin's post–World War II Soviet "modernization" initiatives. *Chaheriz* long predate the Soviet period and were widely used throughout the Caucasus Mountains, as well as in many Middle Eastern and Central Asian countries as a reliable source of freshwater, and yet this technology was declared obsolete under Stalin and abandoned in favor of the introduction of piped water systems. Just as most of the government institutions and social safety nets that helped to prevent a significant problem with trafficking in Soviet times deeply disadvantaged Armenian women like Liana, the advent of Armenian independence meant that there were no more state funds to maintain and repair the pipes that had been installed nearly fifty years before. The result was that people living in the region had only sporadic access to drinking water, despite the existence of vast reserves of pure mountain spring water that flowed freely underground in the abandoned *chaheriz*.

Although the connection between dilapidated water systems and sex trafficking may not be initially apparent, the two share structural similarities that underscore how the trade in women's bodies is very much connected to broader social and institutional realities that impact all Armenians, regardless of education, class, or gender. The most obvious of these is the irony of outsiders teaching local people what is best for them. IOM implemented the USAID-funded project both by consulting elderly men in Meghri who still remembered how to build *chaheriz* and by researching the technique in local historical archives to find remnants of a technology almost forgotten under Stalin.

The end result of the project was the provision of drinking water to 250 families. But this huge success was simultaneously complicated by a number of issues that speak to the inequalities and hierarchies inherent in the aid process. Whereas USAID and IOM saw the small amount of money paid to workers who reconstructed the *chaheriz* as fair because the families of the men who worked on the project would benefit from the water it would eventually supply, the workers themselves felt cheated and angry that their labor was not better compensated. Similarly, it eventually became clear that the village mayor believed that USAID and IOM staff members were actually spies sent from Yerevan by Western European and American companies to assess ways to steal Meghri's mountain springwater, a sentiment that could not have been in more direct opposition to the agencies' belief that they were empowering local people.

That a donor-initiated project as innocuous as the reconstruction of a water system that would benefit an entire community was the subject of such suspicion and resentment reveals that donor efforts face serious challenges even when they do not deal with culturally taboo topics such as prostitution. After all, if providing free drinking water in a project in which locals were freely consulted can become such a controversial issue, what hope do already stigmatized and marginalized women such as Liana have of receiving fair and just treatment from donor agencies and the Armenian institutions they support? Meetings and discussions about the future of the region's water supply were notable in that local women were conspicuously absent from decision-making processes. The few women whom I did encounter in Meghri were either serving food to men or standing silently in the background of meetings in their male family members' homes. This lack of inclusion of women in important structural aspects of community life was also evident in that the few income-generating jobs that existed were only for men. It is fairly easy to see how in this context a woman without male family members to support her might be receptive to an ill-explained offer of employment abroad.

The same sense of hopelessness that leads women like Liana to accept such a proposal was also evident in the men living in Meghri who were frustrated by the lack of employment opportunities and of infrastructural support facilities such as health care and social welfare services. This sentiment was especially evident in such a far-flung region of Armenia, which is closer to Tehran than it is to Yerevan and in which all industry had closed soon after the country's independence. Residents of Yerevan often associate the remote regions of Southern Armenia with Stalin's forced relocation of its experienced stone masons to Siberian work camps to facilitate the construction of new projects in inhospitable terrain. Meghri and its surrounding areas were replete with abandoned factories full of rusting machinery, faded images of Lenin painted on the sides of buildings, and even an unfinished set of train tracks lining the border—complete with an empty train car that would never go anywhere.

Armen and I silently watched this desolate scene pass by the window of our jeep as we edged closer to Armenia's southern border with Iran, where uniformed soldiers in high pillboxes followed our progress with their automatic weapons. Armen and I began to discuss the politics of what we were doing in the context of his usual work of writing grant applications to donor agencies. Armen had trained as a filmmaker in Moscow before the collapse of the Soviet Union and, like most other Armenians, had been forced to reinvent himself professionally in order to find a job in a weakened post-independence economy. "Hey, Susan," he asked, "do you know who paid for this road we are driving on?" I shook my head in deference to his encyclopedic knowledge of which donor governments and agencies had financed specific infrastructural elements of Armenian life, ranging from dairy farms to university programs. Such information is far from trivial in a country where donor aid and (sometimes) the conditions under which it is given are normal topics of discussion for ordinary people.

"Our grandchildren paid for it!" Armen exclaimed and then smiled mysteriously before explaining that the road had been built with a loan granted to Armenia from the World Bank, an international organization that has been heavily criticized for its role in making countries with weak economies even poorer by issuing loans that often cannot be paid back for generations, if at all. We stopped for coffee at a small outdoor café on the side of the road and sat staring back at the heavily armed border guards who eyed us suspiciously from their sentry posts. Russian soldiers still patrol particularly sensitive border regions that were formerly under Soviet control, and jeeps with Russian military insignia are as common a sight in the mountainous region of Armenia adjacent to Iran as the empty factories and half-built train tracks left behind by the sudden removal of Soviet centralization and abandonment of infrastructure. Armen lit a cigarette and blew smoke in the direction of the spectacular mountain landscape dotted with Russian military vehicles. "Well," he began, "there are plenty of Russian soldiers here, so there is definitely sex trafficking going on." Injecting the unique sense of humor that he often used with me at least in part because of the horrified expression I usually reacted with, he lit my cigarette and then noted, "Well, Comrade Susan, if we run out of money this weekend, we can always sell you to the soldiers."

Black humor such as this is often used by people in positions where they are subject to prolonged psychological stress, such as police and military officials, in order to cope with the brutality they experience secondhand on a daily basis. My own status as a voluntary consultant to IOM garnered its share of black humor at staff meetings that dealt specifically with sex trafficking. For instance, bored colleagues sometimes interrupted discussions on definitions of victimization with "Susan is a victim of trafficking, because she receives no pay for her work in another country." Another example of the use of such humor occurred when IOM officials were unable to contact a woman who was believed to have become a victim of trafficking. Suspecting that she had been returned to Dubai, a colleague commented, "Well, at least someone is making some money. We certainly aren't." Jokes told about sex trafficking by colleagues at IOM as well as ordinary Armenians often echoed the focus of Soviet-inspired humor on an understanding of the world as a space of cruelty and suffering that individuals need to accept in order to simply survive.

The most salient aspect of the Soviet joke is that embedded in it is something far from amusing: the acceptance of institutionalized indifference. As Armen and I tried to practice the Armenian custom of reading each other's futures by examining the shape of the residue left behind when our empty cups of Turkish coffee were turned upside down onto their saucers, he began telling his collection of Soviet-era jokes specific to the region in which we were traveling. We had both heard rumors that the workers would be angry and perhaps volatile when we gave them the salaries USAID had deemed adequate, and we worried that we were conspicuous as urban people in a border region that had been at war with neighboring Azerbaijan in the not-too-distant past. Two jokes in particular stood out from his monologue, both of which drew on stereotypes of the mountainous region of Southern Armenia known as Karabakh as home to a stubborn, resolute people. I soon realized that each was quite different in scope and yet made reference to regimes with more in common than is initially apparent:

> So the tractor operator robs the village mayor, who insists on death as a punishment. The people are very upset by this, because there is only one man who knows how to operate this particular piece of farm machinery.

> After much debate, the village mayor calls a meeting in which he announces, "Okay, so we're going to kill the electrician!" When the towns-people respond in shock to the innocent electrician's death sentence, the mayor explains his rationale: "We have two of those, and we only have one tractor operator."

This typifies the formula of the Soviet joke and its stock characters, including the incompetent, irrational political figure and the helpless people who are at his mercy. Though designed to elicit laughter, the Soviet joke's underlying theme is that of life in a surreal and irrational universe in which humanity is subsumed under a faceless and Kafkaesque bureaucracy. I was still very new to the idea of hilarity arising from the grotesque when Hans held his farewell dinner for all of the IOM staff members at CCCP (as USSR is written in Cyrillic), an expensive restaurant in a downtown Yerevan basement that had been deliberately decorated to resemble a Soviet workers' cafeteria. Long, rough wooden tables were haphazardly covered with slippery red oilcloth, and the stark, unpainted walls were punctuated with large propaganda paintings of Stalin ensconced in gilded frames. An Armenian IOM employee sensed my distinct discomfort as I sat on a bench directly opposite a particularly menacing portrait of the mustachioed dictator responsible for the murders of untold millions during his rule. "You see, Susan" the IOM employee said as he said down next to me, "we used to live behind what the West called the iron curtain, but now you could call it 'the irony curtain,' the way we joke about our painful past."

A lively discussion ensued laced with much hilarity about the decor of CCCP, with many Armenian staff members joking about their own stories of hardship and suffering by adding a clever punch line to what was clearly a very painful memory. A woman in her late forties laughed about singing "Strangers in the Night" to her shivering baby when there was no electricity or heat in their building in the winter, and her story was followed by a man who announced that he was avoiding women altogether because they only brought bad luck to the men in his family. He described his soldier-grandfather walking home to Armenia from Germany at the end of world War II, only to find that his wife had married another man, and his father's imprisonment and eventual death in a Siberian labor camp after divorcing his third wife. "With that history," he exclaimed, "how can I ever win?" The more the people seated around me at the table laughed, the more I had to suppress the urge to burst into tears. It seemed so grossly unfair to me that individuals should have to endure so much senseless, irrational suffering that the only way to exorcize such painful memories was to laugh about them.

The notion of irrationality becomes particularly salient when Soviet-inspired humor is used to frame other, more recent events. Armen also used the genre to tell a fictional tale featuring the national stereotypes of the stubborn Karabakh resident, the lamenting Russian, and the spoiled American:

> So an American, a Russian, and a man from Karabakh are all about to be shot. The American says, "Don't kill me! I'm so rich and my life is so good!" The Russian says, "Oh, woe is me, I suffered so much under communism, please cut off my head instead to make sure that I die!" Then the man from Karabakh says, "All right, shoot me, but first get that American bastard to fix the tractor his aid organization sent, because we haven't been able to plough our fields all year!"

This passage makes use of the genre of Soviet humor to detail a much more recent state of affairs in which the interests of donor governments have come to dominate even mundane aspects of Armenian life, glossed in this example as the broken American tractor and the unploughed Armenian fields. The core theme in both of these examples is the absence of human logic, whether in the form of an obstinate mountain man who uses his last moments of life to curse the aid agency that donated the broken tractor or in the case of the innocent electrician sentenced to death to satisfy the village mayor's desire to punish almost anyone for the burglary of his home. Institutionalized indifference is embedded in both of these examples as part of an attempt at making sense of a world devoid of justice, meaning, or individual rights.

It remains important to underscore the agency of individuals whose seemingly illogical fates and reactions are described in the Soviet joke—an agency that may not be immediately apparent because the genre follows its own logic. After all, what did the man from Karabakh have to lose by speaking out when he knew that death was inevitable and pleading for mercy would be futile? By extension, how was the mayor featured in Armen's first joke to maintain authoritarian control over the villagers and simultaneously ensure the harvest if he killed the only tractor driver? The key principle that underlies the logic of the Soviet joke deals with the exercise of agency, resistance, and control: the man from Karabakh uses his last moment of life to exercise a rare moment of free speech, whereas the village mayor follows his illogical train of thought to what seems to be a completely logical conclusion. This "logic" was foremost in our minds as we arrived in Meghri.

We stayed in Meghri for two nights to negotiate the controversy over the USAID payment to the workers. We were guests of the village mayor, whose house was surrounded by the pomegranate trees for which the region is particularly well-known in the rest of Armenia. The village mayor was polite but distant and seemed unwilling to engage in conversation until we ate dinner together in his garden, where the heady fragrance of pomegranate blossoms perfumed the mountain air. He asked us a few halting questions about what water tasted like in Yerevan and asked me directly about the quality of water in the United States. We responded politely, but we were uncertain why he was asking such questions and were hesitant to inquire further while we were guests in his home. Something about us was obviously bothering him, and so I broke the awkward silence by describing our work with victims of trafficking from his region of the country who were rumored to be sold as mistresses to wealthy and much older men from Tehran. The village mayor nodded politely and said that he had also heard about this and that it was very sad. Even so, he remained distracted until he had finished his fourth glass of vodka, at which point he leaned very close to me and whispered conspiratorially, "You know, I am going to buy Meghri's economic independence with water. You can't steal it from us, because it's ours."

Armen and I suddenly realized that his earlier questions about water were contextualized in his belief that we were part of some broader conspiracy to somehow steal this precious resource and profit from it. "We had the best water in all of the Soviet Union," the village mayor continued, extolling the purity and crisp taste of his region's springs. Not quite sure how to respond to this quasi accusation, I politely asked him about his strategy to economically empower Meghri by selling its water. "What do you mean?" he asked, as his face took on an expression of genuine disbelief, and I realized that the kind of infrastructure that would be necessary to collect, bottle, and market the spring-water had not occurred to him. Clichéd as it may sound, the language and practices of independence and a free market still held a kind of magical aura in this distant and out-of-the-way place. The village mayor quickly regained his composure by pouring us both another vodka and said confidently, "Someday you will also drink the pure waters of Meghri in your country, and then you will think of me," and winked. In a more serious tone, he added, "In Soviet times our girls never went to Iran as prostitutes. This shouldn't be."

Darkness was beginning to descend on the orchard, and although Armen and I were eager to meet the workers to give them their salaries, the village mayor's disturbingly clear connection between his naïve plan to get rich selling water and the growth of sex trafficking following the advent of a market economy had truly distressed us. In Meghri, it seemed, we were not only on the margins of Armenia but also on the edge of grasping something terrible: how the introduction of free-market capitalism and donor aid had transformed everything from drinking water to women's bodies into commodities for sale.

Armen and I arrived at the town square just after the time we had promised the laborers we would be there, and as we hurried toward them, we could see that their expressions were already locked in a combination of suspicion, curiosity, and overt hostility. Gender norms in Armenia mandate that men handle most economic transactions, so I stood quietly as Armen explained to the workers that USAID had done a great thing by reconstructing the *chaheriz* and that although perhaps the men were not going to paid a great deal for their work, everyone should be extremely happy that all of the families in Meghri would now have access to clean drinking water. The men began to shift a bit before one suggested that we continue the conversation in a nearby house. Armen nodded, and we entered the screened porch that clearly belonged to the man who had spoken first. I could just barely see a group of women who had discreetly positioned themselves near the door that led to the kitchen, but before I could invite them to join us, the owner of the house raised his voice and pointed an angry finger at Armen.

"You aren't Stalin!" he shouted. "We won't work for you for nothing!" The other men nodded silently as he described in painstaking detail the back-breaking labor that had gone into digging the *chaheriz* and learning how to build it from elderly men who were often not certain whether they themselves correctly remembered the technology. Armen listened politely before firmly reasserting that we had been issued a certain sum of money by USAID and could not give them any more, but before he could finish, one of the men thrust him against the wall and held a knife to his throat in anger. Hoping that this gesture was only a threat designed to see whether Armen could produce more money, I quietly stepped outside as the shouting between the men intensified. The silence outside the house was extremely eerie, almost as if the entire village were straining to hear what was happening inside.

The sun sets quickly in the mountains, so the village was in absolute darkness as the moon slowly rose over the Caucasus, highlighting the peaks in a brilliant purple-blue. As I stood in the cold night air, there did not seem to be much difference between the rocky soil of Armenia and the same earth that rested under the boots of Iranian soldiers patrolling the other side of the border. The sense of accrued hopelessness was almost palpable in the region and transcended generations: grandparents had been forced laborers in Stalin's Siberian camps, parents had lived through the austerities of Soviet times in a far-flung corner of the USSR followed by war with Azerbaijan, and the laborers' desperate actions seemed to demonstrate that even younger people may not have hope for the future. It seemed that it would be so easy be for a young woman from Meghri to agree to an offer of a better life in Tehran, Turkey, or almost anywhere, without even asking too many questions. I shivered as I thought of the silent women I had seen tucked away in the kitchen listening to their desperate husbands fight over their pathetically low salaries, and I realized that this very sort of thought process and lack of hope and of alternatives sets the scene for vulnerability to sex trafficking every single day, all over the world.

The tension was beginning to mount inside the house, and the shouting was impossible to ignore when a strong hand suddenly wrenched my shoulder in the direction of its owner. Terrified, my eyes struggled to focus in the dim moonlight before I realized that it was the village mayor, who was reeling a bit from the effects of the additional glasses of vodka he had clearly consumed after we had left. "You see, Susan," he slurred, "I forget to tell you that we don't have anything in Meghri except pretty girls and water, so we have to be careful. Everybody wants to steal them from us." I was too stunned to speak and stood in awkward silence until the intoxicated village mayor doubled over in hysterical laughter at his own words and stumbled off into the darkness, just as Armen emerged from the house to announce that the workers had grudgingly agreed to accept the money USAID had sent with us.

Embedded in both the Soviet joke and the mayor's black humor is an acknowledgment of both perceived inferior status vis-à-vis those in power and a lack of hope that life will improve. This cultivated sense of irony was met in equal portion by nostalgia for the economic and social security of the Soviet era relative to the situation in contemporary Armenia. Discussions about sex trafficking often included statements such as, "in Soviet times this never happened," implying that although freedoms may have been curtailed, at least women's bodies were not for sale in a free-market economy. Some individuals were convinced that life for the vast majority of Armenians had been infinitely better prior to independence, with this nostalgic quality-of-life index ranging from better-tasting food to job security to a general sense of well-being. "In Soviet times people were more interesting," a typical observation would begin, "because you would finish university and get assigned to some job, and you didn't have to worry about anything. People were more interesting then, because we had so much time to read literature." This sentiment is implicitly juxtaposed with the contemporary Armenian reality that job security and the leisure time necessary for self-cultivation are foreign elements in the free-market economy.

Such humor is by no means confined to rural areas such as Meghri that have been especially devastated by a lack of employment opportunities. Indeed, cultural events and individual conversations in the urban center of Yerevan are often imbued with the same sense of hopelessness. I attended a performance by jazz musician Arto Tuncboyacian, who is best known for singing in an unintelligible language he invented himself as an expression of alienation and isolation. Tuncboyacian had just begun an interlude, halfway through his performance, to draw attention to a table of large men in identical dark suits and black sunglasses seated near the stage. "In Armenia," he began, still beating a drum to create a rhythm for his words, "some people don't have anything, while others profit from their poverty. This is the reality of our poor Armenia, where we can't even walk down the street without falling into a hole." The audience laughed at this reference to the ostentatious display of gold watches and expensive liquor at the men's table juxtaposed with unlit Pushkin Street outside the venue, where, before the show, audience members had to jump carefully over deep trenches that had been dug and left unfilled months ago by municipal workers. "Well," Tuncboyacian sighed before taking a sip of Armenia's most famous beverage, "In Armenia we don't have anything, but at least we have cognac!"

The most marked instance of Soviet nostalgia I encountered in Armenia occurred at a barely functioning pomegranate wine factory several hours' drive from Yerevan. The pomegranate has a special place in Armenian folk culture as both a symbol of fertility and a semi-religious icon; it is said to contain one seed for every day of the year under its sharp outer edge that resembles a tiny crown of thorns. As a curious natural metaphor for life in the form of fertility, and death symbolized by the crown of thorns worn by Christ in his martyrdom on the cross, the pomegranate is a quintessentially Armenian symbol used at important rites of passages such as weddings. Prior to independence, pomegranate wine was manufactured in great quantities in a southern factory that proved unable to function efficiently in the absence of Soviet subsidies. The factory I visited was a wooden construction consisting of two rectangular buildings that contained the machinery necessary to process millions of tiny succulent seeds into the bright red fermented liquid. The machinery had long since fallen into disrepair, was rusting in parts, and did not seem likely to last much longer.

I bought an inexpensive bottle of pomegranate wine in a recycled plastic liter bottle that still bore the label of a commercial brand of water and stood outside the factory, the side of which was entirely covered with an enormous propaganda painting. Lenin's face featured prominently in the upper right-hand corner as the sun, under which happy, well-fed children danced in the shade of a lush grove of Armenian pomegranate trees. "You see that it wasn't always this way," the factory manager who had just handed me the plastic bottle smiled and said. "In Armenia we used to have pride."

Armenian negotiations of a system in which collapse and implosion threaten to become permanent conditions demonstrate how institutional power sometimes takes on such momentum that it engenders an entire genre of black humor as a coping mechanism. Unfortunately, the Soviet joke continues to mirror everyday life for many Armenians almost two decades after independence, and the almost incomprehensibly tragic case of Liana's false imprisonment resembles nothing so much as the Soviet joke about killing one of the two innocent electricians rather than the guilty—but irreplaceable—tractor driver.

This sort of bitter irony is also evident in statements by the officer of the US Department of State Bureau of International Narcotics and Law Enforcement Affairs, who has admitted that Armenia is in "a real mess" as a consequence of the culture of dependency that has been created by US donor aid. The shared conviction among IOM staff members, the traffickers, and their victims alike, that justice had not been served in the Uzbek trafficking case similarly highlights how sex trafficking operates precisely because of the presence of inefficient and insufficient local and international institutions in Armenia. The most significant conclusion to be drawn from the Armenian example, however, is that the complex webs manifested in the articulation of power sometimes become Byzantine enough to disadvantage both the powerful and the powerless.

4

Bosnia-Herzegovina: NGOs, Donor Aid, and the Establishment of Post-Conflict Civil Society

GENDERING WAR AND ITS CONSEQUENCES

"Money wasn't worth anything during the war, so instead we had cigarettes and sex," said a woman in her mid-thirties who had survived the years of the siege of Sarajevo. "If you had one of those things to sell, then you could survive." She had introduced herself to me just minutes before when we were both alone and waiting for friends at an outdoor café in Sarajevo. Then she proceeded to give me a completely unsolicited list of reasons why I should not worry about my safety as a foreigner in Bosnia, because it had been over a decade since the war. "It is true that we live in a country full of war criminals," she smiled quixotically, "but here in Bosnia you can feel safe." I did not know how to respond to her statement, inasmuch as I had already been consistently humbled and overwhelmed by the frequency with which Bosnians I barely knew shared their personal war stories with me.

Before I began my research, I decided not to bring up the war in conversation, out of respect for the people who had survived such notorious brutality, and yet the topic proved to be both inescapable and popular with almost everyone I spoke with. People seemed eager to have a stranger listen to their memories of violence, perhaps because they were certain they would never see me again and aware that their Bosnian friends might not want to hear about such a dark topic.

I was often struck by how a walk past some specific location with one of my Bosnian acquaintances on a beautiful, sunny day would suddenly prompt a spontaneous tale of horror and deeply personal grief from a person I barely knew. On the drive home from a picnic in the countryside, a woman pointed out the car window to the Sarajevo Zoo and told me how, during the war, all of the animals were released because the zookeepers had run out of food. She then recounted how the inmates from the nearby mental asylum had been turned out for the same reason, and it was impossible not to imagine the surreal scene of zebras and schizophrenics wandering the shelled streets of Sarajevo during the siege. As we sat outside at a café in the old Turkish quarter of the city, a Bosnian woman I was having dinner with pointed to a nearby building under restoration and fluttered her fingers through the air like rain to demonstrate how the burned pages of the millions of books kept there since the period of Austro-Hungarian rule had wafted throughout the city for months after the National Library was burned by Serb nationalist troops. Just as the traffic in women in Armenia could not be separated from the socioeconomic devastation caused by the collapse of Soviet Union almost two decades before, the effects of the war in Bosnia were far-reaching and impossible to ignore.

STATE-SPONSORED RAPE ON TRIAL

Radovan Stanković was a Bosnian citizen and a soldier in the Miljevina Battalion of the Foča Tactical Brigade under the command of the Bosnian Serb paramilitary leader Pero Elez (ICTY 1996). He was an ordinary ethnic Serb from Foča, located approximately 34 miles southeast of Sarajevo, who abruptly rose to a position of authority when his town was seized by ethnic Serb forces in April 1992. Ethnic Serb paramilitary troops acted quickly after the takeover to detain Bosnian Muslims, many of whom were forcibly imprisoned in their former homes, apartments, motels, schools, and community centers. Many Muslim women were separated from their husbands, fathers, and children and locked in private homes and apartments that were used as brothels run by, and for the exclusive use of, ethnic Serb soldiers.

Stanković was responsible for the operation of one such private home called "Kamaran's House," which held at least nine Bosnian Muslim females against their will and forced them to work as prostitutes for ethnic Serb soldiers. He not only assigned women and girls as young as twelve to be raped and beaten by specific soldiers but also imprisoned at least one young woman whom he repeatedly raped without allowing her contact with anyone but himself for three months in 1992 (ICTY 2005). In addition to this sexual enslavement, Stanković forced the Bosnian Muslim women and girls to wash uniforms worn by the men who had killed their families, made them cook and clean, and regularly informed them that they would be murdered when the soldiers no longer found them sexually desirable (ICTY 1996).

Stanković was charged in June 1996 under the Geneva Conventions with four counts of crimes against humanity, including enslavement and rape and four counts of violations of the laws or customs of war, including rape and outrages on personal dignity. He was originally scheduled to be sentenced by the United Nations International Criminal Tribunal for the former Yugoslavia, a court in the Dutch city of The Hague specifically designed to prosecute soldiers such as Stanković who were responsible for atrocities committed during the war. The court was meant to bring justice to victims in a destabilized society, as well as to deter future war crimes, by limiting its jurisdiction specifically to the prosecution of war crimes committed in the territories of the former Yugoslavia between 1991 and 1995. The ICTY differed significantly from a national court in that it was staffed by international judges and could try the accused for crimes under both national and international law, in the hope of reducing bias related to the war and ensuring accountability for crimes committed. It was established in 1993 by UN Security Council Resolution 827 to address "widespread and flagrant violations of international humanitarian law occurring within the territory of the former Yugoslavia, and especially in the Republic of Bosnia and Herzegovina, including reports of mass killings, massive, organized and systematic detention and rape of women, and the continuance of the practice of 'ethnic cleansing,' including for the acquisition and the holding of territory" (ICTY 1993).

The ICTY was established to prosecute individuals who committed war crimes as defined by the Geneva Conventions, a series of four post–World War II treaties signed in Geneva regarding the treatment of civilians and prisoners of war during periods of conflict. War crimes are limited to acts against persons or property, including extensive destruction not justified by military necessity, violations against the laws or customs of war, such as attacking undefended populated areas; crimes against humanity such as torture and rape; and genocide, broadly defined as the creation of conditions of life designed to bring about the physical destruction of a specific group of people. ICTY cases are heard by three judges, none of whom are from the same country, and follow the UN definition of "international human rights standards" that prohibit trial in absentia, presumption of guilt, or imposition of the death penalty.

It was seven years before Stanković was apprehended by the NATO-led Stabilization Force (SFOR) in Foča in 2002, after which he was immediately transferred to the ICTY prison in The Hague. Transcripts from the Stanković hearings make it very clear that the judges did not believe his crimes were of sufficient importance to be tried by an international criminal tribunal. Efforts were made from the inception of his case to transfer Stanković to be tried by the Court of Bosnia-Herzegovina in Sarajevo, much to the dismay of the accused (ICTY 2002). The transfer was a controversial decision given that his was the first war crimes case to be remanded to Sarajevo; in light of his crimes, it is not surprising that Stanković was adamant that he would not receive a fair trial in a predominantly Muslim city less than one hour's drive from the place where he had ordered, supervised, and engaged in the rape of at least nine Muslim women. At the hearing that announced his imminent transfer to the court in Sarajevo, Stanković engaged in numerous outbursts during which he called the ICTY's decision a "feudal decree" and described Bosnians as "Ustashe Mujahedin" (fascist Muslim terrorists) and "the Jamahiriya" (in this context, a disparaging term for an Islamic religious court). Stanković became so disruptive that the ICTY judges ordered his microphone to be switched off on several occasions when his invective became particularly vituperative (ICTY 2002).

By all accounts, every effort was made by the ICTY to ensure that Stanković's rights would not be violated when he was tried for the repeated rape and brutalization of underage girls and adult women (ICTY 2005). On November 14, 2006, Radovan Stanković was sentenced in Sarajevo to sixteen years in prison for the egregious abuses he committed by forcing girls and women to become prostitutes for ethnic Serb soldiers. It was decided that he would serve his sentence in his hometown of Foča, where his crimes were committed. He began to complain of ill health after just six months in Foča prison and requested to be taken to the hospital, which prison authorities arranged. On May 26, 2007, en route to the hospital, rapist and sex trafficker Radovan Stanković escaped into a waiting car, which most Bosnians believe transported him to safety in a sympathetic Serbian town. Not a single shot was fired by either prison guards or his accomplices. This shocking news warranted exactly one paragraph on page 16 of the *New York Times*. It was titled "Bosnia: Convicted War Criminal Escapes" (5/26/07: 16).

The Stanković case raises serious questions about justice and the rule of law not only in Bosnia, but also in the international community, given that his transfer to the Sarajevo Court was designed as the first UN and ICTY endorsement of the country's ability to enforce the law over a decade after the war. His escape is understandably a matter of extreme sensitivity in Bosnia, and Judge Shireen Avis Fisher at the War Crimes Chamber of the Court of Bosnia-Herzegovina in Sarajevo was adamant that the Stanković case was a matter of extreme disappointment. "The people of Bosnia and Herzegovina have been let down by this," she insisted. "This court should never have started without a prison. We don't choose the prison, the Ministry of Justice does, and clearly they have made choices based on ethnicity to ensure [adherence to] human rights standards."

Judge Fisher's statement confirmed the suspicions of many Bosnian Muslims that Stanković was sent to his hometown of Foča to serve his sentence because of the threats and violence that ethnic Serb inmates have faced at a non-majority-Serb prison. The Court had hoped to comply with what the UN and other international organizations term *international human rights standards* by ensuring that Stanković would not face such discrimination and abuse in prison because of his ethnicity and status as an ethnic Serb war criminal. Nonetheless, a Bosnian Muslim employee of an international organization put Judge Fisher's analysis somewhat more colorfully when he privately explained to me that if Stanković had been placed in a predominantly non-ethnic-Serb prison, "the Muslims would have cut off his balls and laughed while he died."

Judge Fisher stressed the need for a separate prison to house war criminals, not only to ensure that such egregious breaches of the justice process would not recur, but also to engage in a process of what she called "community rehabilitation." Stating that such a prison would cost approximately sixteen million euros (which she characterized as "peanuts" compared with other donor aid initiatives), Judge Fisher expressed frustration at the lack of funding the Court received and described how she had faced major difficulties in locating donor funds amounting to $2,500 to purchase three computers for defendants to review their case files. "This is not a sexy, showy issue," Judge Fisher explained. "Bill Gates does not want a plaque with his name on it at a prison. And so that's why we don't have one." She noted that her greatest hope was to see such a prison constructed in order to engage in a process of personal rehabilitation and community impact that could be specifically focused on war crimes. It remains to be seen whether donor funds for such efforts will be forthcoming.

Human rights consultant to IOM and former Organization for Security and Cooperation in Europe employee Susan Stamper was adamant that the Stanković case represented "a huge failure" and "an embarrassment" on the part of the ICTY and the Court of Bosnia-Herzegovina. Stamper had done extensive work for IOM in designing a provisional witness protection program for victims of trafficking, and she shared my concerns about the safety of women who had courageously testified before the Court about the rapes and other forms of violence they had endured when they were trafficked into forced prostitution under the direction of Stanković and others. "Perhaps nothing will ever happen to those women who were so brave to testify," she sighed, "but they will always worry." More notably, she also tacitly confirmed the belief of many Bosnian Muslims that Stanković's escape had been part of a carefully orchestrated plan to send a clear message to Bosnia that ethnic-Serb war criminals could not be effectively prosecuted. "They allowed him to go, and now they will be very well-off," she said in reference to the prison guards who at the time of writing were still being questioned about their failure to fire shots as Stanković sped away from police custody.

The use of rape as a tool of war is certainly nothing new, so in this sense perhaps the ICTY was correct in its assessment that the Stanković case was too minor to warrant their full consideration. However, this decision raises pressing questions about definitions of, and responses to, the traffic in women, because one of the most horrifying aspects of Serb nationalist actions during the war was the establishment of what are known in Bosnia as "rape camps" (such as the one administered by Stanković), where women were separated from their male family members and then subjected to rape, torture, and forcible impregnation as part of a deliberate attempt at genocide. It has been documented that such camps were systematically and centrally orchestrated from the Serbian capital of Belgrade and that six months before the war officially began in 1992, barbed wire and posts had already been erected at sites that would later become Serb-administered internment camps (UN Security Council 1994).

The practice of state-sponsored rape was intended to destroy the core social institutions of its victims and to instill terror so extreme that entire communities would refuse to return to their place of origin. There is evidence that in some cases, Serb soldiers were under orders to forcibly impregnate non-Serb women and then expel them from Serbian-held territories when they were about to give birth (UN Security Council 1994). These women often had no functioning socioeconomic support networks when they were released from such camps, because many of their families were dead and health care was unavailable. Rates of suicide and infanticide among the women who were forced to give birth to the children of Serb soldier-rapists were extremely high, a terrible fact which underscores the effectiveness of rape is as a genocidal strategy.

In 1994, the UN Security Council compiled under the direction of Chairperson M. Cherif Bassiouni, a report titled "Rape and Sexual Assault" that examined allegations of rape as a war strategy in 57 Bosnian villages, towns, and cities and 18 Croatian locations. It named 162 detention sites in the former Yugoslavia where women were imprisoned and sexually assaulted, 88 of which were run by Serbs, 35 by "unknown sources," 17 by Croats, 14 "allegedly by Muslim and Croat forces together," and 8 by Muslims as part of "ethnic cleansing" campaigns designed to homogenize the ethnic composition of certain areas (UN Security Council 1994, 6). The UN Security Council report identified a number of systematic patterns at work in the rapes of both Bosnian and Croatian women which indicate that they were part of an organized strategy designed to humiliate and terrorize specific ethnic groups, particularly Muslim women. These tactics included sexual assault in public or in front of family members; the detention of women, with clear communication of the intention to impregnate by both senior military officers and low-ranking soldiers; and the use of broken glass, guns, and truncheons as tools of sexual assault (1994, 12–25).

Although the Security Council report is based on 1,100 reported cases, the methodology employed in gathering this information indicates that this number is probably grossly underestimated. It was based entirely on three sources: a database of evidence at the International Human Rights Law Institute at DePaul University in Chicago, 223 interviews in Croatia, and the analysis of interviews and findings by governments submitted to the Security Council, many of which were based on evidence provided by refugees. It is self-evident that this methodological strategy left out a significant number of victims who remained in Bosnia following their internment in "rape camps"—victims who may not have reported the crimes committed against them because of the shame and stigma associated with sexual assault and an understandable fear that at-large war criminals such as Radovan Stanković would harm them if they disclosed this information.

The UN Security Council Report is disturbing in that it clearly documents the use of rape as a tool of war, and even more unsettling is the conviction of the vast majority of Bosnians that UN peacekeepers from Canada, France, New Zealand, and Ukraine were complicit in perpetuating the traffic in women by patronizing Serb-operated brothels, the best-known of which was Sonja's Kon-Tiki on the outskirts of Sarajevo. This location had been a restaurant prior to the war and was quickly converted to a brothel that housed young Muslim and Croat women who had been captured by Serb soldiers and forced into prostitution. This circumstance later became the focus of an informal inquiry by UN officials, which was promptly dismissed because "there were no grounds for pursuing it" (Ferguson 1993, 3). The abuse of girls and women at Sonja's Kon-Tiki was by no means perpetrated by minor officers and low-ranking soldiers alone; Bosnian video footage described to me by workers at several Sarajevo-based international organizations and NGOs shows at least one senior member of the UN forces in Sarajevo in conversation with Bosnian Serb leader Radovan Karadzić outside Sonja's Kon-Tiki in the clear light of day.

Such incidences were the subject of a 2002 US congressional hearing at the House of Representatives titled "The UN and the Sex Slave Trade in Bosnia: Isolated Case or Larger Problem in the UN System?" (US Congress 2002, 107th Congress), which sought expert and eyewitness testimony on the involvement of soldiers in patronizing Serb-operated brothels filled with trafficked women. The most poignant testimony was provided by Ben Johnston, a Texan who had been blacklisted by his employer, the US-based private security contractor DynCorp, for reporting the "sale," to his male colleagues, of adolescent girls as young as twelve as live-in companions and sexual partners. Johnston, who is married to a Bosnian woman, provided a brief but heart-wrenching account of how his career prospects had been destroyed because of his refusal to accept the behavior of his co-workers. He (perhaps unknowingly) drew on the US counter-trafficking policy's rhetoric of "zero tolerance" in noting, "I can assure you that the only zero tolerance that DynCorp had was anybody that tried to stop them from [what they were] doing they got rid of because they had zero tolerance for anybody that would stand in their way of slavery" (US Congress 2002, 27).

Attention to the traffic in women in Bosnia dates to the advent of international involvement in the war, and, like many other social issues, gradually became addressed solely by the international community. Most Bosnians insist that trafficking was not a problem before the war, in a manner strikingly similar to the pervasive Armenian belief that prostitution did not exist in Soviet times in the same way it does in the country today. Although efforts to hand over responsibilities for combating trafficking to the government of Bosnia are ongoing, it seems quite likely that the international community will continue to play a significant role in the counter-trafficking activities described in this chapter for many years to come.

It remains to be seen how history will make sense of the use of women's bodies as sexual objects by both sides during the war in Bosnia, and what this pervasive disregard for both international law and basic human values in all cultures reveals about the traffic in women. Radovan Stanković and the hundreds of others like him who continue to evade capture and prosecution by the world's most powerful organizations are now in their late thirties, and some of their youngest victims are just now entering their twenties. Bosnia remains a postwar nation that most of the people I spoke to insisted was in desperate need of assistance in gaining a tenuous hold on civil society.

THE IMPACTS OF POST-WAR DONOR FATIGUE

The phrase *donor fatigue* had been in tense circulation in Bosnia for several years prior to my arrival, and many NGO leaders were beginning to worry that financial support for their activities was not as forthcoming as it had been in the years immediately after the war. Not surprisingly, representatives of international organizations and donor governments had quite a different understanding of this problem. First Secretary of the Swedish International Development Agency (SIDA) Dr. Joakim Molander explained that although it was understandable that Bosnian NGOs that had become dependent on Western donor governments and aid agencies after the war were frustrated by the inability of the Bosnian government to financially support their activities, the situation was unavoidable. "After the war," Dr. Molander said,

"Bosnia-Herzegovina was the largest recipient of per capita foreign aid in the world, and such a situation is not sustainable."

Most other Western European workers at international organizations and most donor governments simultaneously insisted that the Bosnian government needed to begin to take responsibility for counter-trafficking and bemoaned the fact that the overburdened and sensitive nature of political appointments in Bosnia does not empower government officials to position the traffic in women as a serious issue. Politicians are answerable to an electorate that see trafficking as a less urgent problem than more general issues such as high unemployment and lack of government services. The government minister who was responsible for dealing with efforts to end the traffic in women in Bosnia was also responsible for a number of other issues, including migration and foreign affairs, which made it highly unlikely that he could devote sufficient attention to trafficking.

Fadila Hadzić, director of the Bosnian branch of the pan-Eastern European NGO La Strada, succinctly expressed the Bosnian view of this problem by noting, "international organizations think trafficking is now the responsibility of the state, but we have no state." Hadzić and I spent several hours discussing her considerable efforts to obtain financial support for the shelter she manages for victims of trafficking in the city of Mostar, which itself had been devastated during the war and was later largely rebuilt with international donor funds. She expressed considerable frustration with the lack of money for education and professional training that could help victims of trafficking reintegrate into society by providing them with employment opportunities. Hadzić felt that because most Bosnian NGOs were formed during the war to distribute emergency assistance, a precedent of generalizing organizational profiles remains in place, and a fair amount of resistance to specialization is encouraged by the need to compete for donor funding. If an NGO chooses to focus on a single issue, for example, it may miss out on opportunities for donor funds in more specialized areas, which in turn discourages NGOs from unduly restricting their activities to a specialized issue. Hadzić insisted that this needs to change if NGOs are to have a real impact in a given area, but the need to attract donor funds just in order to exist significantly limits the likelihood of reform. Lack of state support necessitates that NGO staff spend a significant amount of time soliciting financial support, the lack of which further disadvantages women who are unable to receive the kind of education and assistance that could help them become economically self-sufficient. Women who lack a means of self-support are at significant risk of trafficking, which is why some of the women in Hadzić's shelter had worked as prostitutes intermittently between their attempts to find other types of employment.

It is true that the limited scope of professional opportunities in Bosnia significantly reduces the likelihood that former prostitutes can find other employment, but shelter directors were adamant that receiving education or training in a practical field such as hairdressing could potentially benefit women. "If we don't give them hope for a better future," one shelter director explained, "they will feel that life is not even worth living." This underscores a sharp divide between the real situation of Bosnia as a postwar nation with a struggling economy and the ideal situation of the reintegration of former prostitutes into other sectors of society. Shelter directors and staff were quite clear that the greatest hope for self-sufficiency in an area other than sex work existed among very young women who could still go back to government-supported public school and form a peer group of nonprostitutes. "For the others," one shelter staff member explained, "all we can do is offer limited hope since we don't have a lot of money to help them to improve themselves."

Yet this recurrent lack of life choices could not account for the agency demonstrated by women in shelters run by Hadzić and others, because even the women who had experienced the worst life circumstances did not see themselves as victims. Sabina, a thirty-five-year-old Bosnian woman who was housed in a shelter for victims of trafficking when I met her, framed her life story with the twin themes of the war and a human desire for a better life despite difficult circumstances. I had been sitting in the shelter's waiting room and was absorbed in writing field notes after my meeting with its director when Sabina abruptly sat down next to me, narrowed her eyes in an expression of curiosity, and asked, "Who did this to you?" I looked at her in surprise for a moment and tried to ascertain what she meant before she pointed to my eyebrows and exclaimed, "This! Who did this beautiful thing to you?" I immediately took out a pair of tweezers and a small mirror from my bag and offered to shape her eyebrows like my own, thinking that at least it would temporarily ease the unrelenting boredom of shelter life for her.

We went to sit in the kitchen at the back of the shelter, where light filtered in from the afternoon summer sun, and she sat down as I tweezed her eyebrows. This sparked a discussion in Bosnian with several other women in the room that Sabina translated into our mutual language of French for me. "Hey Sabina," one of the women said, "this woman came from America to be your beautician?" Sabina thought this was funny, as did I. "Women will do anything to feel like human beings," she said, perhaps in reference to the cramped conditions at the shelter, in reference to the lack of activities to occupy time, or as a comment on our shared bond over well-shaped eyebrows. Like most Bosnians I met during the course of my research, she provided supporting evidence for her argument from her experiences during the war. She told me how she had risked Serb sniper fire to wash her red Italian dress in the river behind her apartment building near the front line—a story I had heard in numerous variations from almost every Bosnian woman over thirty.

"It's necessary for survival," she explained as she turned her face to the left to admire her newly shaped eyebrows. "Unless women feel that they are worth something, they cannot survive." I told her about my grandmother's childhood in a New York brothel operated by her mother and about how the money they earned supported their small family of women through the Great Depression. I talked to Sabina about how, when my grandmother was in her late eighties and close to death, she would still exclaim, "I love men!" for no particular reason, and I mentioned how paradoxical I felt this attitude to be when voiced by someone who had grown up with women who sold sex as their only route out of poverty. "Why?" Sabina asked me. "Maybe she just appreciated that they were the ones to help her when no one else would."

Sabina's powerful connection between prostitutes' clients and economic empowerment made me rethink my associations of sex work with oppression, and yet her notion of "help" may have been partially drawn from her knowledge of the funding difficulties faced by the shelter. The word *shelter* is somewhat of a misnomer in societies where state support is not provided and the short-term nature of donor funding means that such organizations may have to close at any time. The resulting temporary nature of shelters is a source of anxiety for women such as Sabina and the directors of these organizations alike. Mara Radovanović, director of the northeastern Bosnian shelter for victims of trafficking known as Lara, expressed considerable frustration that almost no funds were provided for assistance to the women housed in her shelter. She echoed Hadzić in lamenting the ad hoc nature of locating financing for such activities in the absence of state or donor funding, and she also explained that she was in constant fear that her shelter would have to close.

Both La Strada and Lara are supported by volunteer labor and have very little money to sustain their daily operations. Hadzić explained that the girls and women in the La Strada shelter were fed with groceries brought from volunteers' homes, and Radovanović's situation at Lara was not much different. The latter described her arrangement with a group of German artists who volunteer their paintings for sale at an annual Berlin art auction held to support Lara's activities. Although this is definitely a good arrangement for Lara in the sense that it provides much-needed support, Radovanović was uncertain where future funding would come from if this means of income generation were curtailed.

Funds are desperately needed to help women reintegrate into society through employment-oriented education and a safe place to live, but money is not the only issue. Volunteer psychologist Vildana Milavić has spent several years working with victims of trafficking in the La Strada shelter and was adamant that it takes a great deal of time for girls and women who have been coerced into prostitution to regain the self-esteem and ability to trust that are necessary for a healthy adult life. Like her volunteer colleagues, she felt frustrated that without further education or job prospects, most of the women she had contact with in the shelter will never be able to move out of the situations of social invisibility and economic vulnerability that initially placed them at risk. Milavić emphasized that although the women she treats in the La Strada shelter come from a wide variety of age groups and backgrounds, all of them share a set of marginal life circumstances that often include abuse, poverty, and the low self-esteem that often accompanies these problems.

Milavić's work in the shelter taught her that assisting girls and women is an extremely complicated, time-consuming effort that does not always involve immediate rewards. Most of those housed in the shelter arrive after they are referred from the police station and are in a heightened state of anxiety and fear because of what they have undergone both as prostitutes and in their lives as marginal individuals. Women certainly do not leave the psychological consequences of their past experiences at the door when they enter a shelter for victims of trafficking, and the result is often the construction of a number of elaborate hierarchies among women who live in the constrained environments of shelters. Sleeping space in shelters is often limited, there are few activities available to occupy the women's time, and most of them have grown accustomed to a social environment in which a completely different set of social norms and regulations apply.

The La Strada shelter was hardly unique in the experiences it had with girls and women who were clearly struggling with serious psychological problems. A fourteen-year-old Albanian girl housed at a shelter for victims of trafficking that I visited in a large Bosnian town was code-named "Agatha Christie" by shelter workers (including the volunteer psychologist), who bemoaned the girl's propensity to pit sheltered women and shelter staff against one another by contriving elaborate schemes and telling complicated lies with the skill of a detective novelist. In one particularly disturbing example, the staff psychologist felt extraordinarily proud of the progress the teenager had made in talking about her experiences in a Serbian brothel, and the psychologist announced her breakthrough at a shelter staff meeting. That same evening after the psychologist went home, however, the Albanian teenager approached another shelter staff member and sobbed, "The psychologist made me tell her all about my worst experiences. She forced me to talk about things that hurt me so much. You're supposed to protect me here, because I'm only a child!"

Her accusation deeply worried the shelter staff for obvious reasons, although the girl later apologized and confessed her lie. This deliberate creation of chaos often occurs in shelter situations in which women are kept under high-security conditions for their safety, such as shelters for underage girls, where occupants often have little to do with their time. Behavior such as the Albanian teenager's speaks to the human need to feel in control even in extremely constrained situations, because it is sometimes difficult for sheltered women to understand the shelter staff's belief that restrictions on their movements are "protecting" them. A Ukrainian woman in a Bosnian shelter explained to me that she felt greater stress and a sense of confinement that far exceeded what she had experienced in a brothel. Her disturbing statement underscores the inadequacy of shelters plagued by lack of funding and the need to impose rules on a population already under extreme psychological and emotional stress.

These difficulties are compounded by the negative attitudes that many shelter workers have been socialized to have toward prostitutes, many of which are "confirmed" by behavior such as the Albanian teenager's. "These are not nice women, and that's the bottom line," one Bosnian shelter worker explained to me of the victims of trafficking she dealt with, "but life has made them that way, because life has not been very nice to them." Her statement highlights complicated questions of agency and victimization that have no easy answers and that arise out of deeply entrenched cultural beliefs about appropriate behavior for women who have experienced extremely painful life events and out of ideas about "normal" and "logical" decision-making processes.

I was introduced, in the La Strada shelter, to a woman I will call Jasmina whose life story heartbreakingly corresponds to the traumas experienced in Bosnia in recent years and illustrates how victims of trafficking often seem to have made "illogical" life choices. Her father was an abusive alcoholic whose perpetual unemployment kept the family in constant poverty after her mother died at a young age, so the teenaged Jasmina was already in an extraordinarily difficult life situation when ethnic Serb soldiers occupied her town and imprisoned her in a house where she was forced into prostitution. She became pregnant and had several miscarriages during the months when she was repeatedly raped by soldiers, and when she was released after the war, she had no one to assist her.

Jasmina made her way to Sarajevo, where she eventually met and married a much older Bosnian man who held a Swedish passport. In a horrible turn of events for Jasmina just after the terrible treatment she had been subjected to during the war, she soon found herself sold to a clandestine Swedish brothel by the man she had married. She was twenty-two years old when the Swedish police discovered her situation and eventually sent her back to Bosnia, where she was put in contact with the La Strada shelter. Jasmina's life had taught her that her poverty and lack of social safety nets effectively made her an invisible person who could easily be abused, and it is not surprising that she spent her first six months at the shelter in deep depression.

Jasmina explained that she felt she had no future, was frustrated by her inability to earn an income in the shelter, and missed the love and attention she felt she needed from a man. Jasmina's feelings are entirely understandable, and yet the decision she made in response to them is a bit more complicated; she opted to leave the shelter after six months and quickly met a man who pushed her back into prostitution to support his heroin addiction. She returned to the shelter after a few months of living with him and had the sense that shelter workers had given up hope that her life would improve. I wondered whether Jasmina's life would improve if she had the opportunity to acquire a skill that would make her employable, and yet lack of funding makes this unlikely to happen.

Lack of funding is hardly the only problem faced by shelters, because culture, norms, and stereotypes about ethnic groups can all affect policy formation and distribution of donor funds. I visited a shelter for victims of trafficking in the Dayton Agreement-created ethnically Serb territory of Republika Srpska, and my preparations for this journey sparked a number of discussions that drew directly on Bosnian IOM staff members' memories of the war. Stereotypes about militarized Serb masculinity and a passive, almost victimized Bosnia long predate the war, although ethnic Serb actions during the war clearly reinforced many of them. Many Western European employees of international organizations and NGOs alike also embraced these cultural typologies of dangerous, aggressive Serbs and gentle, submissive Bosnians. A Danish woman who made frequent work-related trips to the Serbian capital of Belgrade told me that once I arrived in Republika Srpska, I would immediately see the differences in the way that the men behaved. "Here in Bosnia," she said, "all of the men are so passive, but the Serbs are just very aggressive and very sexualized. It's in the way they walk, how they look at you, their whole way of being."

The Danish woman's characterization of Serb men's "whole way of being" eerily echoed stories I heard from Bosnian women who had been raped by Serb soldiers during the war as part of a military strategy discussed earlier in this chapter. One woman had recounted how the ethnic Serb man who was her neighbor before the war told her as he raped her, "I don't want to do this, but otherwise they'll kill me. They'll think I'm not a man, that I'm not a Serb." Her story highlights some of the disconnects between Serb ultra-nationalism and ethnic Serbs' relationships with non-Serbs, but it also underscores the kinds of behaviors during the war that continue to inform policy and funding. The director of a shelter for victims of trafficking in Republika Srpska complained that her organization did not receive the same amount of money from international organizations as Bosnian shelters because Serbs had been the aggressors during the war. "They think that we're all Serbs who committed atrocities," she said, "and so what does that mean? Serb girls are not victims of trafficking? That's what they think."

Trafficking is clearly a problem in Bosnia and neighboring countries whether donors deem it a priority or not, and yet the budgetary vicissitudes and areas of interests evinced by foreign governments and aid organizations have as much power to destabilize efforts by international organizations such as IOM as they do to effectively undermine the ability of NGOs such as Lara and La Strada to act. The United States Agency for International Development sponsored a 1.5-million-dollar IOM project between 2006 and 2007 titled "Trafficking in Persons: Prevention and Protection in Bosnia and Herzegovina." It consisted of a series of what are usually termed *capacity-building efforts* because of their intended objective of strengthening ("building") the ability ("capacity") of the Bosnian government to combat trafficking independent of assistance from international donors. Objectives of the project were linked to concrete steps to be taken in order to advance counter-trafficking activities among a diverse group of institutions and individuals, including the state authorities, health and social service professionals, judges, prosecutors, NGOs, vulnerable groups at risk of trafficking, and the general population.

This process resulted in a rulebook that outlined the legal and administrative framework for the assistance of Bosnian victims of trafficking, an agreement on cooperation between all NGOs that deal with the subject, and an understanding that the newly appointed State Coordinator for Combating Trafficking in Human Beings and Illegal Immigration would begin to cover shelter costs. The agreement on cooperation among NGOs was designed to make its signatories "understand that the network approach is essential to ensure that the needs of beneficiaries are met in an effective and sustainable way" (IOM Year One Report to USAID 2007). After all, if the Bosnian state was obligated to fund shelters like La Strada and Lara, NGO workers could focus their efforts on areas other than locating funds to ensure their continued existence.

This agreement on sustainable, long-term cooperation was a major breakthrough, even though it may seem paradoxical that organizations that work independently toward the same goal would have difficulties cooperating. A number of factors work against the ability of NGOs to assist one another in a social environment that forces them to compete for donor aid in order to simply exist. Members of the NGO community in Bosnia at the time of my research insisted they were faced with a serious funding crisis, because donors were no longer as forthcoming with funds as they had been in the period immediately following the war. The implications of this were impossible to miss in conversations with individuals who worked in the humanitarian and NGO sectors and were thus dependent on international donor and government agencies such as USAID for their salaries. Many Bosnian professionals expressed deep concern about how they would support themselves and find work in a depressed economy if these funds were curtailed; there are few paid opportunities available in the social service sector even for skilled professionals.

This sentiment was particularly strong at IOM Sarajevo during the course of my research, when the entire counter-trafficking team was informed that they would have to find new jobs after USAID summarily revoked funding for further activities with just a few months' notice. USAID was emphatic that the discontinuation of funding was due to US government cutbacks in light of the costly war in Iraq. Because foreign aid is typically one of the first areas to be scrutinized in Congress when budget allocations need to be adjusted, counter-trafficking activities in distant Bosnia were no longer accorded high priority in Washington. As a result, the professionals who lost their jobs at IOM following these cutbacks had to explain to prospective future employers that the revocation of funds had nothing to do with their performance, and this was especially difficult because false rumors began to circulate in the Sarajevo NGO and international community that there must have been other reasons for USAID's hasty decision. International donors typically give recipients of their funds at least six months' notice to recipients before funding ceases, in order to ensure that agencies will have enough time to seek out other forms of support. It remains something of a mystery why, on this occasion, the largest donor aid agency from the most powerful country in the world decided not to follow this standard practice.

IOM had in fact been doing a stellar job with the USAID-funded project and had made great inroads into understanding how the traffic in women functions in Bosnia. This understanding is critical to the development of sustainable projects, and one of the most interesting of the numerous IOM activities funded by the USAID grant was an undercover investigative project in which a group of male researchers posed as men in search of prostitutes in an effort to discover how sex trafficking functions in Bosnia and Republika Srpska. IOM faced a number of difficulties in finding a group that would take on the project, and most organizations they approached immediately refused to do so, citing the very real dangers presented by coming into close contact with the organized criminal groups that are believed to be responsible for the majority of the traffic in women in the Western Balkan region. People who engage in illegal activities such as trafficking must constantly change their modes of operation in order to evade the police, and this investigation was an attempt to ascertain how IOM could improve its strategies to respond to trafficking. It was hoped that these undercover activities would help IOM to formulate strategies to improve cooperation between the Bosnian government and NGOs by analyzing the everyday experiences of prostitutes and victims of trafficking, rather than just relying on a set of assumptions about their lives.

The project was subcontracted to a Sarajevo media research firm called Via Media, which assembled a group of male researchers to conduct two months of face-to-face interviews with 122 women who engage in sex work (and were thus potential victims of trafficking) and 94 users of their services in seven regions in Bosnia and two in neighboring Republika Srpska. Methodological strategies employed in the study involved mimicking the behaviors employed by men who seek to buy sex, and the male researchers contacted people they referred to as their "links," who in turn provided access to pimps who manage the schedules of the young women who work for them. The researchers were extremely surprised by the complex security system that made it impossible to ascertain where the points of contact were located. Links initially provided them with a mobile phone number to request a specific type of sexual service or woman, and then they were given another mobile phone number to call in order to schedule a time and location for the sex act to take place. Attempts to trace the calls were futile, because all were made either from a public phone or from numbers linked to prepaid phone cards (no registration of a name or address is required to purchase a cell phone). It was thus impossible to deter-mine with whom the undercover researchers were speaking at any given time, and it was difficult to assess whether the same person was ever contacted on the phone more than once.

The goal of the project was to spend time alone with the women under the guise of procuring sexual services in order to determine how many of them fit the definition of "victim of trafficking." This put the male researchers in the awkward position of having to explain why they had paid for services that they did not want to use once they were alone with the women. Each individ-ual researcher chose to do so by saying either that he was nervous about visit-ing a prostitute for the first time or that he was emotionally hurt and needed some attention because he had just learned of his wife's affair with another man. It is clear that this a problematic research methodology, because the sex workers were not informed that this was a research project and thus could have provided the male researchers with information designed to protect—or even possibly benefit—themselves. Yet it is not clear how the social science principle of informed consent, in which subjects are made aware that they are participating in a study, would work in a relatively dangerous, illegal activity controlled by organized crime.

The research yielded a number of findings that both were enlightening and raised important questions about definitions of, and responses to, the traffic in women. One of the major conclusions of the study was that about half of the women who worked as prostitutes were citizens of Bosnia and Republika Srpska, whereas the remainder came from neighboring Serbia (just under 30 percent), Croatia (12 percent), and former Soviet republics (about 8 percent).

This is especially significant given that most definitions of trafficking, including the influential Palermo Protocol, explicitly specify that an international border must be crossed in order for the crime to be so defined. Nonetheless, 40 percent of the women in the study self-identified as victims of trafficking. Clearly, there is a very real disconnect between official and experiential definitions of the term. "Official" definitions such as the Palermo Protocol focus on borders, the notion of force, and the idea of consent, whereas "experiential" definitions given by women who have been prostitutes often focus on the nuanced, complicated nature of relationships and behaviors that reveal the actual process by which women are pushed into situations in which they are forced to sell sex. Although this may be indicative of the cultural stigma attached to sex work, which might discourage women from openly communicating about their life choices with male researchers they believed to be clients, it also suggests that contemporary definitions of the term are simply not meaningful to women who are coerced into prostitution within their own countries.

The relevance of definitions was also rendered suspect by the responses of women to the question of how they entered into prostitution: 20 percent stated that they accepted the job voluntarily, but an equal number elaborated on this to note that they began to sell sex because they had no other options for income generation. Two groups of women who numbered approximately 14 percent each insisted either that they not known, before accepting the offer of employment, that they were expected to sell sex or that they had been tricked by someone close to them who in turn profited from their sexual labor. An additional 20 percent refused to answer the question, and the remainder stated that they had become prostitutes when their search for work proved futile outside their country of origin. These statistics are telling, both because they reflect how women define their own life situations and because they raise the question of what constitutes victimization. After all, are women who describe themselves as "tricked" somehow uniquely disadvantaged vis-à-vis those who were forced into prostitution by poverty or the abuse of trust?

To complicate the debate on definitions of trafficking further, most of the women stated that they had agreed to work for nothing until they paid a debt to a third party, and yet despite this unfair arrangement, the majority who came from former Soviet republics did not want to return to their home countries. Most of these women said they had explicitly agreed to engage in prostitution in Bosnia or Republika Srpska as a condition of their employment, a finding that reveals the level of desperation in their life situations. Women's responses also revealed the brittle tightrope prostitutes are forced to walk on a daily basis in a highly stigmatized and often illegal activity, the clandestine nature of which makes sex workers uniquely vulnerable to violence and intimidation. This potential for abuse is compounded by the fact that more than half (55 percent) of the women had worked in more than one location in the past year, and a significant number (29 percent) had worked in more than four places. Almost all (84 percent) of the women explained that they were sent to multiple sites to engage in paid sex acts, including hotels, private apartments, and clients' homes. This, or course, indicates that they run a substantial risk of violence in such secluded places where the client has more control. These frequent changes of location also indicate efforts by pimps and traffickers to avoid police detection.

One of the most salient features of the study was just how expensive sexual services are in a country that continues to be in a state of economic crisis. The researchers found that fees for sexual acts ranged from 25 to 75 euro an hour, which raised their suspicion that the market is significantly influenced by the presence of Western Europeans who work for international organizations and foreign governments with a presence in Sarajevo. Women reported working at parties frequented by both Bosnian politicians and Western European employees of international organizations, and the researchers were able to infiltrate two such parties and speak to sex workers and their clients who were in attendance. They noted the presence of cocaine, and when they asked the women whether they were being forced to take drugs, most responded that they were expected to have sex with at least five men in a single night and that self-medication with narcotics made this considerably less difficult.

Some of the weaknesses in the report reflect not only the difficulties in conducting research in an extremely dangerous environment dominated by organized crime and individuals with a significant investment in the traffic in women, but also the complex psychological effects that research of this type can have on individuals. Researchers did not receive training to help them deal with the emotional issues they faced in interacting with women in desperate socioeconomic circumstances. One of the researchers had a daughter the same age as most of the sex workers he spoke to and reported being unable to gather data effectively as a result. Researchers noted that they felt psychologically unprepared to deal with the elaborate networks that characterize the sex industry in Bosnia, and their nervous reactions (described as "reacting too quickly") may have been detected by the taxi drivers, pimps, and numerous other actors who facilitate the exchange of sex for money. These weaknesses point to the need for more in-depth training (which in turn underscores the need for more research funding), but even so, the key results of the study revealed the complexities that surround trafficking in Bosnia and just how many levels of society are either invested in or complicit in its continued existence.

The IOM-directed study made it manifestly clear that there is a great deal of work to be done in the field of counter-trafficking in Bosnia. The one-year project also clearly demonstrated that IOM was making significant progress in combating a phenomenon that at policy meetings is often compared to a dragon with seven heads, to acknowledge that disruption of one aspect of a trafficking network simply reveals another six equally formidable aspects. One of the IOM employees whose job was lost to USAID's abrupt decision was deeply disturbed that the important findings of this study would not be able to influence future IOM policies, because the counter-trafficking program would have to be discontinued for lack of funds. "If I were an American tax-payer," the employee said, "I would be so angry that 1.5 million dollars was just wasted, because we can't do anything with the report or build on the activities that money allowed us to do. It just doesn't make sense." The IOM employee's statement underscores how difficult it is for organizations to sustain their activities while remaining dependent on the whims of foreign donors.

Ever cognizant of this unfortunate reality, IOM Sarajevo had developed a proposal designed to facilitate the eventual handover of all counter-trafficking activities to the Bosnian government. USAID's decision to terminate funds without adequate notice, however, effectively meant that all efforts to do so were halted and that alternative sources of funding could not be located in time to ensure continuation of the counter-trafficking program. The world's leading international organization in the fields of migration and counter-traf-ficking thus found itself in the terrible position of having to end a program in which it was deeply invested. That an international organization such as IOM could be so deleteriously affected by the whims of USAID underscores the marginal position and vulnerability of many NGOs and of the shelters they manage for victims of trafficking. The Bosnian government simply does not have the money or the political will to fund shelters, which forces NGOs to plan their activities solely on the year-to-year basis upon which most donor agencies disburse their funds. The wisdom of expecting concrete results after funding just one year of work in a postwar society that is still struggling to establish a self-sufficient state remains extremely questionable, and, as was the case in Armenia, communities on the margins of society are the most dele-teriously affected by such policies.

THE ROMA: SEX TRAFFICKING, MIGRATION, AND HUMAN RIGHTS

In its fifty years of existence, the Sarajevo suburb of Butmir has never had running water, electricity, waste disposal, or a sewage system. Most of the children who live there do not attend school, and those who do attend drop out before fifth grade because they need to contribute to the family income by begging in the city center or collecting scrap metal for resale. Just a forty-minute streetcar journey from downtown Sarajevo, Butmir is a world away from the expensive Western European boutiques and sidewalk cafés that grace the city center. Nearly all of the homes in Butmir are constructed from plastic sheeting, scrap metal, and other found materials, and open fires are the only source of heat during the winter. Teenaged girls breastfeed their babies while caring for their other young children; most families in the neighborhood ensure that their daughters are married before they reach the age of fifteen. Poverty and lack of health insurance exclude almost all of the residents from access to health care, and the women and children of Butmir have a maternal and infant mortality rate that far exceeds the rest of the Bosnian population. Less than 1 percent of adults who live in Butmir have a job in the formal sector, more than half of the community is illiterate, and the absence of waste disposal forces them to live next to large piles of garbage and human waste. And yet their situation is largely ignored by most Bosnians because they are Roma.

"The Roma prefer to live that way because it is their tradition," explained a Bosnian woman who works for a Sarajevo-based NGO that lists the Roma population as one of its target beneficiaries. She then went on to add, "They are gypsies. They aren't like us." I was shocked by her language and was extremely dismayed when I learned that such discriminatory statements about the Roma are commonly voiced by Bosnians regardless of education and social background, and even those who work for international organizations in the field of human rights sometimes share these views. NGOs typically have a "portfolio of activities" that concisely lists the areas they address in their work, and it is more likely that donor funding will be forthcoming for an agency that can deal with multiple issues rather than a single concern in which it is genuinely skilled. This paradox results from a system that forces NGOs to compete for donor funding to ensure their existence, even if the funding they are competing for is not necessarily within the range of activities they are genuinely interested in. Hence "the Roma" may be included in an NGO portfolio in order to maximize its chances of receiving funding, even though staff members have no expertise in that area. Donors, in turn, may select a particular NGO for funding even if it does not have competency in a particular area, simply because that NGO has previously carried out a project to the donor's satisfaction.

Suada Besić is a Roma woman who helps to coordinate the political activities of the Council of Roma, an organization that lobbies the Bosnian government and advocates for the civil rights of Roma people. Her experiences with this kind of institutionalized discrimination have taught her that even those with a great deal of education or a prominent position often feel quite free to share their unfortunate opinions about her community. "People have so many prejudices about Roma women, like we all love sex and have twelve kids. It's shocking, but I hear this all the time, even from people who work for international organizations," she said.

Besić described several instances in which she felt a distinct personal and professional obligation to educate her colleagues about prejudices they did not even know they had. On one occasion, she was on her way home from a conference on human rights when the organizer began to make jokes about what he perceived to be the promiscuity of Roma women. When she told him that his behavior was extremely inappropriate for a human rights professional, he responded by saying, "It's just a joke; it doesn't mean anything." Besić recounted how discrimination against Roma women (and the community in general) sometimes comes in the less overt forms of patronizing attitudes evinced by her colleagues. A woman who manages a highly regarded women's NGO in a Bosnian town hugged Besić when she first met her and exclaimed, much to Besić's anger and embarrassment, "How great, an educated Roma woman!" It is not particularly difficult to understand how Besić's colleagues might see her as a novelty, given the low levels of education and institutionalized discrimination that most Roma people face in Bosnia and, indeed, throughout all of Eastern Europe.

The Roma, who are often referred to by the pejorative term *gypsies*, are easily the most marginal ethnic community in Bosnia. Most of them live in settlements of fifty to sixty families located on the outskirts of cities and towns, where they are extremely vulnerable to police abuse, racially motivated violence, and the whims of the state. There were discussions among Sarajevo municipal officials at the time of my research about relocating the Butmir settlement to a region outside the city limits, and because the Roma do not own the land they live on, they have almost no legal rights to object to such government initiatives. Many, if not most, Bosnians regard the Roma as unwanted outsiders and petty criminals who are bound by strange and backward cultural traditions that seem to belong to another era. When I asked Bosnian and Western European workers at international organizations and NGOs about common stereotypes regarding the Roma, the adjectives used in their answers were always they same: *dirty, uneducated, backward*, and, tellingly, *not European.*

These attitudes toward a group of between 40,000 and 50,000 people who live in Bosnia are unfortunately not new, and they derive at least in part from the Roma's history of social exclusion from decision-making processes and even general social life. No written records exist to document their history, but it is commonly believed that the Roma left India in the Middle Ages to settle in southern Greece, where archaeologists have unearthed evidence of early Roma settlements. Registration records from the Ottoman period in Bosnia demonstrate that by the mid-1800s, most Roma had already begun to live in permanent settlements, which contradicts the common contemporary notion that they are an itinerant population. Conflict always produces a state of heightened insecurity about identity, and historically, Roma in the Western Balkans have been severely persecuted and forced to declare themselves as of either Serb or Croat ethnicity. Roma identity was effectively eradicated on paper by this strategy of enforced self-identification with one of the two predominant ethnic groups in the region, and it is estimated that slightly less than 30,000 Roma were murdered in the territories of the former Yugoslavia during World War II alone. The Roma continued to be a marginal and impoverished population at the outbreak of the war in 1992, when many Roma men were forced to clear mines and many Roma women were coerced into prostitution by soldiers (UNHCR 2004).

The massive population movements that took place both during and after the war affected everyone in the Western Balkan region, and it is not surprising that Roma were doubly disadvantaged by their lack of education and the widespread social discrimination against them. Many fled from their homes during the war and did not return, although it is crucial to note that the lack of accurate demographic data on the Roma makes it difficult to ascertain the extent to which this occurred. Bosnian census records from 1991, the last year such a census was conducted, did not count "Roma" as a separate ethnic category, so most were registered as Muslim, Yugoslav, or "Other" (UNHCR 2004).

This lack of demographic data speaks to the marginalization of the Roma community as a whole, and the discrimination faced by this group intensified problems that were experienced by the entire Western Balkan region during the war. Even during peacetime, Roma face a lack of civil registration and personal documentation (especially for children), have no formal property rights, and experience difficulties in accessing health care, education, employment, social welfare, adequate housing, and state infrastructure. Roma people thus faced additional obstacles when the conflict deprived all citizens of Bosnia of their rights. Many Roma cannot vote because they do not have proper identification to document their citizenship. They cannot run for office for the same reason, nor can they register their children in schools. The cost of such documentation is often cited as a reason for their not obtaining it. And indeed, the Roma are an extremely economically marginalized group: one Council of Europe report stated that the unemployment rate among the Roma is nearly 99 percent (Sarajlić and Kiers 2004). This high figure does not mean that the Roma do not work but, rather, that they are absorbed by the informal sector of the economy and involve themselves in activities on the fringes of society by performing seasonal work, begging, or collecting unwanted materials (such as scrap metal and secondhand clothing) for resale.

Levels of formal education are universally low for Roma communities throughout Eastern Europe, but girls are even less well educated and often leave school in third or fourth grade as a consequence of cultural perceptions that daughters need to be protected in order to prepare them for early marriage and childbearing. Children of both genders are often forced to contribute to the family income, which makes them unlikely to progress far in formal educational systems. Roma families are often evicted from their homes because they do not have documentation of ownership, even in regions where they have lived for hundreds of years. And yet, fearful of the violence and harassment they often face from law enforcement officers, they do not report these abuses. Bosnian authorities have adopted laws and measures to help remedy the situation, including the decision to establish a national advisory board for Roma, adoption of an action plan on the educational needs of Roma and other national minorities, and enactment of the law on the protection of national minorities, but it remains to be seen whether these steps will help change pervasive negative stereotypes about the Roma.

Workers I spoke with at NGOs that support the Roma were strongly critical of such policies and actions, because they did not include provision for a budget to implement any activities. Consequently, many remained convinced that such government initiatives would have with very little impact on individual lives. One woman at a Sarajevo-based NGO asked, "If more than half of all Roma women are illiterate, how can they become aware of their rights?" and another bluntly said, "We have a lot of paper, but no ability to act." Suada Besić from the Council of Roma was quick to emphasize the difference between policy and action: "We have 40 Roma NGOs, and of those only about 20 have the capacity to do anything. Of those 20, just a few have the equipment necessary to do something with." She explained that strict cultural norms about the separation of unrelated men and women and proscriptions against female independence severely limit the ability of Roma women to participate in politics or civil society. One Western European employee at an international organization further noted that Roma women are doubly victimized because "their human rights are violated in their families as girls and women, and then their rights are further violated by society because they are Roma."

It is clear that the traffic in women follows a path of poverty, desperation, and inequality, and the depth of the challenges faced by the community places Roma girls and women at significant risk for exploitation. However, the pervasive social problems evident in the Roma community underscore the crucial fact that the traffic in Roma girls and women cannot be effectively examined without considering the historical factors and human rights abuses that push the entire community into a marginal position. The Roma represent an extreme case of socioeconomic deprivation, but it must be acknowledged that the traffic in Roma women cannot be separated from the poverty, illiteracy, and social inequality that frame their lives. An official from the Council of Roma underscored this reality in a particularly evocative manner:

> I was at a conference on Roma rights, and a Roma representative from an NGO stood up and said that he had eight kids and his family was very poor, so that when he goes to work or to conferences he puts the kids on the bus and sends them out to beg in the street. People were very angry at him for violating their human rights, but he explained that there was no other way to support his big family. Now, how can we even begin to talk about sex trafficking when these are the realities we are faced with as a people?

The Council of Roma representative's statement speaks to the complicated issues that arise when just one aspect of a community problem is addressed. In asking how it is possible to genuinely consider the traffic in women when there are so many other issues of pressing concern, the Roma representative highlighted why it may be helpful to incorporate discussions on the subject into larger dialogues about human rights and violence against women.

Many Bosnians were quick to explain to me that the Roma engage in cultural practices that most Bosnians (who often self-identified as "European" in contrast to their view of the Roma) found offensive, particularly the marriage custom in which, to use the terminology most commonly employed in Bosnia, a Roma man "buys a wife." However, representatives from the Council of Roma contested this point of view and were adamant that Roma marriage customs did not differ significantly from those of neighboring communities. These representatives felt that the tendency of many Bosnians to characterize the payments given from the groom's family to the bride's family as a "sale" were very much in keeping with stereotypes about the Roma as an unscrupulous and conniving people. Nonetheless, one IOM employee said that whenever a minor girl is exchanged for money, it constitutes what she described as "a clear case of trafficking," and many others echoed her sentiments in reference to the early age at which most Roma couples marry.

This is particularly interesting because what some speak of as "tradition" is characterized as "abuse" by many human rights professionals, who feel that this cultural practice is actually nothing more than a culturally sanctioned form of trafficking in women. Moreover, this perspective is complicated by the commonly shared belief that, to use the words of one woman who worked for an international organization, "That's how the Roma are, and they aren't going to change." Others insisted that because this "traffic" in women largely for the purposes of begging and marriage seemed to be confined to the Roma community, there was not much that could be done about it. The only point of agreement on the issue seemed to be that it was very difficult to gain access to the Roma for purposes of data collection because of the closed nature of settlements and the lack of real social contact on an equal basis between

Roma and Bosnians. State Coordinator for Combating Trafficking in Human Beings at the mission of the Organization for Security and Cooperation in Europe (OSCE) Gabrijela Jurela rather eloquently summarized this point of view on the Roma by noting that "the insularity of the women protects them from being trafficked by outsiders, but it also harms them because they can't leave their closed communities."

These debates about cultural practices and definitions of trafficking have at least subtly informed most of the Roma-related initiatives in Bosnia, and they highlight particularly sensitive points of tension for Roma people in relation to Bosnian society at large. Romanian Florin Cioaba, who is widely known as the Roma King, made a speech about state attempts throughout Eastern Europe to legislate against elements of Roma culture (such as early marriage). At an OSCE conference he said, "If you tell us to change our customs, we will be more strongly for them." Representatives from the Council of Roma echoed these views in defense of their decision to refuse a European Commission project that would have infused communities such as Butmir with a great deal of much-needed infrastructural support. According to Suada Besić, the Council of Roma's rejection of the decision was based on the failure of the European Commission to include the Roma even in projects ostensibly designed to assist them:

> The problem is that the EU countries don't want to listen to us. We stopped the European Commission (EC) project because they didn't want to involve us, and when we spoke to the NGOs [that] they wanted to use as implementing partners, they had never even heard about Roma problems and yet the EC had planned to fund those NGOs as implementing partners! EU means inclusivity and if Bosnia joins it will benefit the Roma, but they also have to be able to listen to us.

Ironically enough, Besić's depiction of the Roma as a target group, rather than as equal partners in projects designed to improve life for all Bosnians, was not so different in substance from Bosnian complaints about the attitudes implicit in many Western European initiatives to prepare the country for the possibility of joining the European Union.

BOSNIA AND THE POLITICS OF EUROPEAN UNION ACCESSION

Every morning as I walked to the IOM office in Sarajevo, I passed a conspicuously placed blue billboard that read, "Sarajevo: E.U.ropean Way" above the circle of yellow stars marking the European Union flag. The billboard was part of larger efforts by the European Commission to promote Western

Balkan political stability and the possibility of European Union membership for Bosnia; these efforts also informed many of the policy initiatives and discussions on the traffic in women at the time of my research. The billboard was placed at street level on the corner of a central thoroughfare where it could be seen by hundreds of passersby on their way to work in Sarajevo's central business district, and it hung just below the ruins of a brick building that had been destroyed by a Serb mortar attack during the war. Roma children often hid behind what remained of the building's walls to evade police capture, and the older ones periodically emerged from their hiding place to leap over the billboard and onto the street in front of pedestrians to beg for spare change.

One particularly beautiful morning in July, I was just about to turn the corner with a group of Bosnians who were also on their way to work when several aggressive police officers began shouting angrily and pushed a group of about fifteen of us against the wall by the billboard. The reasons for their actions became immediately clear when a line of large, expensive black cars with small flags from various European Union countries fluttering on their antennae drove around the corner onto the main street at alarming speed. Their tinted windows made it impossible to see who was inside, but one thing was eminently clear: if any of us had ignored the police and crossed the street, we would have been run over and quite likely killed. A group of Bosnian women took issue with this for obvious reasons and began to complain loudly to the police as the motorcade of ten vehicles sped past us, and it was at least a full five minutes before we were allowed to move. When the Bosnian police waved to signal that we could continue on our way, an older man standing next to me noticed my large laptop bag and conservative professional dress, which may have led him to believe that I was an employee of one of the numerous Western European aid agencies or embassies in Sarajevo. He gestured toward the blue EU billboard and smirked, his eyebrows raised as he looked me directly in the eye. "European way?" he asked sarcastically.

The Bosnian man's reference to the EU motorcade's complete disregard for our safety on a Sarajevo street characterized the skepticism evinced by many Bosnians about to the possibility of EU accession. Almost everyone agreed that joining the EU would dramatically improve the economy and help the country to be self-sufficient, but a parallel narrative made it clear that many Bosnians believed that European Commission funding of civil society initiatives (including counter-trafficking programs) was patronizing at best and, at worst, informed by Western European perceptions that Bosnians were incapable of responsible governance.

My discussions with Bosnian workers at international organizations and NGOs were almost always split into two completely separate narratives. Workers would first spend an hour or so with me explaining their organization's official stance on the benefits of EU membership for Bosnian efforts to end the traffic in women. Then, after patiently explaining this, Bosnian professionals would often transition to their real feelings about the subject, as one woman succinctly did by lighting a cigarette and proclaiming, "That was for your book where you can use my name. The rest of what I say is just for you to write down that some Bosnian told you this." This particular woman then completely changed her stance on the subject of the EU and stated, "I would like to tell the EU to fuck off. They grade people in Western Europe, because there they think that the farther south you come from, the less you are worth."

This consistent parallel narrative, in which individuals voiced statements they did not wish to be publicly identified with yet wanted me to be aware of, made me feel distinctly uncomfortable and gave me the sense that I was somehow responsible for reducing highly educated professionals to, as the unnamed woman put it, "some Bosnian." These tense politics of fieldwork and the debates over European Union membership were further complicated for me in Sarajevo when I had an unexpected visit from an old friend who is now a professor at Oxford. I was eager for a few days away from my research, but within hours of his arrival, I found myself retracing what Bosnian acquaintances had called "the war tour" as they walked me around Sarajevo after I arrived. I showed him buildings that had been partially destroyed by Serb mortar explosions and the walls of apartment complexes scarred by sniper fire, watching him react with the same combination of disbelief and grief that I had during my first walk through Sarajevo.

My friend's position of privilege was difficult to reconcile with the stories I had heard from Bosnian women who were eager to emigrate to Western Europe via marriage or jobs that were often far beneath their skill and education level, and I could not stop thinking about the unnamed woman's observation that "they grade people in Western Europe" as I listened to him speak. "It's so sad, what happened in this part of the world," he said as we stood by the shell of an abandoned helicopter covered with graffiti. "You know, most of my friends have married Eastern European women in the past few years. It's pretty much that he thinks, 'I want a wife,' and she thinks, 'I want to marry somebody who makes a lot of money.'" Underneath the helicopter's missing door someone had written, "War is only fun if you have a gun, and most of us don't," and I suddenly felt overwhelmed by the inequalities of gender and citizenship that were so much a part of everyday life in Western Europe that my friend could summarize them so concisely in just one sentence.

I attended a conference in Sarajevo titled "Fighting Human Trafficking in the Western Balkans," which had been organized by the European Forum for Democracy and Solidarity, an organization founded in 1993 by several Western

European branches of the Social Democratic Party. The European Forum has eleven Social Democratic foundations and eighteen Social Democratic political parties on its steering committee, and it regularly organizes conferences and seminars designed to, as its informational literature puts it, "support the transformation and democratization processes in Central, Eastern, and South Eastern Europe and the Caucasus." This particular conference was dedicated to discussions on how governments could successfully combat the traffic in women. It was attended by several Bosnian, Albanian, Serbian, and Bulgarian members of their respective parliaments; numerous heads of NGOs; a significant number of Western European politicians; and the Democratic Stabilization and Social Development Sector head of the European Commission Delegation to Bosnia.

The conference began with a speech by Anita Gradin, who was Sweden's first representative to the EU, on issues related to trafficking and irregular migration, and Gradin spoke eloquently about her professional experiences encouraging legislation and action on the topic in Western Europe. When a Bulgarian politician asked Gradin if she believed a common European police force might help Eastern Europe to protect women from trafficking, she responded that the sovereignty (which she glossed as "integrity") of individual countries needed to be respected. Then she proceeded to admonish the Balkan and Eastern European politicians in attendance by saying, "I can't see that you could go along with this anyway, because there are so many problems which you have still not solved today." In a slightly strange shift of topic, she then suggested that perhaps the politicians from non-EU member states could follow the EU example of creating an "International Day of Human Trafficking." Gradin's speech was followed by an overview of Belgian counter-trafficking initiatives by the founder of the NGO Payoke, Patsy Sorenson, who also stressed the need for increased government involvement in counter-trafficking in Bosnia.

Dutch moderator Olga de Haan then transitioned to the Western Balkan regional leaders' speeches by emphasizing that the conference had been specifically designed "for Western Social Democratic party exchange of information with Bosnian and other Social Democrats." De Haan's description of the day's events as an "exchange" was quite idealistic: because of several extended coffee breaks and a lengthy lunch, the session initially scheduled as an entire afternoon of dialogue among Bosnian NGO representatives, politicians, and Western European Social Democrats lasted less than one hour. Over lunch, individuals quickly divided themselves by geographic allegiances to either Eastern or Western Europe, and I joined a table of two Austrian women who were active in politics. When I asked them whether the counter-trafficking discourse presented by European Union countries in forums such as the conference was really informed by concerns about border security, organized crime, and illegal migration, one of the women shook her head and told me,

> What you need to understand is that these people are really acting like children. They don't learn German and they don't follow rules. One woman from Nigeria in a shelter for victims of trafficking in Vienna keeps taking the metro without a ticket and getting caught and also working illegally. How can you ever expect to receive asylum when you don't integrate, when you choose not to integrate?

When I asked the Austrian woman whether the Nigerian trafficking victim she described had received any kind of training or assistance to help her adjust to life in such a different country, her prejudices were revealed to be the product of assumptions rather than actual experience with "these people" she had spoken so confidently about just minutes before. "Well, I've never actually been to the shelter," she said, a bit affronted. "I've just heard all of this from others who know."

The post-lunch time slot was dominated by a speech by Michael Docherty, head of the Democratic Stabilization and Social Development Sector from the European Commission Delegation to Bosnia. De Haan introduced Docherty by asking whether he believed that the prospect of EU membership for Bosnia could be what she described as "a catalyst for development." "Yes," Docherty emphatically answered before beginning his prepared speech in English, which was simultaneously translated into Bosnian for the benefit of the vast majority of NGO representatives and politicians who were not fluent in the language of the conference. Docherty strongly argued that Bosnia had not done enough to implement counter-trafficking measures. He began by using a highly localized Scottish metaphor in his description of the current situation:

> Trafficking is a little bit like the Loch Ness monster. Everyone believes it exists, but no one knows its exact dimensions. The prospect of accession to the EU suggests that the EU can be a catalyst for development, but there has been very little progress made over the last two or three years and there is a limit to the effectiveness of the tools we can give. However, it is important not to rule out the possibility of EU accession or there will be no incentive to change. Only greater social and economic development can help, and frankly, I think Bosnia-Herzegovina has taken its eyes off the ball.

Docherty detailed how the European Commission had invested more than sixty million euros over the past few years in helping Bosnia move toward the possibility of EU accession. He also mentioned that the draft European Commission Stabilization Agreement with Bosnia had three specific articles related to trafficking, which dealt with organized crime, illegal migration, and regional stability. Docherty clearly positioned the traffic in women as part of what he called "the whole fight against organized crime, which flourishes in a weak state." This is perfectly understandable given his position as an official whose job is to facilitate the possibility of EU membership for Bosnia, but this point of view ignores the reality that the traffic in women cannot exist without the presence of significant gender inequality.

Bosnian Social Democratic politician Besima Borić was quick to follow Docherty's speech by adding that victims of trafficking "most often come from socially excluded and abusive families, and Social Democrats are interested in ending this exclusion in the interests of EU accession." Only twenty minutes remained at this point in the conference, and de Haan was growing visibly frustrated with the lack of dialogue between NGOs and Bosnian politicians. "What goals can we set for today?" she asked emphatically, before suggesting that NGOs tell the Bosnian government what counter-trafficking measures they would most like to see implemented. Many development professionals lament the lack of cooperation between NGOs and the state in Bosnia and contend that because NGOs have been supported largely by international aid agencies and donor governments since the war, there is little incentive for them to cooperate with a state that does not set aside funds for their activities. It was not surprising that the brief exchange that followed between NGOs and politicians was fraught with tension.

Ljiljana Raičević of the Shelter for Women and Children in Montenegro responded to de Haan's call for solutions with a reference to Borić's summary description of victims of trafficking. Raičević was rather accusing as she said, "As is usually the case when politicians speak, we learned nothing," which prompted de Haan to remind her that only constructive criticism was welcome. "But no one is doing their job, from the politicians to the police!" Raičević continued this line of criticism before de Haan, employing a tone reminiscent of an exasperated parent, interrupted her and said that everyone was in agreement that corruption is a problem in Bosnia, but the central question of the conference was how this reality could best be addressed. Raičević then crossed her arms over her chest, leaned back in her chair, and did not speak again. De Haan filled the awkward silence that followed by asking whether any NGO leaders had questions for what she termed "their Western European colleagues."

Highly respected NGO leader Selma Hadžihalilović, of the USAID-funded STAR Network of World Learning, gently but directly raised the point that many NGOs perceive suggestions that they should cooperate with the Bosnian government as a criticism of their abilities and then went on to ask how any progress could be made on the issue when the government could not even afford to pay the phone bills in police stations and social work offices. Hadžihalilović had astutely used a single example to underscore the depth of problems faced by the Bosnian state, and her words stayed with me as I left the conference venue and walked onto the empty suburban streets of Ilidža, which is also home to the Roma settlement of Butmir described in the previous section. I had not been in Sarajevo for very long, and I wondered if I had perhaps misinterpreted genuine Western European concern for victims of trafficking as patronizing arrogance. I felt angry at the Western European organizers for not ensuring that Bosnians had adequate time to present their points of view, frustrated with what I felt was the paternalistic tone taken by many of the Western Europeans in attendance (some of whom did not even bother to put on their simultaneous translation headsets to hear what Bosnian leaders had to say in their native language), and more than a little disappointed that Bosnian NGO representatives had not chosen to challenge these attitudes.

I met with Hadžihalilović a week later to talk about her perceptions of the European Forum Conference, and she was visibly frustrated by what she described as an event that "was really just all about EU accession." She situated the conference within the broader context of emigration from Bosnia:

> These attitudes make me not want to enter the EU, because the EU has a problem with migrants. I have no problems with migrants, with people looking for a better life. Who is the EU to say that you can't have a better life? Unskilled Bosnian workers wait in line at the Western embassies for a three-month visa to have two meals a day and share a toilet with fifteen other men in their barracks for 1,200 euro a month, even though the Embassy people laugh in their faces. There is the European way and the EU way. Citizens of Europe will talk about art and freedom, but then when it comes to the EU way, for us it's Fortress Europe.

Hadžihalilović's critical distinction between what she glossed as "the European way" and "the EU way" highlights the coercive powers of poverty and economic instability to make individuals choose migration even under undesirable circumstances. This perspective was not shared by most Western European employees of international organizations and donor agencies, who were much inclined to support initiatives such as the European Forum conference as a positive step toward what they hoped would be the future engagement of the Bosnian government with efforts to end the traffic in women. First Secretary of the Swedish International Development Agency Dr. Joakim Molander appeared genuinely disturbed by my question of whether the idea of "Fortress Europe" (a phrase used to describe the restrictive immigration policies of EU countries) implicitly informed Western European donor initiatives outside the EU. "We never use this kind of language," he said emphatically, "and we never take 'Fortress Europe' into account, because we are genuinely trying to reduce poverty."

Molander's perplexity regarding my use of "Fortress Europe" speaks to a number of communicative and cultural gaps between Bosnian and Western European staff members at IOM and other international organizations regarding the future of Bosnia and the best ways to combat the traffic in women. Fortress Europe is a phrase used to describe the restrictive immigration policies that characterize the countries of the European Union, particularly the more affluent nations of Western Europe that seek to discourage immigration altogether. The complex interplays between East and West in a postwar nation that is still largely dependent on Western donor aid for basic support underscore how individuals are sharply constrained by the roles they are allowed to play in their organization or, indeed, their society. There were a number of striking differences among IOM staff members who self-identified as "Bosnian" that highlight divisions within the "local" community itself.

Bosnian IOM staff member Rada had become a refugee at age ten when the war broke out and grew up with her family in San Francisco, California. Rada spoke fluent Bosnian and clearly had a deep love for the country of her childhood, but she was also very much an American woman who planned to return to law school after a few years in the country, as was the case with many individuals who still called themselves "aid workers" over a decade after the war. Rada often privately commented on how she resented that the Chief of Mission (who, like me, did not speak or read Bosnian) consistently had a Bosnian who had spent the war years in the country read her work. "What" she complained on one particularly poignant occasion, "I'm not a Bosnian because I spent the war in the West?"

Rada's rhetorical question is not as transparent as it may initially seem, because although culturally she self-identified with Bosnia, her option to leave the country at any time with her American passport clearly placed her in a position of privilege vis-à-vis Bosnian citizens who worked at IOM. Bosnian IOM employee Jasminka, for example, struggled to support her two children and her perpetually unemployed, alcoholic husband and found herself constantly torn between her overwhelming desire to help victims of trafficking and her obligation to strictly follow the rules of the organization in order, as her family's only source of financial support, to remain employed. The need to maintain a steady source of income was often cited as the reason for seeking out a job with an organization that receives significant amounts of donor funds, and many Bosnian employees of such institutions candidly explained that although it was nice to be able to help those in need, their main motivation in taking such a job was to support themselves and their families. This is completely understandable, and yet it also helps explain some of the disconnects between victims of trafficking and those who work to help them in both Bosnia and Armenia.

Suada found herself in a tense bind when her fiancé lost his job and she became the sole income earner in their small family. I often wondered if her vociferous (albeit private) criticisms of all Western European and North American aid organizations as unwelcome and near-imperialist interlopers in Bosnian affairs stemmed at least in part from the stress of her life situation. "They're all a bunch of little kings once they come here," she explained to me, "but in their own countries, they're complete shit and no one cares about them." Although Suada's sentiments were hardly extreme and were in fact voiced in other forms by many Bosnians I spoke to, such views were almost never expressed in front of Western Europeans in positions of power. I was privy to such comments only because I had strongly voiced my opinions about the subject with my Bosnian colleagues at IOM, which evidently resonated with their views to the extent that they felt comfortable sharing similar sentiments with me.

This parallel dialogue in which Bosnians work for organizations dominated by Western Europeans that largely operate by Western European rules, and yet privately criticize this arrangement among themselves, explains Molander's confusion about "Fortress Europe." Molander resembled many other Western European professionals in his perception that Bosnians and Westerners were working "in partnership" with one another toward ending the traffic in women. However, most Bosnians felt that this "partnership" was one in which they had to play by rules they did not invent. This situation created a number of strange overlaps between the personal and the political that revealed the tense dynamics between East and West that often lay just below the surface of interactions between people from these regions.

I was leaving the office one day when a group of Bosnian women who worked for IOM stopped me and offered me a cigarette. We stood talking for a few minutes about how hot the summer had been, and our conversation eventually turned to the progress I was making in my research. "Susan," one of the women asked me, "will you put our pictures in your book?" I felt deeply touched by this question and told her that I would definitely try to include such a photograph, but before my sense of sisterhood in the field could establish itself in my mind, she added a response that elicited much hilarity from the rest of the group. "Wonderful!" she exclaimed in mock joy, "Now we can all find rich American husbands who will feel sorry for us poor Bosnians when they read our stories!" I felt profoundly unsettled by a comment that served to underscore the deep divisions and power inequalities between Eastern Europe and the countries of Western Europe and North America that frame everyday interactions between Bosnians and Westerners.

Despite these divisions and inequalities, the enduring reality is that Western aid and assistance continue to be desperately needed in Bosnia. Dr. Molander explained that organizations like SIDA are essential in a postwar state that is still struggling to coordinate thirteen administrative zones and lacks essential government departments such as a Ministry of Health or a Ministry of Agriculture. He spoke of how many donor projects that could have benefited poor Bosnians had been halted or significantly delayed because of continued divisions between ethno-religious groups. The problem, he said, was that programs designed to strengthen the Bosnian state were often sabotaged by Republika Srpska, the ethnic-Serb-dominated entity that Molander noted "doesn't want a strong Bosnian state." These administrative difficulties were compounded by the problematic nature of defining the traffic in women, and Dr. Molander made it clear that limiting the scope of donor efforts to trafficking means that women who do not meet the highly specific criteria for being a "victim of trafficking" in Bosnia are sometimes turned away at shelters that would otherwise be able to assist them. "This is horrible and should not happen" he said, "and so SIDA is trying to label the issue as violence against women to help all women in need, while working together with the country."

The complexities inherent in interactions between state governments and international organizations are manifold, and a senior IOM Sarajevo official explained that it was absolutely necessary for governments to be involved in counter-trafficking measures. She used her previous experiences at IOM Turkey to demonstrate how the US government had successfully used a combination of donor funding and political pressure to change the prevailing attitude among Turkish government officials that victims of trafficking were unworthy of attention. "These are positive aspects" she stated, "but the judgmental and divertible part is problematic." Elaborating on this point, she explained that if governments do not view the traffic in women as a political issue, the result is a vicious cycle in which "traffickers know that there is no risk, so then there is no development, no education, and this triggers and creates more vulnerability." This way of thinking about the traffic in women strongly encourages national legislation against this activity and the prosecution of traffickers, and it places a high value on the power of the rule of law to improve the life situations of poor women.

My conversation with Gabrijela Jurela of the Organization for Security and Cooperation in Europe seriously undermined the activist critique that governments and international organizations are interested only in protecting Western European and North American borders. Jurela contended that "if this were just about borders, then there would be more of a focus on smuggling than on the traffic in women" and gave the example of how the 1999 European Union Stability Pact was instrumental in providing an incentive (via the threat of sanctions) for the Bosnian government to introduce counter-trafficking legislation. She described her own work acting as a liaison between the OSCE and the Bosnian government office that deals with trafficking and irregular migration as part of a broader effort to build a stronger Bosnian state. "People want to resolve everything with trafficking as an individual program," she said, "but it needs to be linked to other programs and to complement other strategies if it is really going to be effective."

Despite their differences of opinion, everyone I spoke to agreed that positioning the traffic in women as an important human rights issue presents significant challenges. The main points of contention were more often than not tied to individual experiences and occupational roles, so that whereas employees of international organizations and aid agencies were more inclined to stress the successes of counter-trafficking efforts, activists tended to highlight their failures. These disjunctures underscore the complexities inherent in addressing a global problem that most deeply affects poor women but simultaneously affects governments, activists, and international organizations alike. Examining these various points of view in their entirety and hearing how people involved in all levels of counter-trafficking activities were deeply invested in ending the problem forced me to interrogate my own views on the subject. I had initially believed that sustainable solutions to the problem could be arrived at only through initiatives at the local level, but my experiences with the numerous individual actors who influence counter-trafficking policy in Bosnia taught me that almost everyone who deals with the traffic in women genuinely believes that it is a terrible violation of human rights that must be stopped. It is essential to note that the differences between approaches to counter-trafficking lie primarily in how the issue is framed; an activist who considers national sovereignty to be a major issue is likely to resent international efforts to end the traffic in women in his or her country, whereas a policymaker who sees great value in legislation and donor funding to local populations is likely to see the activist's point of view as a nationalist impediment to real change. It remains to be seen whether these differences in opinion are profound enough to undermine efforts to more effectively address trafficking in women.

5

India: Rethinking the Traffic in Women

What struck me first about the Bombay neighborhood of Kamathipura was its vibrancy. Every lane seemed to ready to burst with an insistent vitality that almost resembled a human pulse in its rhythmic combinations of voices, Hindi film songs distorted by tinny speakers, and the periodic calls to prayer from a mosque in the distance. A city of eighteen million people, Bombay is twice the size of New York City and has at least as many migrants who arrived in search of economic opportunities and a better life for their families. It is not surprising that very few of the women who work in Kamathipura, a neighborhood infamously known as Bombay's red light district, are actually from the city itself. India is a nation of over a billion people, which means that the country almost always qualifies as one of "the world's largest" in any statistics related to population size, and its red light districts are no exception: Kamathipura is both the biggest and the oldest area dedicated to prostitution in all of Asia.

A historian at Bombay University who specializes in studies of urban planning explained that the neighborhood had originally been designated as a central location for British soldiers to visit prostitutes in the colonial period. Racism and taboos surrounding intimate relationships between people from different ethnic backgrounds encouraged the unofficial British government policy of allowing a select number of white women from poor families to migrate to their colonial territories as sex workers. Many, if not most, of these women probably would today be termed *victims of trafficking*, given the distance they had migrated and their presumed inability to dictate the terms of their work following their arrival. This kind of migration is part of an international pattern facilitating the increase in prostitution in areas with the large military bases and widespread economic inequality that also characterized Bosnia both during and after the war.

The population of Kamathipura became predominantly Indian following independence in 1947, but the purpose and character of the neighborhood remained the same. Women who frequent the nearby cloth market of the same name are often quick to criticize what they perceive to be the high rates of crime and drug abuse encouraged by the presence of prostitutes, a common complaint heard throughout the world in reference to associations between illicit behaviors and the women who are forced to engage in them because of their poverty and life circumstances. The elaborately hand-embroidered brocades and expensive raw silks of the cloth market, however, are far beyond the reach of most women in Kamathipura, many of whom are forced to buy their food, clothing, and other personal necessities at inflated prices directly from the *gharwali*, or "madam." She, in turn, profits from the sale of each item by pushing her workers ever deeper into debt.

This system is common throughout the world, and in the language of most counter-trafficking organizations it is known as "debt bondage." Debt bondage does sometimes consist of a real debt that the woman has incurred to the trafficker, who may have paid travel expenses and the costs of authentic or fraudulent documents, as well as charging a fee for assistance in finding work. It is far more likely, however, that a woman's debt to her trafficker has been either inflated or invented in order to coerce her into effectively working for nothing. The trafficker perpetuates this indebtedness by overcharging for necessities such as food, and otherwise capitalizing on a woman's lack of knowledge about costs in the area where she is working or on her inability to make her own purchases because her mobility is restricted.

Yet it is equally important to note that debt bondage does not necessarily indicate a lack of agency or even a woman's perception that she has been unfairly treated by the individual who keeps her earnings. Many women I have spoken with who were victims of trafficking by most definitions noted that they were indebted to the person who had paid for their travel expenses, clothing, and other necessary objects before they engaged in sex work, and that this debt necessitated a period of repayment. The logic involved in this way of thinking is strikingly similar to the psychological processes employed by many Americans who rationalize significant credit card debt as a temporary disadvantage en route to a better life. Many victims of trafficking with whom I have spoken were adamant that the handover of their earnings or, in some cases, direct payment from client to pimp, was simply part of a repayment plan that would eventually allow them to earn an income of their own. The chief problem regarding this generally arose when there was disagreement between the sex worker and the person to whom the money was owed, or when she and her debt had been "sold" to another person. The unregulated nature of such an exchange thus creates a situation that minimizes, but does not complete negate, individual agency.

Kamathipura features a very public display of sex for sale at all hours of the day and night; prostitutes stand behind the barred windows of buildings that are often incorrectly described as "cages" in articles by visiting journalists from both within and outside India. This is quite evocative, but it is important to note that the vast majority of urban Indian homes have bars on their windows as a consequence of the high cost and impracticality of glass in a tropical climate. It is nonetheless understandable that so many who visit the neighborhood in search of a story rather than a paid sexual encounter might feel that the girls and women are somehow imprisoned when they see the general conditions in which they live. Garbage collection is only sporadic, large yellow-toothed rats can be seen everywhere scavenging for food, and small children defecate openly next to unfiltered taps used for drinking water. Yet images of gods and goddesses are everywhere, small sticks of incense burning beneath them as a marker of respect, and the brilliant blues and pinks of the buildings are themselves interspersed with tiles bearing the images of Hindu deities at waist-level as part of an effort to discourage men from urinating in public. Damp saris and sheets wave at passersby from the laundry lines of open hallways, as do women and girls in various states of undress. It has been estimated that anywhere between 50 and 75 percent of them are HIV-positive.

The women who live and work in Kamathipura are predominantly South Asian, because the majority of the traffic in girls and women in India occurs domestically. Some are the children of sex workers who have been initiated into their mother's trade because of a lack of other options, and others come from families too poor to care for them. Many were brought up in desperate poverty in Nepal, which left them no choice but to migrate to relatively affluent India in search of work, and some were sold to traffickers by their family members who otherwise faced economic destitution. The delicate features and fair skin that characterize most people from Nepal are considered very beautiful in India, which creates a market in places such as Kamathipura that directly capitalizes on the poverty of a small Himalayan kingdom that has been plagued by Marxist insurgencies and economic instability.

The extremely public presence of sex work in the Kamathipura neighborhood seems paradoxical in a country with laws against prostitution, and yet this irony is able to sustain itself through carefully maintained arrangements between the police and the *gharwali*, who manage the brothels. Weekly bribes to the police are called *hafta*, the Hindi word for "week," and ensure that the police allow the illegal sex industry to function. These bribes also supplement the police officers' low salaries, which would otherwise be insufficient to support a family. The police do conduct regular raids on brothels. They remove underage girls, as well as mature women who explicitly state that they are being held against their will, and resettle them in shelter homes or government centers that specialize in caring for abused girls. One such government center, Asha Sadan, is discussed later in this chapter as part of a broader focus on how perceptions of immorality can forever stigmatize even very young girls who were forced into prostitution against their will.

Nearly all *gharwali* have been sex workers themselves at some point in their lives and were able to leave prostitution only by making a conscious decision to profit from the sale of other women's bodies and spending enough time in the sex industry to develop the social connections that enabled them to procure a group of younger prostitutes. This strategy is part of a complex psychological process through which an individual learns that survival is a matter of protecting one's own self-interests, and it is not difficult to understand how women who have been abused as prostitutes would prefer to be in a position of relative power as *gharwali*. After several years of work as prostitutes negotiating the whims of clients, most *gharwali* are shrewd businesswomen who, because of the illegal nature of their activities, are experienced in dealing with law enforcement officials. Police actions are necessary in order to reduce the traffic in girls and women, but these raids are also cruelly ironic, given that no one of any age or social background really wants to stand behind a barred window soliciting strange men for sex in Kamathipura.

THE POWER OF SOCIAL INVISIBILITY TO SUBJUGATE

Journeying approximately twelve hours south of Bombay to the state of Goa reveals a very different and more clandestine form of trafficking that underscores the scope and geographic range of organized criminal activities. This book has repeatedly demonstrated that in the majority of cases of forced prostitution, the perpetrator is known to the victim, but a significant amount of the traffic in women is controlled by organized criminal syndicates. Goa has long been well-known throughout Western Europe as an inexpensive vacation destination with beautiful beaches, spectacular Portuguese architecture, and a population that has grown accustomed to the strange sight of white tourists lying nearly nude on Indian beaches in hopes of darkening their skin. The state also has a reputation with relatively privileged Indian men as a place where the morals and behaviors of their home communities do not apply and where alcohol is inexpensive and freely available. The combination of a large foreign and domestic tourist population has, not surprisingly, resulted in an increased demand for prostitutes.

Goa is not at all comparable to the oft-described situation in Thailand, where the sex industry is extremely well organized and visible; instead, most exchanges of sex for money tend to be hidden away, just as they are in other areas of India outside Bombay. For about the past ten years, Goa has had a not-undeserved reputation as a destination for pedophiles from Western

Europe, despite efforts by the government of India and numerous NGOs in the region to encourage the prosecution of perpetrators. Just as in Kamathipura, police salaries are not at the level where officers are able to refuse bribes. Middle-class Western European tourists bring with them to Goa a level of wealth that far exceeds what an Indian police officer would earn in a year, and the lack of police respect for the migrant laborers (and their children) who are the victims of the majority of sex tourism cases also does not encourage enforcement of the law. A more recent development in Goa has been the introduction of Eastern European prostitutes, many of whom are quite likely victims of trafficking. These women are extremely visible as a result of their physical differences, and their presence has unfortunately convinced many Indian male tourists that all unaccompanied white women with Slavic features are prostitutes.

I first noticed an unusually large number of young Slavic women in Goan bars and restaurants in 2007, and when I asked Goan friends about this new population of white visitors, they all immediately answered by saying, "Russian mafia." Most Goans are Catholic, and the degree of religiosity present in the region results in extremely conflicted feelings about the presence of hundreds of very young women who were assumed by everyone I knew to have been forced into a situation of exploitation by men who were glossed as "Russian mafia." Sexuality is not a topic of open discussion in most Indian communities, so Goan women in particular used interesting language to describe these Slavic women. "Poor things," one woman said as we walked past a small group of scantily dressed young Slavic women smoking and feigning interest in conversation with three middle-aged North Indian tourists at an outdoor bar. "Their country fell apart and now they have to lay down with those black fellows."

The North Indian tourists were of medium complexion not so different from that of the women I was walking with, so this disturbing comment should be read in the context of the prevalent color prejudice in India. The according of higher status to lighter-skinned persons underlies the common usage of the adjective *black* as an insult. Presumably, then, the woman's observation was intended more as an assessment of the men's low character and outsider status than as a description of their skin color. She went on to distinguish Goan culture from the rest of India by saying, "These Indians all want fair-skinned girls, but Goans couldn't be bothered. We like our own kind." This follows a pattern exhibited in many countries, in which trafficking is almost always thought to be someone else's problem. Although its existence may be acknowledged, it is very rare for individuals to accuse their own community of encouraging or engaging in it. The Goan women thus effectively absolved their community of responsibility for the young women's welfare by situating blame either with the North Indian tourists or with what they believed were non-Indian organized criminal groups they referred to as Russian mafia.

Activists may take the Goan women to task for their refusal to intervene in the situation described above, and yet it is crucial to mention the complexities involved in attempting to assist a woman one suspects may have been forced into prostitution against her will. I took a group of fifteen undergraduate students from a small liberal arts college to my research site in Goa in January 2007 as part of a service learning project that focused on child sex tourism. I was forced to confront the traffic in women shortly after our arrival in a way that made me question my own humanity and also made me understand why most people choose to ignore the issue. There is a highly visible traffic in young women from Russia and other former Soviet republics to Goa, and even though I had informed my students of this, I was not adequately prepared for what happened one evening when I took one of my students to the doctor's office in the Goan town we were visiting.

The waiting room was located on the large veranda of the doctor's house and was full of some thirty Goans when we arrived. My student and I took a seat and were watching passersby on the street outside when an unsavory Indian man slowed his motorized scooter just enough to practically push an extremely thin and sickly Slavic teenager from the backseat. He sped away as she stumbled onto the veranda and sat huddled in the corner, shivering under a shawl. Her skin was a sallow, yellow shade, and it was clear that she was seriously ill. All of the Goan people in the waiting room cast sidelong glances at her, because it was impossible not to notice that something was very wrong; however, no one did anything. I was similarly paralyzed even though I felt I understood the dynamics of the situation, as did the others in the waiting room, judging by their reactions and noticeable embarrassment. I thought about the welfare of my fifteen midwestern students and my responsibility for them, of the possibility of retribution from her pimp if I tried to help, and of the stigma I would acquire from the perspective of community members I had spent several years building relationships with in my research on labor migration. I wondered whether many of the others in the room were thinking similar thoughts, with obvious variations depending on their life circumstances. And I wondered whether they were thinking about the risks to which they might expose themselves if they acted to help her. Perhaps that was why they, like me, did nothing.

As the Goan women's pity for the Russian prostitutes in the bar and the paralysis of everyone (including myself) in the doctor's waiting room demonstrates, there is a deep cross-cultural stigma attached to women who perform erotic labor. I began to understand this the moment I followed ten other women out of a dressing room swathed in a soft blue glow onto a rectangular dance floor, the small artificial gems adorning the women's tight sleeveless blouses, called *choli*, catching and reflecting the light as they moved in single file toward the circle of waiting men seated against the walls of the room. I had just spent the past two hours speaking to these women, who support themselves and their families by dancing for men. We talked as they dressed for a night of work in a tiny backroom at an establishment I will call Heera, which was then the most expensive and well-known dancing girls' bar in Bombay.

DANCING GIRLS AND STRUCTURAL ADJUSTMENT

Women at Heera were almost always completely covered by the *choli*, which most Hindu women wear underneath their saris, and a loose-fitting ankle-length skirt known as a *ghaghra* or a *lengha*. The next section will illustrate that this costume has deep historical roots in dance traditions from North India and would not be entirely out of place at a wedding or other formal event in a large Indian city. Women at Heera follow the Indian cultural norm that dancers of all kinds perform barefoot in order to maintain maximum control over their movements. Dancers at Heera, which means "diamond" in Hindi, are extremely privileged compared to the girls and women in Kamathipura because their working conditions are safer and more lucrative. They are not expected to have sex with the men who watch them perform, although, as is the case in many such establishments all over the world, many of the dancers do engage in informal relationships (which may include sex) with regular clients as a form of additional financial support. However, even dancers at Bombay's most exclusive institution are not entirely immune to the kinds of violence that sex workers often face, because the common social perception is that their occupation places them just one step away from prostitution.

Backstage at Heera, women with playful, seductive names such as Bobby, Khushboo, and Ruby fastened their shimmering *lengha* low on their waists and laced colorfully embroidered *choli* closed tightly at their backs. They helped each other to unbraid their long hair so it would swing as they danced, and the spirit of conviviality backstage might have led an outsider to believe that the women were relatives. Yet it was well-known that certain women with the fair skin and long, straight hair favored by most Indian men were very popular, and such women resented having to share their income with others who did not meet this standard of beauty. Dancers evinced a combination of extreme toughness and cultivated vulnerability that reflects the tightrope they are forced to walk as women who engage in a socially stigmatized form of work. "*Aache lagte hain, hamari zindagi* [You think our life is so good]?"

asked one of the younger women sarcastically as soon as I entered the room, before switching to English and whispering, almost in admonishment, "This is the only way we have to survive."

Cigarette smoke has a way of hanging in the air in a certain kind of light, so that it almost seems to be a solid, albeit transparent, object suspended in time. As my eyes began to adjust to the darkness of the dance floor, and the men's faces in the audience gradually began to take on a more recognizably human form, the men all seemed to be shrouded in the still, eerie smoke that formed a protective wall around them. Because they have to work in shifts of eight hours or more, the women conserve energy by standing in groups and swaying seductively to Hindi film music, smiling at the men in the audience as they approach them to exchange a few words of conversation. Words like *mera dewaana* (my male lover) and *meri jaan* (my female beloved, literally my life) take on a distinctly different tone as they are uttered simultaneously in the Hindi film song lyrics playing in the background and in the conversations between undulating women and their male clients.

I was privileged during the time I spent at Heera to earn the trust of three women whose names and key life details have been changed here, in order to protect their privacy and ensure their safety. All of the women I spoke to insisted that they and their families would be ostracized if their neighbors knew what they did to earn an income. At least five dancers told me that they would probably be sexually assaulted by low-ranking gangsters in their respective communities if their occupations were public knowledge. Indian cities are not so different from rural villages in that neighbors generally know a great deal about each other's personal lives, so maintaining a facade of respectability while staying out all night is not an easy task for an unmarried young woman. Most of the dancers commuted long distances from their suburban homes to work at Heera, which is located in the more affluent southern section of Bombay. This section functions as the city's business district and is home to the families who have benefited the most from imposition of the International Monetary Fund's structural adjustment policies. These policies further widened the already vast gap between rich and poor in Bombay, which pushed some women into establishments like Heera and neighborhoods such as Kamathipura.

Structural adjustment programs have been employed in over seventy countries around the world that are in significant debt to the International Monetary Fund. They consist of two phases, both of which are aimed at reducing account deficits: short-term macroeconomic stabilization and the implementation of structural reforms deemed necessary by the IMF (Rangarajan et al. 1994). These reforms specifically amounted to devaluation of the rupee by 23 percent, the institution of a new industrial policy more conducive to foreign investment, government disinvestment in potentially profitable public sector areas, the introduction of private banks, a liberalized import/export regime, cuts in social spending to reduce fiscal deficits, and amendments to laws to support all of these reforms (Chopra et al. 1995). Although these policies did little to help the poor, they vastly altered the commodity and consumption choices available to those with disposable income. Thus they were part of a pattern that mirrors the further marginalization of already disadvantaged groups throughout the world following the implementation of structural adjustment programs.

One of the most salient features of structural adjustment is its encouragement of foreign direct investment at almost any cost, and as a result, many US credit card companies and banks chose to relocate their customer service divisions to India following the implementation of IMF policies. India was particularly attractive as a destination because of its highly educated English-speaking population and its extremely low labor costs. These outsourced US businesses are known as "call centers" in India. The majority of their workers are young females who have just graduated from college, a fact that most call centers attribute to what they perceive as women's superior communication skills and ability to work long hours at monotonous tasks.

Women are particularly sought after as call center employees because they are more willing to accept monthly salaries that are sometimes equivalent to just a few days' earnings at a minimum-wage job in the United States, although this "willingness" is also a reflection of a lack of other employment opportunities and the understanding that they will stop working after marriage. Call centers operate at their highest volume during US business hours, so the time difference of ten and a half hours between India and the United States means that their Indian employees report to work at 11 p.m. and return home just before dawn. The feminization of low-paid labor in the call center industry, which is considered respectable work for middle-class women, ironically allowed most of the dancers at Heera to avoid stigmatization (and possible violence) by convincing their neighbors that they were actually call center employees.

One individual's life can by no means be considered representative of an entire population of women who do the same kind of work, but stories that three women at Heera shared with me do illustrate a level of marginalization shared by the vast majority of women who work in similar establishments. From a suburban Miss India aspirant to a North Indian single mother to a teenaged Nepali girl brought to Bombay by a relative who told her family that he would find her a job in an office, the women at Heera all had complicated lives that were not always in keeping with general understandings of the traffic in women. More often than not, their stories centered on the twin themes of economic marginality and a lack of real choices.

The routine involved in male/female interaction at a dancing girls' bar is profoundly about the performance of gender and can be most succinctly described as the use of women as objects with which to demonstrate male power and prestige. From the entrance of women into the room filled with men to the transfer of money from male patron to female performer, the entire encounter is suffused with the performance of masculine power and feminine vulnerability.

The routine begins when women enter the dance floor in a group to the sound of more erotic genres of Hindi film music and then begin a series of intricate hand motions and gentle sways of their hips that mimic dance forms popular in contemporary Hindi cinema. Men stay seated on cushioned chairs against the wall with tables in front of them, bundles of ten- to fifty-rupee notes (worth between twenty cents and one US dollar) in their hands or within easy reach. Nearly all of them are drinking alcohol and smoking cigarettes (which, despite their deleterious health effects, remain symbols of male afflu- ence in India). The vast majority of men arrive in groups, which testifies to both the generalized acceptability of male patronage and the social nature of this activity for men.

Dancers begin by approaching groups of men who consciously demon- strate their willingness to spend large amounts of money through their con- spicuous display of expensive bottles of imported American liquor on the tables in front of them. When I asked one young woman how she decided which men were likely to prove the most lucrative, she responded by making reference to a popular imported brand of scotch, saying "[m]ein sirf Black Label types ko jaati hoon [I approach only Black Label types]." Other women agreed that this was an admirable strategy. After a brief exchange of conversa- tions and compliments between the men and the dancers, at least one of the men in the group is obligated to hand a bundle of rupee notes to a uniformed male attendant. This individual functions as an intermediary for the exchange of money between the men and women and is also responsible for its redistri- bution to dancers at the end of the night. The exchange of money between the two men is followed by a stunning display that attracts the attention of almost everyone in the room and prompts applause at its conclusion.

The dancer begins by positioning herself close to the uniformed male atten- dant and then starts to spin rapidly in a circle with her hands raised high above her head, her *lengha* rising and fanning out around her lower legs to reveal her bare feet and the small silver-belled chains fastened around her ankles. Her long hair covers her face and swings through the air as the male attendant begins to shower her with the male client's rupee notes, which rain down over the dancer's body until the money the attendant has been given by the male patron is gone. The entire audience is transfixed by this process, and the more money a man gives, the longer the performance lasts. The message underlying the dancer's actions does not necessitate complex analysis, although a famous Bombay-born writer who accompanied me to Heera while he was visiting from New York City was quick to joke, "You know how in the US, porn movies have a 'money shot'? That's our Indian money shot." His reference to ejaculation, known in the adult film industry as "the money shot" because its occurrence marks the end of the movie, was more than a little disturbing and caused me to interrogate my own gendered perspective about what had seemed to me a difficult and skilled performance by the dancer. It occurred to me, after listening to his comment, that other men in the bar may have seen the showering of rupee notes over the woman's head in a similar way.

I met women at Heera who came from a fairly broad range of ethnic backgrounds, but they shared the common trait of structural marginality. Nearly all of them were migrants to Bombay, except for a few suburban dancers who had grown up in the city but did not have access to the same kinds of class privilege as those who live in the southern neighborhoods surrounding Heera. As part of their work personae, all the women had adopted playful, seductive names that in an Indian context imply a sweet and accessible femininity, such as Bobby, Khushi (Joy), Sapna (Dream), Ruby, and Khushboo (Perfumed One). As a uniquely Bombay phenomenon that does not exist in other Indian cities because of strict cultural prohibitions against the public display of sexuality, dancing girls' bars such as Heera hire a very specific type of woman who is young, fair-skinned, and able to tolerate constant comments and propositions from male patrons. The women who worked at Heera came from regions as diverse as Nepal, Rajasthan, and Bengal, and yet all were strikingly similar, exhibiting fair skin, long, straight hair, small, delicate features, and, of course, youth.

As is the case in the rest of the world, the amount of money a woman earns in a Bombay dancing girls' bar depends on the kind of establishment in which she works. Salaries are calculated through tips from male patrons divided at the end of the evening and can be as low as 3,000 rupees (62 US dollars) per month in some bars, whereas at Heera women earn closer to 50,000 rupees per month (just over 1,000 US dollars). These women are often the only wage earners in their families, and they sometimes send their income home to families who believe that their daughter is earning money in a "respectable" office job rather than in a bar. The profit that is earned from their bodies, however, is far greater: at Heera, the owners paid a weekly bribe of close to 15,000 rupees (over 300 US dollars) to the Bombay police in order to ensure "protection," which is a euphemism for official tolerance of their activities. Businesses such as Heera were legal when I began my research in Bombay, and yet police capitalized on their social marginality and ties to organized crime and money laundering by insisting on frequent bribes. Heera's owners, in turn, also benefited from this arrangement because it assured them of police protection from rival gangsters who might try to damage the premises or persuade particularly beautiful dancers to work at their establishments instead. The large sums of money they were able to pay thus effectively turned the police into a private security force to guard their business.

The first dancer to approach me at Heera was Bobby, a tall woman in her early twenties from a suburban Bombay neighborhood that was at least a two-hour journey via public transportation from Heera. I remember wondering what it must be like to leave Heera's opulence to sit on a run-down commuter train for a long journey home in the early hours of dawn, and I asked her what motivated her to travel such a distance. Her answer surprised me. "I want to be Miss India," she smiled broadly within five minutes of introducing herself. The Miss India pageant is a cultural phenomenon in Indian cities; the winners are seen as India's ambassadors to the world and often go on to very lucrative Hindi film careers. Bobby had unsuccessfully tried to enter the pageant three years in a row as part of her master plan to become an actress in Hindi films, and she was concerned that she might have been rejected because, as one of the pageant organizers who met her in Heera flatly informed her, "prostitutes can't represent the country." Bobby had been crushed at this callous remark, particularly because she saw herself as a skilled performer who was trying her best to support herself in a country where it is highly unusual for anyone to live alone, especially a young and unmarried woman.

"It's not easy for girls like me," she stated emphatically in English as she brushed her long hair in front of a tiny, streaked mirror backstage. Bobby wore the tightest, most heavily embroidered *choli* of all, and she employed the most risqué dance forms almost as if she were auditioning for a Hindi film. As we spoke I realized that this was no accident. "What am I supposed to do?" she asked almost defensively as she applied another layer of thick eyeliner, "Get married to some office clerk and be happy making *daal-roti* [lentil soup and flatbread, a typical Indian meal] for the rest of my life? I'm a middle-class person, but I have big dreams. For girls like me, it isn't easy to break into films, and while I'm waiting for my opportunity, I have to support myself. To be perfectly frank, this is the only chance I have to make something of my life." Bobby's ambitions and great beauty made her one of the most popular performers at Heera, and her flawless self-taught English was a definite asset in interacting with powerful men who were from a class background very different from her own. Although she was the woman who was most like the sisters and wives of her clients because of her fluency in English, Bobby's work as a dancer notably rendered her unmarriageable in any Indian community.

I admired Bobby's courage to follow her dreams and fearlessly flout social convention when I first met her, but I was horrified when I learned more about her life situation. She explained that several months prior to our conversation, a gangster from her suburban neighborhood had knocked on her door and, with a cruel smile on his face, explained that he knew everything about her work at Heera. Bobby described standing stunned and petrified in her doorway as he calmly proposed two solutions: either he could tell everyone in the neighborhood and almost definitely expose her to sexual violence by local hoodlums, or she could pay him roughly 75 percent of her monthly salary in exchange for his silence. This was hardly a choice, and Bobby agreed to the arrangement despite the fact that the remainder of her salary just barely allowed her to pay for her daily commute to Heera and maintain the small suburban room she rented. "I'm left with almost nothing at the end of the month, but that's my situation, and I can't quit doing this because then he'll tell everyone everything about me. Things will get better for me, but what can I do in the meantime?" she asked rhetorically before following several other women back onto the dance floor.

According to most definitions of trafficking, Bobby was a victim because of the debt bondage her neighbor's threat had placed her under. She was unable to quit her job because of the implicit threat of sexual violence that would ensue, was not allowed to keep much of her salary, and was powerless to do anything to improve her situation. However, Bobby clearly did not see herself as a victim and was adamant that she remained in control of her life despite a grossly exploitive situation. Bobby is not unlike many other women throughout the world who are coerced into performing erotic labor for someone else's benefit. She clearly believed that because it had initially been her choice to engage in such work, she was somehow responsible for the abuses that followed. The complex realities of Bobby's life serve to complicate ways of thinking about trafficking and raise deeper questions about how women like her could be helped out of such unfair situations.

Bobby resembles many other women whose lives are described in this book in that she shared her story with me only because of the life realities she felt we had in common. I first visited Heera with a male author (as described earlier) and did not return until the Fulbright-Hays dissertation research fellowship I had been awarded was unexpectedly suspended (along with all of the other Fulbrights that year) after I arrived in India. This suspension occurred because of a US State Department ruling that arose out of concerns that India and Pakistan were on the brink of a nuclear war in 2002. The impact on my life was devastating. I had no money to return to the United States, very little money in the bank, and no close friends in Bombay with whom I could stay. In short, I was in dire straits. In a highly unusual turn of events from a research perspective, I returned to Heera and found that Bobby remembered me from my first visit to the bar.

Bobby became my friend, offered to lend me one of her dancing girls' costumes, and freely shared her much-needed life advice with me. The other women at Heera opened up to me quite readily as well, because of our shared language of Hindi and similarities in age, but also because of our shared origins in poverty and marginal circumstances that were beyond our control. Bobby sat with me on numerous occasions and matter-of-factly explained the benefits and pitfalls of her work, noting that although she earned a great deal of money, she was also exposed to exploitation. She was concerned that I would be even more likely to find myself in a troubling situation because I was a conspicuous, fair-skinned young foreigner, and she encouraged me not to perform at Heera unless I had exhausted all my other options for self-support.

Bobby's description of her decision to become a dancer was strikingly similar to discussions I had with topless dancers in the United States, many of whom cautioned me that I was not emotionally strong enough to handle the experience. As one US performer explained to me after she learned how little money I survived on as a graduate student, "Look, the money here is good, but there are some lines that once you cross them you can't go back. That's why we get so mad when people think that we're whores, because dancers don't get paid for sex even though ignorant people think that. If you think about doing this, you have to remember that there are strings attached." She went on to explain, as did Bobby, that I would need to surround myself with a great deal of emotional armor in order to perform. My Fulbright-Hays fortunately came through by the end of the month and solved my money problems, but I will never forget the extremely frank conversation Bobby and I shared in the back of a Bombay dancing girls' bar—or how it felt to be young, female, poor, and alone in a foreign city.

My own extremely minor experiences of course pale in comparison to those of most of the other women I met at Heera, who were in much worse situations that showed little sign of improvement. I met Khushboo when she approached me backstage and sweetly asked, in quiet and extremely formal Hindi, if I needed to borrow a costume to perform in because she had an extra one to lend. "I know what it's like to be in a new place and not know anyone," she whispered after making her offer. Khushboo explained that she had been abandoned by her husband shortly after the birth of their first child. She did not know where he was, and he did not provide her or her child with any financial support. To complicate matters, Khushboo's roots were in conservative North India, and she and her mother felt that it would create more scandal than it was worth to return home. Khushboo's father had died several years before, and thus, lacking a strong male support system, the small family chose to remain in Bombay. "I came to Bombay shortly after marriage," she explained, "and soon became pregnant. In a strange city where I knew no one, it was just one step from my husband never being at home to him actually leaving me and my child. My mother and younger sister, suspecting that something was wrong in my marriage, came to Bombay and we decided that it is best to stay here rather than returning home."

Going back to Lucknow as a new mother with no husband was simply not an option, she explained. "In Lucknow, people talk. Even when a woman has a husband, there is no question of her working, so imagine what people would say if we three women went back alone, with a small baby. This is the only option available to me right now." Khushboo was beautiful in a North Indian way, with high cheekbones and gray-green eyes that placed her heavily in demand with men at Heera. She showed me a picture of her mother and seventeen-year-old sister, and the resemblance was unmistakable. When I asked about her younger sister's future, Khushboo was emphatic that she did not want her to enter into the profession. "I paid for my sister's dowry," Khushboo sadly smiled. "We haven't found a groom yet, but I have saved the money nonetheless. I am determined that my sister will not live a life like mine." Dowry is an illegal but extremely prevalent cultural practice in India that involves the transfer of valuable gifts and money from a bride's parents to the family of her new husband, and some radical Indian feminists have provocatively described it as "buying a groom." Dowry nonetheless remains a requirement for many North Indian marriages, and Khushboo saw her responsibility as the family's sole earner to provide her sister with close to a year's salary in order to help find a good husband. As she left the dressing room to spend the night dancing for strange men in order to add to the money for her sister's dowry and to support her small family of women, it seemed to me that in many ways, Khushboo was representative of almost all the structural inequalities facing women who find themselves alone with small children and few job skills.

I met Ruby when she asked me for a match with which to light her cigarette. "I know smoking is a bad habit," she smiled apologetically, "but I feel like it makes me seem older, and that protects me here. They leave the older girls alone." Ruby would not have been out of place in a school uniform, and I estimated her age at around fifteen—far too young to be in Heera legally. The bribes paid to the police, however, ensured that she would be able to work for as long as the owners were able to continue payments. She sat down next to me, twirling her glass bangles around her wrist as she told me about her life far away from her home village in Nepal. "My family thinks I work in an office. In Nepal, people aren't so worldly. I've been here for one year now and I don't know if I will go back, because people may suspect. We call AIDS 'the Bombay disease' in Nepal, because so many girls come back to their villages sick, but I don't like to think about it. Everyone knows that Indians like Nepali girls. If I go back and they ask me questions, how will I answer? What do I know about office work?"

Ruby put out her cigarette and told a story that is heartbreakingly familiar in regions as geographically and culturally disparate as Nepal and the republics of the former Soviet bloc. "One of my uncles approached my father and told him that he could use his connections to find me a job in Bombay. My family is very poor, so when that uncle offered money in exchange for my work, how could my father refuse? We are seven daughters, and that is something difficult for a father." Ruby fit the definition of a victim of trafficking in almost every way. She had not known that she would be performing erotic labor, she was unable to return to her place of origin, and she had effectively been sold by her desperately poor family in Nepal. Ruby was resigned to her life situation in many ways, but I could not help wondering what the future held for her or the thousands of young women exactly like her. I also questioned whether it would make any difference to her life if she knew that definitions constructed by powerful international organizations and her own government defined her as a victim who deserved state protection.

Definitions aside, Heera was just one of 2,000 dancing girls' bars in Bombay that employed over 800,000 women before the government of India forced their closure on May 18, 2005. The decision was celebrated by Indian religious conservatives, government officials, and feminists alike as a concrete step toward women's empowerment, and it was widely cited as proof of social intolerance for institutions that exploit female sexuality. It is true that for women such as Bobby, Khushboo, and Ruby, performing erotic dances for men is a way of life that negatively affects their psychological health and safety at very real levels, and yet their other options for economic self-sufficiency are severely limited by their social class and gender. The closure of the dancing girls' bars may further a certain conservative Indian political agenda, but it does precious little to help the women whose lives are destroyed by the loss of their jobs.

The question of what will happen now that the bars have been closed remains. Because there are no social safety nets or broader structures in place to absorb women who live on the margins of society, dependent on male patronage for their very survival, the next step for all three women would probably be the brothels of Kamathipura. More succinctly put, the real question is this: When the state decides to enforce publicly lauded measures designed to reduce the traffic in women, what is the real impact on women such as Bobby, Khushboo, and Ruby?

Institutions like Heera do not exist in a historical or cultural vacuum and are necessarily informed by social norms and practices that long predate their existence. The closure of bars such as Heera was devastating for women whose survival depended on them, but this imposition of state authority on women's sexuality and lives is by no means new. In fact, the government of India's actions are remarkably similar to those taken by British colonial officials in the country almost 140 years before. This is exceptionally notable given the way in which prostitutes have so consistently been used as tools throughout the world to further a wide variety of political agendas, and the striking frequency with which this has occurred warrants some discussion.

The dance form known as *mujra* emerged in the 300-year period of Central Asian Mughal rule in North India, and it strikingly resembles the performances by women at Heera. Characterized by its soft eroticism, *mujra* was performed by courtesans called *tawaif* who were an integral part of life in the Mughal court. *Mujra* as a style of performance originated under the Mughal emperor Jahangir and truly flourished under Shah Jahan, who commissioned the Taj Mahal and invested enormous amounts of funds and resources in building palaces to house the *tawaif* who were most proficient in *mujra*. Yet in just a few hundred years, the word *tawaif* devolved from a term describing a woman of great talent who could sing, dance, and recite Urdu poetry with enormous skill to a word synonymous with *whore*.

Originally operating from mobile encampments, *tawaif* women were members of organized troupes that would create a settlement to occupy during the time that one of them had a patron. This system can be considered a temporary relationship between a wealthy older man and a *tawaif*. When North Indian cities such as Lucknow and Kanpur became centers of Mughal power, *tawaif* began to attach themselves to courts and also established permanent settlements in which to perform their art. The way in which *mujra* was performed is almost identical to the manner in which dancing girls' bars function today. During a *mujra* performance, dancers spent the evening in the center of a room ringed by a seated male audience and very similar to the arrangement of the stage at establishments such as Heera.

Tawaif became an important part of urban life in the Mughal period, and the rules for entry into the profession were quite strict. Mothers passed their skills and their established relationships with families of patrons to their daughters, who in turn taught the sons of such families music and Urdu poetry. *Tawaif* are often thought of today as women who sell sex, but at the height of Mughal power they were the only women who had access to education, had the right to interact socially with men, and often wielded political influence thanks to their close ties to powerful men. Many women in their profession had to learn to survive in environments fraught with intrigue, so it is no wonder that politics came easily to them.

The decline of the term *tawaif* from a word denoting studied professional to a near-euphemism for prostitution is closely linked to the end of the Mughal Empire, which had been the profession's largest employer. Centers for *tawaif* performances known as *kotha* were rife with political discussion in the early to mid-1850s, and many *tawaif* were active participants in the events surrounding the mutiny of 1857. *Kotha* became an easy target for punishment by the British colonial administration after the rebellion was quelled, and many *tawaif* were victimized by government seizure of their property and by new public health regulations and zoning laws designed to depict them as social nuisances detrimental to society's moral well-being. As has happened so often in history, women who had the most insecure political position of all the actors involved were punished the most severely.

The mutiny of 1857 was a turning point in Indian history in innumerable ways, and the political climate of the time was one in which survival in the public eye was anything but easy. The growing All-India Congress Party routinely received generous donations from *tawaif*, and yet its leaders denounced *kotha* as immoral centers with no place in the independent India they were trying to create. Gauhar Jan, a *tawaif* who later became the first South Asian singing star of the twentieth century, was often requested to leave Congress Party meetings by "respectable" female members. This political transition to Indian independence thus marked the end of a system that offered women performers a real social role and the beginning of their social ostracism.

Some *tawaif* were able to survive this transition by branching out into the nascent recording and film industries; an example is the iconic film star Nargis, who was trained by her *tawaif* mother. When their talents were no longer desired in the wake of a collapsed Mughal system that could not support them, however, the vast majority of *tawaif* became prostitutes because there were no longer any other avenues of economic support open to them. Those *kotha* that managed to survive had by mid-century become brothels and were subject to raids by the police, which further encouraged their closure. *Kotha* that remain open today number only about a dozen, and many of them are essentially similar to dancing girls' bars, with the additional assumption on the part of male patrons that sexual services are available for purchase. In fact, a rumor circulated throughout Delhi in 2000 that adolescent *mujra* dancers were being trafficked to London to work as prostitutes for South Asian immigrants. English police were encouraged to investigate by a Delhi human rights group and soon discovered that numerous Indian restaurants and bars that advertised themselves as venues for the performance of *mujra* in British cities were in fact functioning as brothels. Most of the dancers were deported to India.

This is hardly surprising given that such women, as we have seen in the case of the closure of Bombay dancing girls' bars, are often the first to be punished for perceived social ills that extend far beyond their own activities at the margins of society.

SOCIAL CLASS AND "MORAL DANGER"

If international organizations, states, NGOs, and individuals all play a direct or indirect role in facilitating the traffic in women, social class also functions to subvert well-intentioned efforts to assist women who are discursively constructed as "at risk." India is sharply distinguished from the Eastern European case studies presented in the previous two chapters because of its political stability and long history of active, vibrant civil society organizations, and yet the country's endemic class inequalities sometimes inject a problematic tone of rescue and redemption into efforts to assist. It is almost self-evident that those with greater class privilege have more time, resources, and energy to devote to social causes, and yet this reality also carries with it the possibility of patronizing class-based behaviors and assumptions in relation to subjects as sensitive as prostitution and trafficking.

I spent a day with a group of twenty affluent women who had decided to participate in an activity they designed with the intention of assisting ten teenagers who had been relocated from a Bombay brothel to a shelter that described itself as "for girls in moral danger." All twenty women ranged in age from twenty-six to forty-five and had attended the same prestigious schools in Bombay. Most had pursued a university education in Western Europe or the United States, and none had ever worked for an income either before or after marriage. The ten teenagers these women aimed to help ranged in age from thirteen to seventeen when they were forced into prostitution, and most came from small towns and villages. Many were the children of migrants, some of them had been sold to a brothel by a family member, and very few with whom I spoke had any real hope for the future. The interactions between these two extraordinarily different groups throughout the day revealed much about the kinds of misunderstandings that can arise from differences in social class and thus can undermine efforts to "help."

The day was organized by a thirty-five-year-old woman I will call Deepa, whom I met while interviewing alumni from a former British colonial school in Bombay that now educates the most privileged boys and girls in Bombay. Deepa and I were approximately ten minutes into our discussion of her school experiences when her mobile phone rang, and she began an anxious conversation with the caller about what she described as a "social service day" that appeared to cause her great concern. Deepa gave a series of monosyllabic replies to her caller, who apparently had a great deal of information to relay, after which she exclaimed, "But it's not my responsibility!" The caller continued speaking for a few minutes while Deepa nervously twirled her highlighted hair around her fingers before finally announcing, "I'll settle everything." Deepa snapped her mobile phone shut and leaned toward me with a very serious expression on her face. "Can you help me?" she asked, "I need to organize an event for our charity cases and I had completely forgotten about it."

Deepa was like many women of her age and class background in belonging to a women's organization that met on a weekly basis for lunch, although its members often saw each other at other social functions throughout the week as well. Her organization was like many others that engage in charity work, and this specific women's club had, as Deepa explained to me, "adopted a group of girls in moral danger," meaning that they donated a small amount of money each month toward the food and shelter necessary to support these girls with a modest standard of living. I found her use of the phrase *moral danger* simultaneously fascinating and repugnant, and I agreed to assist the young women in preparing lunch for Deepa and her women's club in order to have an opportunity to interact with both groups. This, I hoped, would give me a deeper insight into the way social class functions to divide communities in a highly stratified society that paradoxically features a great deal of interaction between class groups because women like Deepa frequently hire domestic workers to care for their children and homes.

My involvement with women from Deepa's social background dates to the year I spent in India as a sixteen-year-old after I was awarded a scholarship to study in a country of my choosing. I selected India because it was the most distant geographic destination from the small, impoverished town I grew up in, and I planned not to come back. Other than my many male relatives who had spent time as soldiers on distant battlefields, I was the first person in my family to leave the country. I was forced to confront (albeit internally) a number of class-related issues once I arrived in India at such a young age, and I found myself awkwardly walking a tightrope between the relationships I cultivated with my affluent Indian host families and school friends and the innate empathy I felt for their domestic workers, drivers, and cooks as a result of my own working-class background.

My position as a white foreigner who eventually learned to speak the national language of Hindi with native-like fluency placed me in the uncomfortable position of often listening to wealthy host family members (and later, when I returned to conduct ethnographic fieldwork in India, research contacts) criticize the "laziness" of the poor people who worked for them. As an outsider, I was also the person to whom those very same employees often would describe the low pay, abuse of labor, and demeaning living conditions to which their poverty confined them. Strangely enough, I often knew more about the lives of the poor people who worked for the families I lived with than the families themselves did, despite their having lived side-by-side for years. The difference, of course, was that my own class background had taught me that the "servants" were also human beings with thoughts and opinions, whereas my host families simply saw them as disposable and easily replaced labor. My outsider status no doubt influenced the willingness with which such people spoke to me, because as a foreigner, I was seen as relatively free of the class (and associated caste) constraints that most Indians find themselves operating by in everyday life.

The unfortunate continued existence of white privilege in India over six decades after independence also influenced the relationship I had with people, such that the charity women's group (and many others I met in India) saw it as prestigious to have a white foreigner in their midst, a profoundly problematic issue given my own conflicted stance on class privilege. It turned out that the women's group Deepa belonged to had "adopted" girls who came from Asha Sadan, one of the oldest social service organizations in India. It was founded by its parent organization, the Maharashtra State Women's Council, nearly one hundred years ago to house young women between the ages of thirteen and twenty who are what its brochures describe as "in social distress or moral danger."

Asha Sadan means "The Home of Hope" in Hindi, and the organization houses approximately one hundred females in its shelter, which is located in a Bombay prison. The walls that surround it are covered with barbed wire and topped with broken glass, and one can immediately understand how the teenaged girls who live inside might feel they inhabit a world that perceives them as a social threat. Girls who live at Asha Sadan come from a variety of circumstances, but all have been forced into prostitution at an extremely young age. They include runaways, single mothers, and girls who were rescued from brothels by the police during the frequent raids the city of Bombay carries out in Kamathipura. Until the age of eighteen, the wards of Asha Sadan are provided with a basic education at local government-run schools and vocational training in traditionally female occupations such as cooking, sewing, and hairdressing. The establishment refers to these activities as *rehabilitation*, a word that has the less-than-subtle implications of moral redemption from a sordid life of sin.

It was mid-morning when Deepa and I arrived at a large house in South Bombay and were greeted by a woman wearing a large diamond pendant and an expensive, peacock blue silk sari who ushered us into the central courtyard. Rising population pressures have encouraged the destruction of houses in Bombay to make way for apartment buildings, and real estate developers regularly pay millions of dollars for property such as the one on which this home was built. "The girls are in the kitchen," she said to me slowly and with wide eyes, as though her words had great meaning or were being spoken in a language difficult to understand. After pointing in the direction of the back of the house, where most Indian kitchens are located in such large homes, she led Deepa to sit with a group of elegant women who were already drinking watermelon juice from slim crystal goblets. I entered the kitchen unsure of what I would find, and I was more than a bit uneasy about what seemed the very likely prospect of spending the day watching a group of extremely under-privileged girls cater to the needs of twenty over-privileged women. The pur-pose of the exercise, Deepa had explained, was to educate the young women in behavior and presentation so that, if they were lucky, they could be adopted as live-in housemaids by the kinds of wealthy Bombay people who believe that the way their servants behave is a reflection of their family's social status. "You'll be doing them a big favor in life," she added when I hesitated.

Ten adolescent girls stood in one corner of the kitchen next to an older woman who identified herself as a social worker. Their expressions revealed that this was not a new experience for them, and as they stood there in their identical dull brown uniforms, their oiled hair neatly braided and tied with frayed red ribbons, I felt very uncomfortable with my role for the day. With no prompting whatsoever, almost as though it were expected as a matter of course, the social worker immediately began to tell me extremely personal and no doubt painful stories from each of the girls' personal lives in Hindi, India's national language. She spoke as if the young women were not present, although she did gesture in the direction of the appropriate girl when using her name. Hindi is rather idiosyncratic in that most Indians feel that words associated with sexuality tend to sound crude in that language, and the social worker followed linguistic convention by inserting the English words *rape*, *sexual abuse*, and *prostitute* into her Hindi descriptions of the circumstances that had led each of the young women to Asha Sadan. I remained silent during the social worker's monologue and tried to imagine what the girls were think-ing as the most horrific moments of their lives were recounted to a complete stranger in a flat and passionless tone.

Some of the young women seemed unable to make eye contact at all, while others looked right through me and everyone else in the room. Many of them had colorful names that are typical of women who work in the sex industry in India, such as Shehazadi, which means "princess," or Gulabi, which means "pink." I wondered if these were their real names; most of them had no iden-tity documents because of their minor status, and according to the social worker, a few had refused to say where they came from originally when they entered Asha Sadan. The social worker gestured toward a smiling girl who wore a thin red thread tied around her wrist for good luck and told me that just over one year ago her parents had abandoned her because of their poverty. Frightened and alone, she soon found herself en route to Bombay with an older teenaged boy who promised her that they would get married as soon as she was eighteen. Instead, the boy sold her to a brothel, where she stayed until a social worker's inspection revealed that she was underage. Her name was Anjali and she was fifteen years old. Flavia, who was also fifteen, could easily have been Anjali's sister, judging by the similarities in their life circumstances of abandonment, social invisibility, and betrayal. Many of Flavia's difficulties stemmed from the death of her father several years before, which had pushed her and her mother into a position of social marginality and dependence on other family members, who were also struggling to survive on their own. Flavia's mother was illiterate and had no marketable skills, so she was forced to accept the decision of her extended family that Flavia would be sent away from their small South Indian town to work as a housemaid. It had been clear to the teenager almost as soon as she arrived in Bombay that the job her family had in mind was actually prostitution.

Gulabi, fourteen, and Shehanaaz, fifteen, were introduced together, even though they were standing on opposite sides of the small group. "*Humare ko ek hi house se pakad liya* [They were brought to us from the same brothel]," the social worker explained, substituting the English word *house* for *brothel* and using the guilt-implying Hindi verb for "to catch" (*pakadna*) to describe their removal from the premises by police. Gulabi and Shehanaaz may have worked in the same establishment but were otherwise completely different. The social worker first explained that Gulabi had been sold by her alcoholic father to a broker in Nepal who transported to her Bombay, where she experienced abuse that resulted in her difficulties speaking and making eye contact. Gulabi's mannerisms and posture made her look more diminutive and younger than Shehanaaz, who was thirteen. Because she was adamant that she did not want to tell anyone about her family or her life, little was known about the circumstances that landed Shehanaaz in the Bombay brothel she had lived in prior to the police raid that placed her in Asha Sadan's care. The facts she had revealed to social workers were terrible enough to suggest that Shehanaaz had been brutalized for most of her life, such as the story she told about the time, around her tenth birthday, when she was beaten until she acquiesced to the "sale" of her virginity to a much older man.

It is impossible to have knowledge of a stranger's private pain and not search her behavior for signs of its impact, and for the rest of the afternoon, as I helped the girls prepare and serve a lunch of spaghetti and salad, I was struck by how differently they seemed to have responded to a very similar set of traumas. Some seemed like children much younger than their actual age, such as Anjali who smiled and clung to me throughout the day, whereas others such as Gulabi were very quiet and seemed terrified of life. A few girls behaved like normal Indian adolescents of their age and social background, but most had clearly been emotionally changed by their experience in ways that would have been obvious to anyone regardless of what they knew or didn't know about the girls. Anyone in the room would have sensed that most of them had experienced some kind of serious trauma firsthand. Individuals cope with trauma in different ways, and the kinds of survival strategies they adopt depend on their culture, their socioeconomic class, and, of course, their age. Minors do not have the adult emotional resources to make sense of the world and protect themselves in times of crisis, and underage victims of trafficking often face lifelong impacts of the abuse they have undergone.

Under the watchful eye of the social worker, I helped the girls boil water for the spaghetti and chop vegetables for the salad, as Deepa and her friends sat and discussed their busy social schedules in another room. The girls were eager to help and called out *"Didi! Didi!* ["Big Sister," the normal Hindi term of address from a younger girl to an older woman of the same generation]" every time something seemed even slightly amiss—an indication that they were accustomed to close monitoring. There were at least four occasions during the forty minutes it took to prepare lunch when the social worker berated the girls for minor infractions, such as dropping a knife or spilling some water, and the social worker very loudly advised me to "watch out" for Shehanaaz after the teenager and I exchanged a smile. The atmosphere of control and suspicion that surrounded the girls must have been clearly conveyed, although perhaps they had grown used to it over time. It was decided that each of the girls should carry something to the table to serve Deepa and her friends, who were eager to advise the teenagers on what constituted appropriately servile behavior, and all ten formed a line carrying plates laden with food they had never eaten before.

"Where is the silverware?" asked one of the youngest women seated at the table. The girls remained silent and looked confused, because, like most Indians, they ate their meals using their right hands while seated on the floor and were not accustomed to European-style table manners. Deepa moaned in English to no one in particular, "They're disadvantaged girls, and you have to start at the beginning with them, because they don't know anything." The social worker, who stood near the door to the kitchen listening to the conversation, nodded her head in agreement. "Well, what can you do?" a third woman at the table opined as the plates were laid in front of them. I went back into the kitchen because I was afraid I would say something in admonition to the woman for their bad behavior, and yet as soon as I was alone, I realized that the two groups were so fundamentally disconnected from each other that there was perhaps no way for them to really communicate except through criticism and silence. Shehanaaz entered the kitchen soon after I came to this sad conclusion, her lips slightly curled at the corners in a sarcastic smile. "*Mujhse uphar hain kya, ve log* [Those people think they are better than me]?" she asked rhetorically as her eyes examined my face. Before I could respond, Shehanaaz picked up the plate of fruit the other girls had meticulously cut for dessert and slowly let her saliva drain all over it. She then carried the fruit out of the kitchen to serve to the women's group, turning once before opening the door to give me a huge smile.

Shehanaaz's clear use of one of Scott's (1985) "weapons of the weak" did nothing to change or improve her life situation, and yet it was the only way she could register silent dissent from a system that marked her as a person of little value. After the girls were sent into the kitchen by the social worker to wash the lunch dishes as part of their "training," Deepa and her women's group started a revealing conversation about their perceptions of the teenagers. "Just one of those girls is sharper [more conniving, in Indian English] than all of us put together," one woman said ambiguously, after which another woman more clearly asked, "Does everyone have all of their jewelry? You never know with these types from the street." Deepa sensed my intense discomfort and sought to draw me into the conversation. "Susan," she said so that everyone could hear, "these girls are fourteen and fifteen and they know more about sex than we do in our twenties and thirties." I nodded patiently. "I wouldn't let any of them around my sons," another woman began, before adding "or my husband." A much older woman then caused the entire group to break into explosive laughter when she responded to this by saying, "Who knows, maybe your husband would choose one of them instead of you."

The events of the afternoon served to underscore how normalized underage prostitution is for girls from poor communities, and many of the women's comments and reactions highlighted how such girls and adolescents are highly stigmatized for behaviors that they neither consented to nor wanted to engage in. I was sixteen years old the first time I lived in India, and I will always remember the day another girl who was a few grades behind me in school told me how her mother had slapped her tear-strained face after a visibly pregnant adolescent prostitute approached their car begging for food. "Don't cry," her mother told her, "because if you start crying in this country you'll never stop." It would be dangerous and wrong to suggest that India is home to a population any more callous than those who live in the Eastern European countries discussed in Chapters 3 and 4, because we see many of the same patterns and social invisibility at work in all three case studies. However, none of this mattered to me as I listened to Deepa and her self-satisfied friends discuss the socially productive work they had engaged in that afternoon or as I watched the girls assemble for their return to what was effectively the prison of Asha Sadan. This raises the fundamental question of how the girls could have been genuinely assisted rather than put on display for what was essentially the benefit of another group.

BANKING ON RESILIENCY: IOM INDIA AND THE ERTV SUCCESS STORY

One of the central problems with most of the counter-trafficking efforts discussed in Chapters 3 and 4 is that none offered victims of trafficking opportunities for sustainable and long-term economic support, and yet all of the women whose stories are presented in this book share several things in common: they are poor, they are desperate, and they do not have economic alternatives to prostitution. "Civil society," "capacity building," and the concept of "partners in development" were so commonly invoked by the international organizations, governments, and NGOs that I spoke to in Armenia and Bosnia that it was sometimes unclear what these words meant, especially when viewed in conjunction with the extreme differences in access to power and resources that characterized these groups and the populations they aimed to assist.

Analyses of "development" projects and initiatives throughout the world have clearly demonstrated the dangers in citing how a solution to a problem worked in one country as evidence of how well it could be implemented in another. However, the universality of the conditions that make it likely that women will be coerced into prostitution offers compelling evidence that it is not possible to address the traffic in women without simultaneously dealing with its root causes.

IOM India developed a unique program to address the need to provide economic alternatives to women in the form of its Economic Rehabilitation of Trafficked Victims (ERTV) program, which emerged as part of the solutions proposed for survivors of the 2001 Gujarat earthquake. This adaptation of a program designed for the general population affected by a natural disaster to a project targeted specifically at a population of sex workers raises a number of problematic issues related to the politics that determine what makes a social issue significant. Western European and North American donors and governments first began to address the traffic in women in Armenia following the collapse of the Soviet Union, when it was unclear what form the new government would take. These considerations also accompanied concerns about unwanted migration and the desire to control organized crime, as was the case in postwar Bosnia.

Trafficking received a significant amount of attention from donors and governments both during and after the war in Bosnia, and it continues to be considered a direct outcome of the violence that overwhelmed the Western Balkan region in the early to mid-1990s. Armenian and Bosnian women have been the targets of Western donor assistance in a way that simply has not occurred in India, which has not undergone the same kinds of crises many small Eastern European nations suffered in the 1990s. As was discussed in detail in Chapter 2, the realities of unwanted migration from neighboring countries clearly informs Western European policy on trafficking, and India's geographic distance from powerful donors in both Western Europe and the United States has not made its problems with the traffic in women a great priority to either.

This lack of international response, combined with the fact that most of the traffic in women in India is domestic, thus positions the problem as a national one. The result has been an interesting partnership that links government and civil society in a move to socially and professionally reintegrate women who have been forced into prostitution. One of the foremost principles of the ERTV program is that women who have been coerced into prostitution often, in order to survive, develop inner strength and resiliency that can be productively channeled into other, more self-empowering avenues that could provide a long-term, sustainable source of income. ERTV benefited over three hundred victims of trafficking in its first year of operation alone by taking an approach that combined the expertise and resources of NGOs, corporations, the government of India, and, of course, the women themselves.

Many aspects of the program reflect the conviction that cooperation at both the state and the local level is perhaps the only way to help women create a sustainable future for themselves, and its success in the absence of aid from any international donors demonstrates that effective measures to end the traffic in women clearly can be developed without the assistance of much more powerful countries. This kind of cooperation between government and civil society can occur only in countries that have a strong central government. Hence a program like ERTV could never be a success in Armenia or Bosnia because of their nascent governments and sense of civil society. Nonetheless, it is significant that such a partnership can be established and sustained to assist women who have been coerced into prostitution via a central coordinating institution such as IOM.

The three key aspects that staff members at IOM offices throughout the world see as essential to assisting women through their counter-trafficking programs consist of rescue, rehabilitation, and reintegration. In the Indian context, "rescue" usually consists of the removal of underage girls (such as Shehanaaz and Gulabi) and unwilling women from brothels during police raids. Female NGO workers often accompany the police during these raids to help instill a sense of trust and safety in women who are very likely to be suffering from post-traumatic stress disorder and other psychological conditions created by enforced isolation and violence. The standard procedure then moves to the "rehabilitation" stage, which takes place in a shelter for a period of time ranging from a few days to several months, when the girl or woman is provided with assistance in locating family members to live with. Most girls and women are returned to their families after two weeks in the shelter, in keeping with the South Asian cultural norm of extended-family living arrangements. However, this is often complicated by the fact that many girls and women have been coerced into prostitution by family members, which means that alternative living arrangements and financial support need to be determined for them. The ERTV program specifically targets such women in the belief that financial independence is absolutely necessary to ensure that women do not become victims of trafficking again once they have reached the "reintegration" stage that aims to provide them with a means of self-support.

IOM India describes the government of India as "the largest development agency in the country." This stands in sharp contrast to the situation in Eastern Europe, where governments are still struggling to establish their roles in and responsibilities for tackling social problems in conjunction with NGOs and the many international organizations and donor governments represented in the region. ERTV was founded on the premise of governmental responsibility. Its program is based on the assumption that because the police act on behalf of the government of India, the government has a social obligation to assist girls and women who are rescued from brothels by the police. Despite what many feminists criticize as the patronizing language of "rescue" and "rehabilitation" (because of the lack of agency that each term implies), ERTV celebrates the capacity of such women to succeed as entrepreneurs precisely because of the difficult life circumstances they have survived. The program is rather pioneering in its recognition that the coping mechanisms a girl or woman must develop to deal with trauma and abuse can be interpreted as admirable strengths.

The ERTV program positioned IOM India as a facilitator between multiple institutions and agencies with very different roles in government and civil society in order to ensure that victims of trafficking could develop economic alternatives to sex work. This was especially important in light of the reality that many women throughout the world who survive such a situation later find themselves without other means of economic support, which puts them in exactly the same position they were in before their coercion into prostitution. Many victims of trafficking who are rescued or able to leave are thus either re-trafficked or enter into voluntary prostitution as a consequence of the stigma and shame they feel, combined with the lowered inhibitions they have toward sex work. ERTV focused on creating a sustainable source of income for its participants that would significantly reduce the risk of either outcome happening to a woman again, but the program became a success only because it clearly defined the roles and responsibilities of its key partners: IOM India, selected NGOs, five major corporations, and the government of India.

ERTV owes a great deal to the fact that every corporation in India is responsible for maintaining a social responsibility policy that it is legally obligated to support. IOM sought out highly successful corporations managing businesses that do not require extensive skills training and have numerous franchises throughout India. These include two dairy product manufacturers, coffee shops, beauty salons, and garment manufacturers. The premise was that each corporation's social responsibility policy encouraged it to assist underprivileged groups, including victims of trafficking, and ERTV gave each an opportunity to do so by providing franchises, training, and support to the women. ERTV does not function as a charity, so these services are paid for with micro-credit loans provided to women by IOM and the government of India and managed by an NGO selected by IOM India. In addition to overseeing the disbursement and eventual repayment of these micro-credit loans, the NGOs are responsible for maintaining a special bank account to be used solely to assist additional women through ERTV once other loans have been repaid. NGOs are also responsible for providing support to the new entrepreneurs in the form of social and psychological counseling and help in finding possible locations for future businesses.

The government of India is obviously the most powerful partner in ERTV, and its financial and institutional support is critical to continued success. The government provides funding for micro-credit loans, assistance in locating real estate that can be provided free or at a subsidized rate to support an enterprise, and, most important, lends critical institutional support to an issue that has been highly stigmatized—a legitimizing effect that helps to mobilize community support for women. Government involvement in ERTV underscores just how important state commitment at all levels is to effective measures to support the reintegration of victims of trafficking into the community. ERTV supports this approach by acting as liaison between the main partners in the project, ensuring that the program is sustainable by monitoring the progress of each enterprise, and consulting women who have benefited from the program for advice on future initiatives. However, the most unique aspect of ERTV is the amount of responsibility given to the women it is designed to benefit: the women who choose to participate in the program are considered businesswomen who must repay their micro-credit loans and manage their businesses just as as they would if they had started the businesses independently.

IOM India recognized long before it designed ERTV that victims of trafficking do not share a monolithic set of circumstances that can be remedied with a single set of solutions. ERTV must carefully consider a number of factors in designing sustainable enterprises for women to manage, including the location of trusted NGOs and the resources each is able to devote to the project, the skill level of the individual women who will benefit from the project, the amount of support provided by the government of India, and the potential for success of a corporate franchise in a particular area. Several business models emerged as a result, all of which provide a monthly income that assures a woman financial independence and can be tailored to suit the unique circumstances of each individual woman's life. The most ambitious of these is the corporate franchise, which allows a group of women to manage a coffee house or ice cream parlor and to pay the corporation a set commission on the basis of their sales. This involves a great deal of work and initiative and is popular with women who do not want to return to their natal homes because of the abuse they suffered there. Women who are interested in learning a particular skill and who do not have the self-confidence or level of interest required for a franchise are given the option to work at production centers where they can learn to sew or bind books to sell in the market.

A third option for women who may already have some skills in a certain area is to develop a business plan of their own for a small-scale enterprise such as a beauty salon, taxi service, fast-food center, or mobile restaurant. The final ERTV option provided appeals primarily to women who are able to return safely to their families but still need to earn an income in order to support themselves and their loved ones. This usually involves region-specific activities such as dairy farms, beekeeping, and agriculture. All of the business models have strengths in their own right, but the success of ERTV as a program is due to its clear division of roles and responsibilities between its various partners in order to ensure that women from a highly stigmatized group can be effectively incorporated into the community without fear of the withdrawal of donor funds.

I visited a small Bombay café operated by Anu and Mallika, two former sex workers who had been identified as victims of trafficking by IOM and assisted with the ERTV program. I was initially concerned about the stigmatization of prostitutes and the possibility that reintegration projects would not be particularly effective in the face of community sanctions. Given Bombay's enormous size, this was not an issue for the two women I spoke to, although it might be an issue in smaller areas. Anu and Mallika were very busy when I introduced myself and my book project, but Anu was eager to talk about her experiences as what the ERTV program brands "a success story." Anu was adamant that she was a businesswoman, and she even used the English word *entrepreneur* in her Hindi language description of her work.

I was conscious that most of their customers do not know Anu and Mallika are former prostitutes, and of course I was careful not to broach the subject in public. I had initially worried that neither of them would want to speak to me, yet both of them repeatedly reassured me that if I came back after working hours, they would be very happy to talk to me. We spoke at length when I returned at the appointed time, and Anu emphasized how her independence from her family and the adverse life situations that had pushed her into an exploitive situation in a Bombay brothel were a direct result of her ability to earn her own income through the ERTV micro-credit program.

Mallika, however, was a bit less confident about the enterprise and mentioned that she sometimes worried that one of her former clients would recognize her and humiliate her at the café. Anu immediately interjected that she found this idea ridiculous and reminded Mallika that her former place of work was in a distant neighborhood. She presented the extremely pragmatic argument that because their customers at the café nearly always came with their families, it was highly unlikely that either of them would ever be embarrassed by a former client. Many urban Indians sanction the existence of prostitution as long as men visit them discreetly, and there is some degree of stigma associated with public knowledge that a man has slept with a prostitute. This conflicted view on the subject is by no means confined to India and, in fact, characterizes many societies that simultaneously ignore and revile the existence of prostitution.

Anu explained how she felt confident that she could direct the course of her own future now that she had her own income, and she added that she was teaching her daughter skills that could be used to manage the café when Anu eventually retired. "If I didn't have my own business," she explained in Hindi, "my daughter would end up in prostitution as well, and what kind of future is that?" Mallika nodded before adding that the only downside to working with the public in the same city they had both previously worked in as prostitutes was the danger of being blackmailed for unpaid sex from former clients. Anu had clearly heard this argument from Mallika multiple times and was accustomed to assuaging her fears; in this case she responded in emphatic Hindi, "Mallika, *in logo ko tere shukel ka yaad nahi aate hain* (those people don't remember your face)."

Anu's sense of pride in her work and self-confidence about her and her daughter's future was matched in equal measure by Mallika's worries about the possibility that the past would catch up with her. These very different reactions to the same micro-enterprise project demonstrate that women respond to these programs as individuals. Some wholeheartedly embrace them, while others are not quite certain that the ERTV program promises a chance at a new life for those who want it. Such varying responses underscore how there are clearly no easy solutions or templates that can be effectively imposed to assist women who have been coerced into prostitution.

Nearly all of the cases presented in this book illustrate how women frame their life experiences in a number of ways. Some genuinely feel that they have been victimized and have little hope for the future as a result, whereas others see themselves as independent agents acting to improve their lives to the best of their abilities. What remains to be seen, of course, is whether the various actors and institutions involved in counter-trafficking activities can respond adequately to the manifold factors that inform women's perceptions of their individual situations.

6

Feminist Ethnographic Research in Times of Crisis

The real danger of indifference is not that it grows out of the barrel of a gun, but that it too easily becomes habitual. (Herzfeld 1993, 184)

The critical analysis this book presents of institutional responses to the traffic in women leaves a key question unanswered: How do we tackle a social phenomenon of unknown scale and proportions that directly capitalizes on the failure of societies everywhere to recognize poverty, sexism, endemic power inequalities, corruption, and, above all, the basic human need to live with dignity? Chapters 3, 4, and 5 all present ethnographic examples of the perplexing cross-cultural phenomenon in which institutional power takes on its own momentum in a manner that has the potential to grossly marginalize individuals. Even more striking is the frequency with which economic struc-tures and policy decisions are determined by political institutions and processes designed by those who are far removed from the individuals ostensibly to be helped by such measures.

INVISIBLE AGENTS, HOLLOW BODIES: WHEN INJUSTICE BECOMES BUSINESS AS USUAL

Invisibility was a constant theme in all three countries in which I conducted research throughout the four years it took to complete this project. I had initially believed that the cliché of the "faceless bureaucracy" unfairly absolved individuals of any wrongdoing in their capacity as bureaucrats, yet the longer I spent in the field, the more I realized how limited even the most senior figures are by their inability to institute changes in systems infinitely larger than themselves. I soon recognized that individuals who form the basis of institutions are rarely able to exercise the degree of agency that would render them accountable for the results of policies they create and implement, and thus I began to understand that there is indeed some truth to the idea of institutional anonymity and "facelessness."

Bureaucracy evinces a kind of invisible agency in which a culture with its own rules and codes of behavior emerges in tandem with the needs and responsibilities of the organization itself, and this culture informs the decisions made by those who are tasked with carrying out its daily operations. This invisible agency explains why so many individuals I met in the course of my research simultaneously lamented the inefficacy of efforts to assist victims of trafficking and yet continued to pursue strategies that were clearly ineffective. Part of the reason why such assistance measures often had unintended negative consequences, as outlined in Chapters 3, 4, and 5 is that victims of trafficking themselves constitute a population invisible to most policymakers, who thus fail to see the agency such women demonstrate as part of broader strategies to improve their lives.

The trafficked woman is thus constructed as a sort of hollow body, an empty figure to be filled up with the assumptions of the relatively privileged staff members at most international organizations, governments, and nongovernmental organizations. Simultaneously, victims of trafficking who approach such institutions for assistance find that NGOs can sometimes be little more than hollow fronts for donor funding, that certain governments are more concerned with policing borders than alleviating the economic conditions that necessitate labor migration, and that branches of international organizations can occasionally find themselves ill-equipped to deal with the problem.

The nature of any bureaucracy is informed by the cultural context in which it operates, and international organizations that deal with the traffic in women are no exception. It is impossible, for example, to separate the traffic in women in Armenia from the post-Soviet realities of economic collapse and massive emigration that continue to frame everyday life for most Armenians. I climbed the five hundred steps of the Soviet World War I memorial known as The Cascades every evening after I finished work in Yerevan, only occasionally remembering that it had been named for the enormous artificial waterfall Soviet authorities had never installed. The magnificent panoramic view from the top of The Cascades overlooked the snow-capped peak of Mount Ararat, the Armenian national symbol that, by one of the many cruel ironies of history, remains on the Turkish side of the border.

Armenia has no diplomatic ties with Turkey because of the latter's refusal to acknowledge the genocide in which an estimated 1.5 million Armenians were murdered by Ottoman Turks, and yet the fact remains that Turkey is the country to which most Armenian victims of trafficking migrate in search of work. Some Armenians use the word *Turk* as a kind of expletive that is often employed as a rebuke to someone who is behaving in an undesirable way; to "act like a Turk" means to disrespect or insult in a profound way. Breathless and exhausted from the long climb to the top of The Cascades, I would gaze across the border and think about the cultural and historical weight those women carried with them from unemployment in Armenia to brothels in Turkey.

The view from the back of The Cascades is much less spectacular and reveals an almost stereotypically post-Soviet wasteland in the shadow of such an enormous monument. I remember watching feral dogs wander around an inexplicably placed bathtub filled with a bright orange-red liquid of indiscernible origin, Soviet-built cars on cement blocks huddled nearby, enveloped in rust that made them look as if they might collapse into powder with a single touch. Yet above all of this rose the highest monument of all, a giant statue of Mother Armenia that had been erected in place of the statue of Joseph Stalin that had stood on the same pedestal prior to independence. Many people I met in Yerevan insisted that if I sneaked into the garden behind the National Gallery, I might catch a glimpse of Stalin's enormous concrete head lying in a far corner.

The implications of the post-independence switch from brutal dictator to ancient nationalist symbol on the same pedestal are not difficult to grasp and, in fact, spoke to numerous instances of *plus ça change* in Armenia. The Soviet buildings in Yerevan that had initially struck me as an inspiring and powerful architecture of the people began to look increasingly menacing as I gradually became aware that the same white car always parked outside my apartment building and left when I did, or that my phone line hissed and crackled as a less-than-obvious sign that someone was listening. In retrospect I know that I was very naïve to cry at the beauty of the Soviet propaganda posters that celebrated manual laborers and other varieties of working-class people I had grown up with, and yet the more I listened to Armenians nostalgic for communism's potential for creating class equality, the prouder I became that my class background had sensitized me in ways that made it easier to empathize with the women I met every day as part of my research.

This double narrative of professional curiosity and personal enlightenment was brought to a slow and terrifying halt as I became more involved in efforts to assist Armenian Liana after her ordeal of forced prostitution in the Middle East. The strange phone calls I had started to receive in the middle of the night quickly escalated into direct threats, and when I finally left Armenia with less than forty-eight hours' notice following Liana's false imprisonment, I fully understood why Armenians who lived through Soviet times do not find the same kind of beauty that I did in such architecture. I also began to understand that those enormous buildings were not really about a celebration of the people but, rather, a kind of imposing surveillance that reminded everyone of the power of a centralized authority so massive and far-reaching that it attempted to create a new kind of human being.

Armenians were quick to draw parallels between Soviet-centralized administration and the culture created by reliance on US donor aid, despite the obvious differences between the two economic and social systems. The Armenian representative to the Council of Europe was deeply involved in countertrafficking efforts and spent an evening with me voicing her frustrations about the refusal of the United States and the European Union to assist victims of trafficking in ways that she felt would genuinely help, such as granting visas and funding programs to assist prostitutes. "These people remind me of the Politburo," she said, emphatically using the word for Soviet centralized administration. "They sit quietly and listen, they remember who you are, and if they don't like you, they crush you. They tell you they are listening, that they will form a committee to discuss it. Let me tell you, it's just like in Soviet times— that committee will establish a committee to evaluate its progress and it will report directly to itself."

Armenia's Soviet legacy understandably framed most of the discussions about donor funding and responses to the traffic in women, just as conditions in Bosnia were framed by the devastating war that also resulted in its creation as an independent state. My journey to Bosnia provoked a number of completely unanticipated responses from strangers and loved ones alike, even though over a decade had elapsed since the war and large numbers of Western European tourists were beginning to holiday in Croatia, Bosnia's Western neighbor. "You want to go to Sarajevo?" the airline agent on the other end of the telephone said when I called to book my ticket, "Is that safe?" I initially attributed her question to a lack of current events knowledge but quickly changed my mind when I was asked multiple variations of it as I made my way eastward via Montreal, Paris, and Milan.

I slowly started to understand that these questions about safety and my motivations for traveling to Sarajevo were part of the Western European and North American view of Bosnia as little more than the home of a brutal war in a small, out-of-the way place. Ironically enough, this understanding also informed Western policymaking and the distribution of donor funds in Bosnia, because much of both remains oriented around the principle of basic infrastructure provision. The director of a shelter for victims of trafficking in a mid-size Bosnian town explained her confusion regarding the Spanish government's willingness to pay for the construction of a new shelter and its refusal to contribute funds to manage it. The result, she explained, was that the shelter had no furniture and the women in it were fed with leftovers from volunteers' homes.

It is true that many years have elapsed since the war, yet almost everyone I met who had lived through it was still dealing with the psychological effects of what they had witnessed or experienced firsthand. Jasminka was sent from IOM to pick me up from the airport and help me get settled in my house in Sarajevo, and we instantly became friends and spent nearly eight hours walking around the streets as she provided an ongoing narrative of the city's history. "We say Europe begins and ends in Sarajevo," she said on the street where the Serb nationalist Gavrilo Princip assassinated Archduke Franz Ferdinand in a move widely cited as the spark that ignited World War I and thus shaped the future of contemporary Europe. The "end of Europe," we both understood without her having to explain it, was the failure of Western Europe to live up to its humanitarian ideals by largely ignoring Sarajevo during the years of its siege by Serb nationalist troops.

Jasminka held my arm in hers as we walked throughout the city, explaining the significance of certain buildings that still lay in collapsed heaps as a result of Serb mortar attacks. We went back to my apartment, where we sat smoking Drina cigarettes as I listened to her much more personal geography of the war. Her husband was traveling when the siege of Sarajevo began and was unable to reenter the city, leaving Jasminka to spend the war years alone with her infant son and three-year-old daughter. She described the difficulties of washing and drying diapers in the winter with the windows covered to avoid giving snipers an easy target, and the constant worry about the long-term repercussions of inadequate nutrition for such small children. Tears streamed down my face as she told me how once a week she had to run down the street under Serb sniper fire to buy formula for the baby from the local black-market merchant who smuggled goods into the city through a tunnel near the airport beyond the front lines and sold them at exorbitant prices.

Serb nationalist soldiers surrounded the city during the siege and officially forbade any food or other necessary commodities from entering Sarajevo, as part of an effort to destroy its predominantly Muslim inhabitants. The blockade created an economy in which the black market was the only source of basic provisions, some of which sold for over a hundred times their peacetime prices, and left ordinary people to search their apartments and homes for goods that could be traded to avoid starvation. "Before the war," Jasminka explained in reference to her own experiences surviving the siege, "I bought an Italian furniture set that was much too expensive; we really couldn't afford it, but I couldn't resist. My husband didn't talk to me for three days after I spent so much money. Little did he know that this would eventually save my children and me in the war. Some of it we burned for fuel, and some of it I sold for bread. I don't know what we would have done otherwise."

Bosnians often insist that they no longer see the roofless buildings and hollowed out houses that still dot cities and countryside alike, but nearly everyone

I spent more than two hours with shared with me a deeply personal war story that made this difficult to believe. In many ways, it was as if the siege mentality of the war had taken over and imposed the idea that Western forces were the only hope of assistance, because the Bosnian state remained unable to rid itself of the corruption and ethnic politics that had sustained the war. "The main problem," an official at the Swedish International Development Agency succinctly explained in what is perhaps the saddest synopsis of a national crisis I have heard, "is that we cannot do anything in the absence of a functioning state."

It was impossible to be in Bosnia and not be affected by the depth of postwar problems and ethnic divisions. These were reinforced by the ethnicity-based territories created by the Dayton Agreement as part of a strange Western philosophy in which separation equates peace. When my Bosnian mobile phone stopped working as soon as I crossed into the ethnic-Serb-dominated territory of Republika Srpska, the problem was not reception or services but the refusal of Bosnian and Serb branches of the same mobile phone company to cooperate. I was certainly not alone in my frustrations and heard dozens of stories to this effect, such as one from a Bosnian friend who insured her car at the Banja Luka branch in Republika Srpska and was told at the Sarajevo branch of the same company that she could not pay her bill and would have to travel six hours to Banja Luka for any future transactions.

This deliberate lack of coordination between ethnically divided units created by the Dayton Agreement means that Western European organizations remain the central means of dealing with Bosnian social problems. "Why should we fund your shelter?" Bosnian government officials pointedly ask shelter directors who approach them for assistance and explain that it is the responsibility of a humane government to support all of its citizens. In a striking response relayed to me by one such shelter director, the government official curtly replied, "Then get the EU to do it." In the hollowness of a postwar place where unemployed metalworkers carve intricate designs on expended shell cartridges in hopes of selling them to Western visitors, it was never entirely clear to me how some individuals mark the lines where responsibility stops and oppression begins.

These lines were similarly blurred during a visit to a friend in Bombay who is not an activist and has no inclination toward changing the world. She looked out of her living room window after we finished having lunch and happened to see a small child foraging for food in the garbage that had been left to rot on the street for days during a strike by municipal workers. "At some point," she sighed, "we as the individuals who make up our society have to say to ourselves, 'This is an acceptable way for that child to live.'" In reality, of course, societies never directly ask such weighty questions of individuals, but my friend raised an important point about the mundane choices we make every day that tacitly endorse the continued existence of injustice.

Class inequality frames life in India in an inescapable manner that results from a population of one billion people living side by side in an extreme example of unequal wealth distribution. Shantytowns spanning several square miles surround several major cities, and nearly all apartment complexes have at least a small squatter settlement nearby that houses the domestic workers whom apartment residents need during the day to cook, clean, and care for children. These settlements exist in violation of urban zoning laws and are periodically demolished by bulldozers under government orders, as part of urban beautification campaigns that often coincide with the visit of an important official to the city. Indian journalists and ordinary urban residents alike use the phrase *slum clearance* to describe the deliberate destruction of the huts made from found materials that house poor migrants.

Government orders for slum clearance are kept secret to reduce the risk of violence from angry residents whose families will be rendered homeless by the razing of their squatter settlement. Slum clearance is usually conducted on weekend nights when traffic is lighter and with a significant armed police presence to ensure that residents comply with the order to leave. I was in the passenger seat of a friend's car in Bombay late one Saturday night when a police officer standing in the middle of the otherwise empty street waved us to a stop and explained in rapid-fire Hindi that we should turn around immediately. "Slum clearance *chal raha hain* (is now being carried out)," he said, pointing to a crowd of impoverished families weeping as their homes were crushed into a pile of rubble by a government-owned bulldozer.

We explained that no other road led to my friend's apartment building, and the officer reluctantly let us keep driving past the homeless group, some of whom were wailing audibly. People were darting back and forth across the road in attempts to salvage whatever possessions they could from their destroyed homes, and my friend drove very slowly to avoid colliding with people who could barely be seen in the absence of streetlights. Suddenly the passenger window was hit with a force that partially cracked the glass, and in the dim glow produced by the headlights I saw that it was a sobbing woman cradling an emaciated infant of indiscernible age in her arms. I screamed and my friend suddenly hit the brake, jolting us backward in our seats. The woman outside the window pressed her unresponsive baby against the glass and begged me to take him from her. "Do something; do something!" I started to shout, unsure of whether I was talking to my friend or to myself. "Susan," he replied in a careful monotone voice, "You can't help everyone. When you live with poverty and suffering every day, you have to learn to stop seeing things, or you won't be able to function."

His rationale is both incredibly callous and completely understandable when viewed in the context of the endemic poverty and inequality that frames life in India. This incident took place nearly a decade ago, and yet it could just as easily have taken place today, despite the fact that India has changed enormously since my first visit as an idealistic teenager in the mid-1990s. The International Monetary Fund's structural adjustment policies and the associated austerity measures and removal of import and export controls were implemented in the early 1990s, and within just a few years a stunning number of American and Western European products and commodities were for sale in major Indian cities. The most salient development in this regard was the advent of the "superstore," a sort of miniature mall in which many types of commodities were for sale. Many Indians used the "superstore" as a metaphor for the future of their country, and some even proudly use the term *India Incorporated* to describe privatization initiatives that followed free-market logic by selling formerly government-controlled companies into the hands of individual investors.

For all the excitement surrounding "India Incorporated," it remained impossible to ignore the cruel realities of poverty, as even the most beautifully decorated and expensive boutique in Bombay or Delhi still had a wizened woman who looked much older than her chronological age squatting in a tattered sari as she swabbed the floor with a wet rag. Urban poverty still had its own culture and rules that remained relatively unchanged by the introduction of free-market capitalism; the homeless still paid low-level hustlers a nightly fee to sleep on city streets or railway station platforms; and slumlords still charged poor migrants exorbitant rents for decrepit shacks that might be demolished at any time by the authorities. All of this works in tandem with what is known in India as the black economy, which launders the illicit income of the rich through the Hindi film industry and controls squatter settlements with equal proficiency.

This normalization of poverty is also evident in the evocative names chosen by Indian NGOs that deal with populations ranging from orphans to abused women. A woman who worked for a branch of the United Nations in Delhi once complained to me that this was symptomatic of a mentality that allowed little possibility for genuine empowerment. She described feeling extremely disheartened as she reviewed proposals from hundreds of NGOs that were competing for a special grant made available by her agency. "The names of these organizations are always something like The Home for the Downtrodden and Oppressed," she complained, "But how can people ever stand on their own two feet if the organization trying to help them is calling them 'downtrodden and oppressed,' as if they are weak and helpless?"

This institutional branding of populations as what the UN employee in Delhi described as "weak and helpless" is hardly confined to small Indian NGOs, and all three of the ethnographic chapters presented in this book detail how such characterization works in reference to the traffic in women. If the examples above reveal how societies are shaped by their economic and political crises, numerous cases discussed in Chapters 3, 4, and 5 underscore the frequency with which the intersection of politics and economics has powerful (though sometimes unintended) consequences that alter the course of individual lives. The question remains whether this will continue to be a permanent feature of life in Armenia, Bosnia, India, and any number of other countries around the world.

INSTITUTIONAL POWER, INDIVIDUAL LIVES, AND THE POLITICS OF FEMINIST RESEARCH

Institutional power has clearly taken on its own momentum in the form of US donor aid to Armenia, which has created a system of Armenian NGO dependence on donor support as a consequence of a lack of government funds, a situation that results in what an officer of the Bureau of International Narcotics and Law Enforcement (INL) termed "a real mess." The situation is further complicated by the centralization of power at international organizations and donor agencies in the hands of Western Europeans and North Americans who, despite their long-term postings, do not speak the local language and yet, paradoxically, have the authority to determine local priorities. As the director of an Armenian NGO wryly noted, "Look, if USAID or some other powerful donor says that turtle preservation should be Armenia's number-one priority, we'll all write about our passionate desire to save the Armenian turtles in our proposals for project funding. How else are we going to support ourselves?"

This response is quite rational given the lack of respect many local NGOs feel their priorities are accorded by the agencies that support their activities; if the donors don't care, this line of reasoning goes, why should we? IOM Armenia employee Armine complained to me at length about this kind of attitude on the part of both donors and recipients, following her return from a year of studying International Law in the United States. She noted that this kind of apathy and insensitivity toward trafficked women was appalling to her upon her return to Armenia. But she also mentioned that she would soon be like some of her colleagues, who included "trafficking" in their NGO portfolio of activities in order to increase the chance of receiving donor funding and yet simultaneously considered victims of trafficking "a bunch of useless prostitutes."

Armine's story underscores how idealism can be trampled by bureaucratic systems, yet the almost complete miscarriage of justice that surrounded the case of one victim of trafficking, Liana, highlights how individual actors within large systems also make choices that directly impact others. Liana's seven-year prison sentence as the leader of a trafficking ring after she had approached IOM for assistance following her harrowing ordeal in forced prostitution in Dubai is by far the clearest example of how institutional power can take on its own momentum in a way that renders individual goodwill and dedication almost irrelevant. Liana found herself at the center of a number of institutional forces when she approached IOM, including an Armenian prosecutor's office eager to prosecute a trafficking case. That office found itself subject to considerable pressure from the government and civil society, both of which benefit from significant amounts of US donor aid that can be revoked in the absence of what the US government determines are "reasonable steps" to fight trafficking. Liana and her social invisibility as a prostitute made her an easy target for the elaborate machinations that ensure the uninterrupted flow of donor aid, as well as for individuals in the prosecutor's office who were willing to accept bribes from her trafficker and frame her for the very crime she was victimized by.

The United Nations International Criminal Tribunal for the Former Yugoslavia faced a comparable crisis when it sought to relocate some of its cases to the Sarajevo War Crimes Chamber in order to lighten its own caseload and create a sense that Bosnia had stabilized enough to handle the prosecutions of soldiers who had committed war crimes. The War Crimes Chamber sought to uphold "international human rights standards" to such a degree that it imprisoned Radovan Stanković, a Serb nationalist soldier who had raped and forcibly imprisoned Bosnian Muslim women and girls as young as twelve in Foča, a town near Sarajevo. Imprisoned in Foča because he would face "undue discrimination" if held in a non-Serb-dominated prison, Stanković escaped in May 2007 after serving just six months of his sentence and was presumably transported to safety in sympathetic Serbia. Most Bosnians and Westerners were adamant that he had bribed the Serb guards to allow him to escape, and both groups also agreed that human rights concerns had paradoxically operated in this case to free a war criminal.

Bosnian NGO culture is reminiscent of Armenia with its competition for donor funding that creates a fractious environment in which shelter directors see themselves as rivals rather than peers. "She is a very bad woman. Do not put her in your book," at least two shelter directors said about women who held a similar position at other shelters. "What if people send her money instead of us because they read her name in your book?" The constant and unrelenting stress of managing a shelter or an NGO on donor funds is compounded by an almost complete lack of government support and thus creates a seemingly irresolvable situation in which Bosnia remains dependent on outside support over a decade after the war. Shelter director Fadila Hadzić concisely explained the terrible contradictions faced by international organizations and NGOs alike in the absence of government support, noting that "international organizations think trafficking is now the responsibility of the state, but we have no state."

The Bosnian example demonstrates how even international organizations such as IOM can be destabilized by the termination of funds on short notice by powerful donors from wealthy countries. The United States Agency for International Development gave just a few months' notice that budgetary cutbacks in light of the costly war in Iraq meant that USAID would no longer be able to support the counter-trafficking program at IOM Sarajevo. This extremely short notice meant that no other donors could be located to fund the program and thus resulted in the discontinuation of the only division of an international organization devoted exclusively to the traffic in women in Bosnia. In this case, policy decisions made in Washington, D.C., to prioritize Iraq over foreign aid had a devastating impact on women in faraway Bosnia.

That institutional power can take on its own frightening momentum is much less obvious in India, because the world's largest democracy does not face the deep infrastructural crises evident in Armenia and Bosnia. Yet endemic poverty and class inequality function as institutions in their own right through the elaborate social systems that have developed around both. Chapter 5 detailed how the weekly payments made by the madams of brothels to the Bombay police ensure that their businesses are allowed to remain open, with the simultaneous understanding that although these bribes protect them from being closed, the police must still conduct occasional raids and take underage girls into protective custody. Police officers who take such bribes are encouraged to do so by extremely low salaries that would otherwise be insufficient to support their families. Thus the arrangement benefits both police and madams, despite the fact that prostitution is explicitly prohibited by law in India.

This understanding and collusion between law enforcement and groups who are breaking the law reveals how individuals can subvert the broader structure of government by creating their own system that works in their favor. Such systems are institutionalized to a degree that affects everyday behavior and informs decision making for individuals from a wide variety of social backgrounds in India. I was once stopped for speeding in Delhi, and the friend I was with immediately pulled out a fifty-rupee note (worth a little over one US dollar) for me to hand to the officer in lieu of having to pay a much larger traffic fine. I was initially reluctant to endorse the culture of bribery that sustains so many problematic relationships among citizens, the police, and government, and yet found myself giving the fifty-rupee note to the officer, who then waved me back into traffic without saying anything.

This silent exchange troubled me, even though I knew it was extremely minor in the broader framework of life in India. "I wonder what would happen if we all refused to give bribes to the police," I said to my friend, who scoffed in response that "their children wouldn't be able to eat and we wouldn't be able to get away with driving too fast." His response spoke deeply to the entrenched system that both enforces poverty and endorses class inequality, and as we drove home that night I had the distinct feeling we were all inextricably caught up in a system that only superficially worked in everyone's favor and actually hurt us all.

Structural adjustment programs are perhaps the most tragic global example of the power that large institutions have to shape individual lives with their cutbacks to social spending and their prioritization of foreign investment and open markets at any cost to ensure the repayment of loans to the International Monetary Fund and World Bank. These newly open markets in India introduced satellite television and beauty culture from North America and Western Europe and simultaneously widened the scope of the entertainment industry. Marketing executives sensed an opportunity for greater profits, and cosmetics companies that sponsor extremely popular beauty pageants and films began to emphasize, in their advertisements and related events, how almost anyone could become a star.

Bobby, a dancer at the Bombay bar Heera, was by no means naïve, and yet she genuinely believed that a successful career in Hindi films awaited her if she could just make the right contacts. The seemingly disparate examples of free markets and aspirations to stardom evinced by performers in Bombay dancing girls' bars are eloquent testimony to the powerful rhetoric employed by neoliberalism, with its claims to universality and competition among equals that are carefully concealed beneath the glossy exterior of free-market capitalism and commodity culture. Yet it is equally important to note that although Bobby was able to sustain dreams of media success, there are far more girls and women who have not benefited at all from the rhetoric of competition among equals. Conversely, they have become even more dependent on independent organizations such as Deepa's women's group (described in Chapter 5) as cutbacks in government social spending render many social welfare programs incapable of offering assistance.

One of the most fascinating and troubling realities of the traffic in women is that it is both a universal phenomenon and highly localized in nature. It would be illogical to suggest that trafficking is a new phenomenon, and the discussion in Chapter 2 on the American and European "white slavery" panics of the late nineteenth and early twentieth centuries underscore how much of the contemporary counter-trafficking discourse has been employed before. Yet labor migration has reached a historically unprecedented level within the past century such that accepting an offer to work abroad not only has been normalized in many countries of the world but also has become an absolute survival strategy employed by many families.

Globalization has opened up new avenues of both legitimate and illegitimate trades, which overlap much more than is immediately apparent, and the enormous contemporary scale of the traffic in migrant labor, organs, and women is inseparable from the economic and political processes that create large populations of poor people who have limited options for income generation. The advent of neoliberal economic systems in many countries in recent decades has encouraged the development of commodity culture. And it has also exacerbated socioeconomic inequalities in a way that has increased the frequency with which individuals themselves become commodities available for sale.

I have been consistently struck by how often countries that have relatively newly adopted free-market economies also feature highly sexualized advertising, whether in India following structural adjustment or in many former Soviet republics following the collapse of communism. One day an Armenian friend and I were in my Yerevan apartment watching a popular Russian music television channel on which a woman wearing a bikini made of diamonds that barely covered her very large breast implants was undulating provocatively on the hood of a shiny black Mercedes as she lip-synched to a popular song with a chorus that translated as the rather unsubtle "I love money." My friend was in her early thirties and regarded her adolescence in Soviet Armenia as worlds away from the country in which her daughter was growing up. "Sometimes I think that we're making up for all those years under communism when we couldn't really buy anything," she said, as she shook her head at the semi-nude woman undulating on the screen. "But not in [a] good way."

There are clearly audiences eager for this kind of entertainment and many women and men who enthusiastically embrace the images it presents of gender and class as an empowering message about opportunities presented by capitalism. Yet the fact remains that the increased mobility of global capital and decreased restrictions on labor regulations have also opened up other routes of "opportunity" that previously did not exist. It is nearly impossible to ignore the bitter irony that the young women who dance for men's money in Bombay bars often explain their nightly working hours to their curious neighbors by pretending that they work in a call center, one of the hundreds of outsourced customer service divisions of North American businesses that have sought cheaper labor in English-speaking India. Both forms of work are almost exclusively performed by women, neither is seen as a long-term or sustainable job by the women who engage in it, and both are poorly paid relative to the amount of work performed (and, in the case of dancing bars, relative to the risk incurred).

One of the countless paradoxes of globalization is that many women workers at call centers and bars feel that they are improving their lives by earning an income, even if they know that they are forced to work in an unfair system on someone else's terms. This hope for a better future is part of the reason why women agree to terms of work that are recognized as illogical by more privileged individuals, such as not knowing the nature of the work they will perform in another country, incurring large debts to travel abroad for a low-paid job, or thinking of sex work as a temporary strategy to earn an income before moving on to other things with acquired savings. Women exercise agency even in opting to migrate on someone else's terms in hopes of improving their own lives, because they are in situations that offer them few, if any, other options, given their lack of education, their debt, and/or their inability to support their children.

Yet these women are also following the logic of a free market in choosing migration as a survival strategy, especially in accepting the principle that some degree of risk is necessary in order to generate a profit. Participation in a free-market economy at any level necessitates that such individuals change their way of thinking about the self in relation to the rest of the world and accept the foundational capitalist principle that individuals are assigned value and worth on the basis of their access to resources. The normalization of labor migration, especially when it occurs under terms unclear to the migrant herself, is a direct result of a globalized world in which borders have become both more flexible and more restricted.

It is clear that wealthier nations simultaneously need labor migrants and seek to control the conditions under which they are admitted to their countries of destination. This is hardly a new phenomenon, and the review of literature in Chapter 2 demonstrated how nineteenth-century discussions of "white slavery" occurred in a time of unprecedented female labor migration and thus sought to restrict the movement of poor and working-class white women by creating moral panics that often drew on racist stereotypes about "others" who were eagerly waiting to push innocent women into sexual exploitation. Although the term has changed to the more racially inclusive *sex trafficking*, the language of slavery remains the central trope in discussions of efforts to end the problem by members of Congress, international organizations, human rights activists, and policymakers alike.

The key differences among these diverse parties lie in how trafficking is distinguished from prostitution, although it was never fully clear to me how the two differ, given the focus on "force, fraud, and coercion" that frames most definitions. After all, if poverty and lack of education are considered coercive agents in women's decisions to engage in prostitution, then nearly all prostitutes can be defined as victims of trafficking. Definitional differences end when it comes to descriptions of the migratory aspect of trafficking; almost everyone agrees that the traffic in women involves an element of movement that generally takes place across an international border.

Borders thus remain one of the central themes of discussions about trafficking at the international and policy level in all countries, but concerns about policing national perimeters were particularly salient in Bosnia because of the ongoing debates about European Union accession. Chapter 4 underscored how disconnects arise between countries that import and those that export labor. We saw how, in the European Forum for Democracy and Solidarity conference, Western European diplomats consistently emphasized the need to increase border control and efforts to discourage organized crime in order to reduce the traffic in women, whereas Bosnians in attendance emphasized the need for economic improvement in order to limit the push factors of poverty and unemployment that encourage migration in the first place. This is precisely why Bosnian activist Hadžihalilović distinguished between "the European way" and "the EU way," the latter of which she characterized as "Fortress Europe."

Western European donor aid designated for the improvement of Bosnian border control is often couched in the language of improving postwar stability, yet most Bosnians are aware that at least part of the underlying motivation is to limit westward migratory flows from their country. This is but one example of how donor aid functions as a means to exert influence on national governments, sometimes in less-than-obvious ways. The power of the US Trafficking in Persons Report similarly works to undermine national autonomy in Armenia and elsewhere on US terms. Countries that do not meet US minimum standards not only risk losing US donor funds but may also face opposition to some assistance from international financial institutions such as the International Monetary Fund and World Bank (US Dept. of State 2004, 28).

The result of the cultural construction and definition of sex trafficking on largely Western European and North American terms is that the idea of "victimization" has become institutionalized despite the agency demonstrated by women identified as victims of trafficking. Many women I spoke to who met most of the various definitions of *victim of trafficking* did not see themselves as helpless and robbed of their humanity, and yet this is the kind of language used to describe them in policy documents prepared by governments, international organizations, and NGOs. Instead, most of the women saw themselves as actors and agents who sought to improve their lives by making a choice to migrate, even if their only option was to do so on someone else's terms.

I sought to position myself at the center of these sometimes confusing and contradictory definitions and practices related to policy via my research methodology as a consultant and ethnographer, which itself raises a number of issues about the politics of ethnography. I was accorded more respect, attention, and assistance as part of an institution than I would have received as an outsider, which doubtless influenced the amount of data I was able to obtain. Institutions are societies in their own right, and my fieldwork as an IOM consultant helped to reveal some of the internal contradictions between policy and practice that would otherwise have been obscured. It is clear that my gender, age, and size affected how people treated me; I often felt adopted by older women who sought to mentor me and a bit intimidated by much older men in positions of power, who sometimes made inappropriate overtures. Yet what worked to create the perception that I was an innocuous character was often immediately deflated when I used the word "feminist."

US Embassy Chargé d'Affaires Anthony Godfrey met with me to discuss the traffic in women shortly after he assumed his position in Armenia. We spoke for about ten minutes before he asked me why I was interested in the issue, and I responded with what I thought was a heartfelt statement in which I explained that the traffic in women was something very important to me as a feminist and a human being. Godfrey immediately stood up to indicate that the meeting was over and curtly said, "Be assured that we will resolve the traffic in women with Armenian sensitivities in mind, not American feminism." I walked home from our meeting certain that I had offended him but without really understanding how.

Two days later, IOM chief of mission Hans Muller smiled wryly at me and asked what I had said to Godfrey. "Why?" I asked, worried that I would provoke the same response in Muller. "He complained to me that you lectured him." I was genuinely perplexed by Godfrey's complaint, and I wondered whether he felt that, because I was only a volunteer consultant, I had somehow overstepped my boundaries in describing my political views to someone in his position. I also had the unsettling suspicion that the word *feminism*, when used by a young woman, had indicated something dangerous to him. I fully understood that the word has different meanings to many individuals, and perhaps I was naïve to believe that Godfrey understood that feminist principles and the inequalities they expose are essential to ways of thinking about the traffic in women. Most of all, however, I remain confused about what he meant when he mentioned "Armenian sensitivities," because the examples of US policy interaction with Armenian women presented in Chapter 3 hardly demonstrate any concern for their welfare as human beings.

Such miscommunication raised profound questions for me about inequalities inherent in the research process, because the salient fact remains that someone like Godfrey was willing to meet with me, even if only briefly, to discuss the issue, whereas an experienced Armenian activist might not have received an appointment. My citizenship, PhD, skin color, and ability to obtain grant funding to conduct research as an unpaid consultant all definitely affected how people treated me, with varying degrees of privilege accorded to me in all three of my field sites. IOM Armenia allowed me to become a full-fledged employee with serious responsibilities during my time in the country, and I sometimes felt a subtle resentment from more senior colleagues who had worked their entire lives to be able to attend the meetings with senior diplomats that I was expected to attend as part of my work.

It is extremely problematic that a woman in her mid-twenties who had just finished a PhD should be able to arrive in Armenia or Bosnia and be positioned as an expert on gender issues, yet it is even more troubling that lack of funds and qualified staff made this a necessity. As a consequence of my years of research experience with the country, my situation in India exposed even more issues related to privilege. And although my own sudden poverty in Bombay, following the temporary suspension of grant funding, made me deeply empathize with performers and even think about becoming one of them in order to pay my rent, I also had more education than they did and knew that the situation would be temporary (of course, so do most other women who perform in such establishments). It is self-evident that one's position as a researcher directly determines the kind of data one is able to obtain, and yet how is one to reconcile the need to conduct ethical research that is also activist in nature, especially when the results are potentially condemnatory?

Anthropology is both the most human discipline and the academic subject that bears the closest relationship to the work of spies. Although informed consent and clarity about one's intentions in speaking to consultants both reduce the risk of misrepresentation and miscommunication, the fact remains that the final power to represent lies with the anthropologist. The ethics of the ethnographic research process were never far from my mind no matter what country I was in, and I constantly questioned myself about whether I was doing the right thing. When I told senior officials in international organizations, governments, and NGOs that I was writing a book about responses to the traffic in women, was I also supposed to inform them of my distinct political position on the subject? Doing so would have certainly cautioned them against talking to me, and yet it seems unethical to pretend that individual beliefs do not inform the kind of ethnography one writes.

I told victims of trafficking stories about my own family history that made them trust me because they believed I was not so different from them, and I explained that my book would discuss how the choices we are forced to make in life are complicated and not always easy for others to understand. Was it unethical to create this sense of trust in one group and not another in the course of my research? Should I instead have presented myself to victims of trafficking as an unbiased person who simply wanted to publish their stories? As is the case with the counter-trafficking officials I spoke to, doing so would probably have prevented them from talking to me at all or reduced the amount of information they shared with me.

The fact remains that it would be ridiculous to assert that anthropologists do not take sides in the course of their research. I fully understood that employees of international organizations, governments, and NGOs were also limited by their social and professional roles, but my strongest sympathies were with the women who were clearly not being assisted, and it was their story I wanted to tell. Part of this ethnographic dilemma stems from questions of agency and oppression in anthropology, and these were never far from my mind in the course of my research. The complex positioning of various actors involved in counter-trafficking often reminded me of a spider's web; just as the question of agency evinced by victims of trafficking is complicated, so is the positioning of people whose professional lives are dedicated to attempts to assist them. The examples of oppression discussed throughout this book are deeply connected to agency evinced by key players and their organizations, almost as if one cannot exist without the other.

I remain convinced of basic human goodness and firmly believe that, if given a choice, most people in the world will opt for the common good. However, this natural inclination toward doing the right thing is seriously complicated by institutionalized processes that depend on hierarchy and inequality for their very existence, and this book is replete with examples of that pernicious effect. Most US taxpayers, for example, would be livid if they knew that USAID's sudden revocation of funds to IOM Sarajevo rendered 1.5 million dollars effectively wasted, even if that amount is quite small compared to the money spent on other issues. Yet the same disappointed US taxpayers may simultaneously believe that their high standard of living might be compromised if the US government did not continue to pursue a foreign policy that sometimes resembles realpolitik in its dispersal of donor aid. The Armenian prosecutors who falsely imprisoned Liana are similarly able to justify their actions to themselves because she was "just a prostitute," but the bribes they received in return also allowed their families to live better lives. This is why some EU citizens admit that living conditions are abysmal in neighboring countries but still believe that unskilled migrants should not be let into their countries, despite labor shortages, because such people "refuse to adapt" or "are not European." And it is why many Bosnians believe it is acceptable for the Roma community to live in poverty because they are "just like that."

It is a truism that it is much easier to accept conditions as they are than to question them. This is why the demand among some men to buy sex from poor women remains uninterrogated. To do so would reveal too many uncomfortable realities that underlie our basic existence and beliefs. After all, it is self-evident that there can be no authority without oppression, no distinction without disenfranchisement, and no success in the absence of the social construction of failure—and that who we are as individual human beings is directly predicated on what we are not. In more everyday terms, this is why women use words such as *whore* to denigrate each other, knowing full well that such a term describes a woman who is so reviled by society that she is rendered virtually invisible. This process also functions at a much larger level at which powerful countries see "development" and "capacity building" as processes that attempt to remake the world in their own image—and inevitably fail to do so because of the lop-sided nature of this construction.

Discussions of sex trafficking, prostitution, and responses to both throughout the world reveal a naked human community trying and failing to make sense of a world replete with incomprehensible suffering amid powerfully seductive individual desires for a better life. Women I met from Armenia, Bosnia, and India who were coerced into prostitution were all victimized by poverty, social marginalization, and a lack of life choices, yet all of them also had hopes and dreams for their futures. Claudia Dias, who led the counter-trafficking program at IOM Sarajevo at the time of my research, insisted that it is wrong to criticize women who take risks by migrating or accepting job offers without fully understanding the terms involved:

> People are entitled to dream. You are entitled to dream to become the President, and this dreaming makes you grow. I think that the cruelest thing is when people question the dreams victims of trafficking had by saying something like "you really thought you could become a model abroad?" When you ask that, you are telling people they are not entitled to dream or to have a tomorrow. There are so many people in the world who have no tomorrow. That's what we from more fortunate backgrounds do not understand.

Dias argues for the basic human dignity of dreams and, in doing so, underscores how hope for the future has a powerfully sustaining function in all our lives. The question that remains is why so many individuals consistently have their right to dream denied and even mocked.

There are no heroes or villains in this book. The characters whose lives and points of view have been presented here are all bound by their professional obligations and limited social roles. They are nothing more—and nothing less—than ordinary human beings caught in a global system that continues to endorse the unequal distribution of power and justice alike.

Postscript

Every day, as human beings and as citizens, we all make choices that support injustice, and yet these are not our only choices. Despite the significant obstacles detailed in this book, we can all play a role in ending the traffic in women. If you live in the United States or are a US citizen, write to your congressional representatives and tell them that you refuse to support temporary US funding initiatives that do not consider local needs and operate on a short-term basis that renders them unable to effect real or sustainable change. Many members of Congress may not be aware of the damaging potential inherent in the practice of funding projects of short duration, rather than long-term programs with a focus on sustainability. Many countries in the world have political representatives who are accountable to their citizens, so no matter who you are or where you live, inform your leaders that they cannot use donor aid as a coercive mechanism to further their political ends, especially when women's lives are at stake. These people rely on you for their jobs; write to them and tell them how you feel about the traffic in women.

You can also volunteer your time. Violence against women exists in manifold forms other than the traffic in women, and chances are you know someone who is being victimized by it. Refuse to accept the commonly held notion that domestic violence is a private matter, because this kind of attitude only perpetuates its existence; instead, make it your business to intervene. Most violent men will not continue to abuse if they know that there are social consequences for their actions, and you can play a role in sending the message that such behavior will not be tolerated. Almost every community has a shelter, a hotline, or a center that advocates for abused women, and you can join them (even if only for an hour or two each week) in their noble efforts to help all women be free of violence and abuse. Never underestimate the power you have as an individual to make a difference in the community where you live.

We can all make activism part of our lives and our social agendas, even if we do not have time to solve all of the world's problems. Men and women need to work together as equal partners for change, and we all have a responsibility to ourselves and to the world to give equality a very high priority. Whether in the supermarket checkout line, in the classroom, or on the job, you can advocate for attitudes, policies, legislation, and empowerment for everyone, regardless of gender, class, race, or national origin. Part of doing this entails the old maxim of "making the personal political" and recognizing that prostitution exists everywhere and that its market is made up of the men who surround us. Not all men are prostitute users, and not all prostitutes are victims of trafficking, but the continued invisibility of sex workers pushes them into situations of increased poverty and marginalization. Carry the names and numbers of organizations that assist sex workers who feel they need help on an equal and nonjudgmental basis, and share them with women who sell sex in your city. If you are a sex worker, share this information with other women who perform erotic labor to ensure that they are able to make free and informed choices about what to do with their bodies and their lives.

The messy realities of human existence, the complicated nature of relationships between men and women, and the inability of international organizations, governments, and NGOs to adequately address the problem means that we all have a choice to make about whether we will be complacent about the stories presented in this book or will work to change them. Sex trafficking is often described by activists and institutions alike as a "global problem with global solutions," and yet we as individuals have the power to make it a global problem with local solutions. It is the continued social invisibility of poor women in communities throughout the world that allows trafficking and many other forms of gendered injustice to continue. Thus the unnoticed Sarajevo roses that we first encountered in Chapter 1 are universal, and we must all choose whether we will take notice and take actions designed to make the world a better place.

References

Note on Internet Citations: Every effort has been made to ensure that the URLs in this book are accurate and up-to-date. However, with the rapid changes that occur in the World Wide Web, it is inevitable that some pages or other resources will have been discontinued or moved, and some content modified or reorganized. The publisher recommends that readers who cannot find the sources or information they seek with the URLs in this book use one of the numerous search engines available on the Internet.

Barry, Kathleen 1996. [1986]. *The prostitution of sexuality: The global exploitation of women.* New York: New York University Press.

Berkovitch, Nitza. 2002. *From motherhood to citizenship: Women's rights and international organizations.* Baltimore: John Hopkins University Press.

Bruno, Martha. 1998. Playing the co-operation game: Strategies around international aid in post-socialist Russia. In *Surviving post-socialism: Local strategies and regional responses in Eastern Europe and the former Soviet Union.* London: Routledge.

Burg, Steven and Paul Shoup. 1999. *The war in Bosnia-Herzegovina: Ethnic conflict and international intervention.* London: M. E. Sharpe.

Chang, Iris. 2000. *Disposable domestics: Immigrant women workers in the global economy.* London: South End Press.

Chew, Lin. 2005. Reflections by an anti-trafficking activist. In *Trafficking and prostitution reconsidered: New perspectives on migration, sex work and human rights.* London: Paradigm Publishers.

Chopra, Ajai, Charles Collins, Richard Hemming, Karen Parker, Woosik Chu, and Oliver Fratzscher. 1995. India: Economic Reforms and Growth. International Monetary Fund Occasional Paper 134. Washington, DC: International Monetary Fund.

Connelly, M. Patricia. 1996. Gender matters: Global restructuring and adjustment. *Social Politics* 3: 12–31.

Constable, Nicole. 1997. *Maid to order in Hong Kong: An ethnography of Filipina workers.* Ithaca, NY: Cornell University Press.

Dekić, Slobodanka. 2003. Sex, slavery and politics: Representations of trafficked women in the Serbian media. *Canadian Women's Studies* 22, no. 3/4: 192–207.

Doezema, Jo. 2001, "Ouch!" Western feminists' "wounded attachment" to the "third-world prostitute." *Feminist Review* 67: 16–38.

———— 2000. Loose women or lost women? The re-emergence of the myth of white slavery in contemporary discourses of trafficking in women. *Gender Issues* 18, no.1: 38–54.

———— 1998. Forced to choose: Beyond the free vs. forced prostitution dichotomy. In *Global sex workers: Rights, resistance and redefinition*. London: Routledge.

Donovan, Bryan. 2006. *White slave crusades: Race, gender and anti-vice activism, 1887–1917*. Chicago: University of Illinois Press.

Ehrenrich, Barbara and Arlie Russell Hochschild. 2004. *Global woman: Nannies, maids and sex workers in the new economy*. London: Owl Books.

Enloe, Cynthia. 2007. *Globalization and militarism: Feminists make the link*. London: Rowman and Littlefield.

———— 2004. *The curious feminist: Searching for women in a new age of empire*. Berkeley: University of California Press.

———— 1990. *Bananas, beaches and bases: Making feminist sense of international politics*. Berkeley: University of California Press.

Farley, Melissa. 2004. Bad for the body, bad for the heart: Prostitution harms women even if legalized or decriminalized. *Violence Against Women* 10, no. 10: 32–40.

Ferguson, Alan. 1993. UN probes abuse claims at brothels in Bosnia. *Toronto Star* 11/4: 3.

Fisher, William. 1997. Doing good? The politics and antipolitics of NGO practices. *Annual Review of Anthropology* 26: 439–64.

Frelick, Bill. 1994. Faultlines of nationality conflict: Refugees and displaced persons from Armenia and Azerbaijan. *International Journal of Refugee Law* 6, no. 4: 581–619.

Gamburd, Michelle Ruth. 2000. *The kitchen spoon's handle: Transnationalism and Sri Lanka's migrant households*. Ithaca, NY: Cornell University Press.

Gradin, Anita. 2007. *History of EU counter-trafficking policies*. Presentation at European Forum for Democracy and Solidarity Conference. Hotel Hollywood, Sarajevo. June 23.

Haynes, Dina. 2004. Used, abused, arrested and deported: Extending immigration benefits to protect victims of trafficking and secure the prosecution of traffickers. *Human Rights Quarterly* 26, no. 2: 26–42.

Herzfeld, Michael. 1993. *The social production of indifference: Exploring the symbolic roots of Western bureaucracy*. Chicago: University of Chicago Press.

Hondagneu-Sotelo, Pierrette. 2001. *Domestica: Immigrant workers, cleaning and caring in the shadows of affluence*. Berkeley: University of California Press.

Huda, Sigma. 2006. Sex trafficking in South Asia. *International Journal of Obstetrics and Gynecology* 94: 374–81.

Hughes, Donna. 2002. The 2002 trafficking in persons report: Lost opportunity for progress. *House Committee on International Relations Testimony*, June 19, 2002.

Huggins, Nik. 2004. "Lilya 4-Ever Movie Review," available online.

International Criminal Tribunal for the Former Yugoslavia (ICTY). 2005. "Tribunal decides to refer the case against Radovan Stanković to Bosnia and Herzegovina." 5/17/05, available at the www.icty.org website.

———— 2002. Transcript of Radovan Stanković hearing. 11/5/02, available at the www.icty.org website.

———— 1996. The prosecutor v. Gojko Janković and Radovan Stanković. IT-96-23/2, available at the www.icty.org website.

———— 1993. Mandate of the ICTY, available at the www.icty.org website.

International Organization for Migration (IOM). 2007. Year one report to USAID. Internal Document: IOM Sarajevo Office. 2001. Trafficking in Women and Children from the Republic of Armenia: A Study. Available online at the www.iom.int website.

Jeffreys, Sheila. 1998. *The idea of prostitution*. London: Spinifex Press.

Keck, Margaret and Kathryn Sikkink. 1998. *Activists beyond borders: Advocacy networks in international politics*. Ithaca, NY: Cornell University Press.

Kempadoo, Kamala. 2005. Victims and agents: The new crusade against trafficking. In *Global lockdown: Race, gender and the prison industrial complex*. New York: Routledge.

Keough, Leyla. 2006. Globalizing "postsocialism": Mobile mothers and neoliberalism on the margins of Europe. *Anthropological Quarterly* 79, no. 3: 431–61.

Lawson, Victoria. 1995. Beyond the firm: Restructuring gendered divisions of labor in Quito's garment industry under austerity. *Environment and Planning D: Society and Space* 13: 415–44.

Lundegaard, Erik.2003. Lilya 4-Ever. *Seattle Times*, available online.

MacKinnon, Catharine. 1990. Liberalism and the death of feminism. In *The sexual liberals and the attack on feminism*. New York: Pergamon.

Mainor, Prudence. 1999. *Commodity trading: A story of the white slave trade*. New York: Prime Time Publishers.

Malarek, Victor.2004. *The Natashas: Inside the new global sex trade*. New York: Arcade Publishers.

Mills, Mary Beth. 1999. *Thai women in the global labor force: Consuming desires, contested selves*. Piscataway, NJ: Rutgers University Press.

Mohanty, Chandra Talpade. 2003. *Feminism without borders: Decolonizing theory, practicing solidarity*. Durham, NC: Duke University Press.

Moodysson, Lukas. 2003. *Lilya 4-Ever*. Sandre Metronome Studio.

Mullings, Beverley. 1999. Globalization, tourism and the international sex trade. In *Sun, sex and gold: Tourism and sex work in the Caribbean*. Boulder, CO: Rowman and Littlefield.

Murray, Allison. 1998. Debt bondage and trafficking: Don't believe the hype. In *Global sex workers: Rights, resistance and redefinition*. New York: Routledge.

New York Times. Bosnia: Convicted war criminal escapes. 5/26/07: 16.

O'Connell Davidson, Julia and Jacqueline Sanchez Taylor. 1998. *Prostitution, power and freedom*. Cambridge: Polity Press.

O'Connor, Monica and Grainne Healy. 2006. *The links between prostitution and sex trafficking: A briefing handbook*. Coalition Against Trafficking in Women and the European Women's Lobby on Promoting Preventative Measures to Combat Trafficking in Human Beings for Sexual Exploitation.

Ortega, Mariana. 2006. Being lovingly, knowingly ignorant: White feminism and women of color. *Hypatia* 21, no. 3: 56–74.

Parrenas, Rhacel Salazar. 2001. *Servants of globalization: Women, migration and domestic work*. Stanford: Stanford University Press.

Peach, Lucinda Joy. 2005. "Sex slaves" or "sex workers"? Cross-cultural and comparative religious perspectives on sexuality, subjectivity and moral identity in anti-sex trafficking discourse. *Culture and Religion* 6, no. 1: 107–34.

Peterson, Karen Lund. 2001. Trafficking in women: The Danish construction of Baltic prostitution. *Cooperation and Conflict* 36, no. 2: 213–38.

Pheterson, Gail. 1993. The whore stigma: Female dishonor and male unworthiness. *Social Text* 37: 39–64.

Rangarajan, Chakravarti, et al. 1994. "India's Balance of Payments: The Emerging Dimensions." Shri Govind Ballabh Memorial Lecture. *Reserve Bank of India Bulletin*. Delhi.

Republic of Armenia. 2005. *Statistics on Annual Migration*. Yerevan, Armenia: Republic of Armenia.

Roe, Clifford. 1915. *The great war on white slavery*. Chicago: Fleming H. Revell.

——— 1914. *The girl who disappeared*. Naperville, IL: World Purity Foundation.

——— 1910. *Panders and their white slaves*. Chicago: Fleming H. Revell.

Rubin, Gayle. 1993. Misguided, dangerous and wrong: An analysis of anti-pornography politics. In *Bad girls and dirty pictures*. London: Pluto Press.

Rupp, Leila. 1997. *Worlds of women: The making of an international women's movement*. Princeton: Princeton University Press.

Safa, Helen. 1995. *The myth of the male breadwinner: Women and industrialization in the Caribbean*. Boulder, CO: Westview Press.

Salzinger, Leslie. 2003. *Genders in production: Making workers in Mexico's global factories*. Berkeley: University of California Press.

Sanchez, Lisa 1998. Boundaries of legitimacy: Sex, violence, citizenship and community in a local sexual economy. *Law & Social Inquiry* 22, no. 3: 543–80.

Sarajlić, Amir and Judith Kiers. 2004. *Report on Council of Europe project: Roma access to employment*. Sarajevo, Bosnia-Herzegovina: Council of Europe.

Sassen, Saskia. 2006. *Territory, authority, rights: From medieval to global assemblages*. Princeton: Princeton University Press.

——— 1999. *Globalization and its discontents: Essays on the new mobility of people and money*. New York: New Press.

Scott, James. 1985. *Weapons of the weak: Everyday forms of peasant resistance*. New Haven: Yale University Press.

Sharma, Nandita. 2005. Anti-trafficking rhetoric and the making of a global apartheid. *National Women's Studies Association Journal* 17, no. 3: 88–111.

——— 2003. Travel agency: A critique of anti-trafficking campaigns. *Refuge* 21, no. 3: 53–65.

Shelley, Louise. 2003. Crime and corruption: Enduring problems of post-Soviet development. *Demokratizatsiya* 11, no.1: 110–14.

Shoquist, Lee. 2003. Lilya 4-Ever. *Reel Movie Critic*, available online.

South Asian Association for Regional Cooperation (SAARC). 2002. Convention on preventing and combating trafficking in women and children for prostitution, available online at the www.saarc.org website.

Spekman, Hans. 2007. *Legalized prostitution: The Dutch experience*. Presentation at European Forum for Democracy and Solidarity Conference. Hotel Hollywood, Sarajevo. June 23.

Tzvetkova, Marina. 2002. NGO responses to trafficking in women. *Gender and Development* 10, no.1: 60–68.

United Nations. 2000. United Nations protocol to prevent, suppress and punish trafficking in persons, especially women and children, supplementing the United Nations convention against transnational organized crime, available online at www.unodc.org.

United Nations High Commissioner for Refugees (UNHCR) Sub-Office for Northern BiH. 2004. *They see us but they don't see us: Report on Roma displaced persons and returnees in Northern Bosnia and Herzegovina*. Tuzla, Bosnia-Herzegovina: UNHCR.

United Nations Security Council. 1994. *Final report of the commission of experts established pursuant to Security Council resolution 780 (1992)*. New York: United Nations.

United States Agency for International Development. 2007. *USAID's family planning guiding principles and US legislative and policy requirements*, available online at the www.usaid.gov website.

United States Congress. 2002 (107th Congress). *The UN and the sex slave trade in Bosnia: Isolated case or larger problem in the UN system? Hearing before the subcommittee on international operations and human rights of the committee on international relations*. Serial No. 107-85

——— 2002 (106th Congress) *Committee on the Judiciary, report submitted on TVPA of 2000*. House of Representatives Report 106-487, Part II.

——— 2000. *Victims of Trafficking and Violence Prevention Act of 2000*. Public Law 106-386. www.state.gov/documents.

United States Department of State. 2006. *Trafficking in persons report*. www.state. gov/g/tip/rls/tiprpt.

——— 2006. *Tier Placements*, available online at www.state.gov/g/tip/rls/tiprpt/2006.

2005. Trafficking in persons report, available online at www.state.gov/g/tip/rls/tiprpt/ 2005.

——— 2004. *Trafficking in persons report: The tiers*, available online at www.state. gov/g/tip/rls/tiprpt.2004.

Walkowitz, Judith. 1996. *City of dreadful delight: Narratives of sexual danger in late Victorian London*. London: Virago Press.

——— 1980. *Prostitution and Victorian society: Women, class and the state*. Cambridge: Cambridge University Press.

Wedel, Janine. 1998. *Collision or collusion? The strange case of Western aid to Eastern Europe, 1990–1997*. New York: Palgrave Macmillan.

Weitzer, Ronald. 2005. Flawed theory and method in studies of prostitution. *Violence against Women* 11, no. 7: 934–49.

Wright, Susan. 2003. *Slave trade: Abducted by aliens, forced into bondage!* New York: Pocket Books.

List of Abbreviations

CATW   Coalition Against the Traffic in Women
EC   European Commission
ERTV   Economic Rehabilitation of Trafficked Victims
EU   European Union
GAATW   Global Alliance Against the Traffic in Women
ICTY   International Criminal Tribunal for the Former Yugoslavia
IMF   International Monetary Fund
IOM   International Organization for Migration
NGO   non-governmental organization
OSCE   Organization for Security and Cooperation in Europe
SAARC   South Asian Association for Regional Cooperation
TIP (Report) United States Trafficking in Persons Report
TVPA   United States Trafficking and Violence Prevention Act
UDHR   Universal Declaration of Human Rights
UN   United Nations
UNPROFOR United Nations Protection Forces
USAID   United States Agency for International Development

About the Author

Susan Dewey is a cultural anthropologist and practitioner of Women's Studies at DePauw University. She has been the recipient of nationally competitive grants from the National Science Foundation and Fulbright-Hays and is the author of *Making Miss India Miss World: Constructing Gender, Power, and the Nation in Postliberalization India.*

Index

abortion 60; impacts of US policy on 71–72

abuse: as a predictor of involvement in sex work 75–78, 151–154, 160; of authority 37, 72, 81, 101, 116; graphic descriptions of in popular culture 51–53; rationalization of, 79, 143. *See also* family; Gyumri

agency: debates on 46–52, 107; definitions of 8–9; examples of 67, 74, 88–91, 104, 176; refusal to see oneself as a victim 78–79, 132–133; topless dancers and 9–10. *See also* Bobby, Liana's story; stigma; Uzbekistan

aid agencies: coercive nature of 67, 72–73, 82, 84, 109–110, 127–128; diversion of funds from 58–59; racism evident in policies of 43–44; temporality of 81, 103. *See also* culture of aid dependency, donor fatigue, European Union, IOM, USAID

Albania: 19, 33; "Agatha Christie" from 106

American Bureau of Moral Education, *See* Roe, Clifford

Anthropology, ethical issues in 179–180

Anu 160–162

Armenia: aid dependency in 81–82, 85–86; brief history of and overview of causes of trafficking in, 13–16; cultural stereotypes about prostitutes in 46–47, 53, 60; genocide in 13–14, 81, 164; legislation on trafficking in 14, 59; migration from and unemployment in 14–15. *See also* Azerbaijan; Ottoman Empire; Turkey

Armenian Sociological Association (ASA) 69

Armine 61–63, 171–172. *See also* IOM

Azerbaijan 13, 14, 71, 86, 90

Banja Luka 168

Barry, Kathleen 48–49

Bassiouni, M. Cherif 100

Berlin Wall, fall of 12, 36

Besić, Suada 115–117, 120

black humor 86, 91; institutionalized indifference and, 92–93.

"Black Label types" 140

Bobby 142–144, 174

borders: control of 12, 33–34, 36–37, 39, 164; trafficking and 3–4, 42, 122, 124, 177

Bombay: dancing girls' bars in 25, 137–142; social inequalities in 22, 149–152, 173–174; *See also* Heera; Kamathipura.

Borić, Besima 125

Bosnia-Herzegovina: abbreviation to Bosnia 16; allegations of UN sexual misconduct in 101–102; brief history of and characteristics of victims of trafficking in 16–21; genocide in 97, 100; legislation on trafficking in 18; NATO-led Stabilization Force in 97; State Coordinator for Combating Trafficking in Human Beings and Illegal Immigration in 109, 120. *See also* rape; Roma; Sarajevo

195

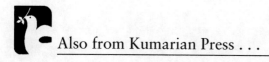

Also from Kumarian Press . . .

Women & Gender

Women and the Politics of Place
Edited by Wendy Harcourt and Arturo Escobar

Progress of the World's Women 2005: Women, Work, and Poverty
Edited by Martha Chen, Joann Vanek, Francie Lund, and James Heintz

War's Offensive on Women: The Humanitarian Challenge in Bosnia, Kosovo, and Afghanistan
Julie Mertus

New and Forthcoming:

Reluctant Bedfellows: Feminism, Development, and Prostitution in the Philippines
Meredith Ralston and Edna Keeble

The World Bank and the Gods of Lending
Steve Berkman

World Disasters Report 2007: Focus on Discrimination
Edited by Yvonne Klynman, Nicholas Kouppari, and Mohammed Mukhier

Peace through Health: How Health Professionals Can Work for a Less Violent World
Edited by Neil Arya and Joanna Santa Barbara

Visit Kumarian Press at **www.kpbooks.com** or call toll-free **800.232.0223** for a complete catalog.

Kumarian Press, located in Sterling, Virginia, is a forward-looking, scholarly press that promotes active international engagement and an awareness of global connectedness.